The Boids and the Bees

Guiding Adaptation to Improve our Health, Healthcare, Schools, and Society

The Boids and the Bees
Guiding Adaptation to Improve our Health, Healthcare, Schools, and Society

A.H. Jones, D.O.
with
Jerry Bozeman, M.Ed.

ISCE
Publishing

3810 N 188th Ave
Litchfield Park, AZ 85340

The Boids and the Bees
Guiding Adaptation to Improve our Health, Healthcare, Schools, and Society
Written by: A.H. Jones, D.O. with Jerry Bozeman, M.Ed.

Library of Congress Control Number: 2009941680

ISBN13: 978-0-9842164-1-3

Printed in the United States of America

Acknowledgements

While the insights that led to this book come from our personal experiences, those experiences would have much less meaning without the education we have received in our respective areas. I would like to thank therefore the professors in the Department of History at the University of Washington long ago for instilling in me an awareness of the importance of context, both for those writing history and for those adapting to it, and the importance and power of ideas.

I would also like to thank the Osteopathic profession for its continuous and often unsuccessful attempts to hold on to the vision that led to its birthing. Born at a time in the late 1800s when frustration with health care was rampant, due to their use of poisonous drugs and harmful practices, the Osteopathic profession gave birth to the idea that the body itself has many means of dealing with illness, and that the physicians role should be to help those processes work better. We hope this book will augment that practice.

Jerry's long experience in education repeatedly led her to see the importance of early child education and the often irresolvable problems that follow emotional trauma in this period. Looking for help to better deal with these problems she found the work of Garry Landreth and his colleagues at North Texas State University and the Association for Play Therapy.

Children lack the language tools to deal with their problems cognitively, but children do play, they do adapt, and they do so toward wholeness. Given the right materials, a safe place, and a caring relationship they are fully capable of playing out their traumas, dealing with them in the play process, and overcoming them. We hope this book will augment this practice as well because the same processes hold for all complex adaptive systems.

Contents

Part I
Living Agents as Complex Adaptive Systems

CHAPTER 6
GO! Defense

Part II
Social Systems as CASYs

CHAPTER 7
Shopping for Healthcare: Shop 'til you Drop

CHAPTER 8
No Lab-Rat Left Behind—Education

CHAPTER 9
A "Boids" Eye View of Society

PREFACE

Without our children and grandchildren this book would not be possible and it is to them that we dedicate it and offer it as consolation for not being there with them more often. They earned this dedication because even when not present with them they are a large part of our context and it is often their problems that provide our greatest challenges—which is how this all began.

Recurrent ear infections in a granddaughter, the recognized and accepted ineffectiveness of medical treatment for this condition when the infections become chronic, and the understanding (that is largely unrecognized by our health care and educational systems) of how this problem can lead to learning and developmental handicaps, prompted us to look for alternatives that could help her. In that process we developed a nasal spray that effectively eliminated her problem by addressing its source in the back of the nose; ear infections are caused by bacteria in the middle ear, but they get there by moving down the Eustachian canal from the back of the nose. That development prompted this book because when we tried to explain it to other physicians we found it difficult because it required thinking differently.

The conventional model of medicine, the one most doctors are trained in, is mostly analytical and mechanical; it sees symptoms as signs of imbalance and uses drugs to restore the balance. So when someone has an upper respiratory problem, that precedes most ear infections and is manifest by a runny nose, we use commonly available cold medicines or prescribed steroids to stop it. Our spray doesn't do this; we thought differently.

Biologists are now pointing out that symptoms occur for a reason and that the runny nose is a successful adaptation that washes the nose and helps us better deal with environmental challenges. Turning it off in this case may not be in our best interest. If the function of the runny nose is to wash out the pollutants that get there, what happens to the pollutants when the washing is turned off? Honoring and supporting this defense made more sense and that is what our spray seemed to do.

This book is about a new way of seeing based on the recognition that we are living agents that can adapt to our environments rather than mechanical creatures that need to be tuned up, regulated, or balanced. We look at some of our adaptations, particularly our defenses, and at how we can support them in ways that make us healthier.

Then we look further at the processes of adaptation: to our physical world by adaptations in our DNA; to our social world, our families, tribes, and communities, by adaptations in our neurons; and in our ideas and the way we see the world by adaptations in our paradigms.

It begins not only with our experience explaining our spray, but with the problem posed by ecologists who have demonstrated that the analytical approach we use to find and fix problems in our cars and other mechanical systems doesn't work to fix ailing ecosystems. If it doesn't work with ecosystems because they are complex systems why should we expect it to work with our even more complex bodies, or any of our other systems? Systems that are living agents, or that are made up of living agents, are called *complex adaptive systems*, and the key word is *adaptive* because all living agents adapt—we call them CASYs.

A prior interest in systems theory led to looking further at these systems and a graduate degree in the history of science and ideas gave perspective. Jerry's experience in early childhood education as a teacher, counselor, and Registered Play Therapist helped us to realize a truth, seen by few that little children with their focus, adaptability, playfulness, and growth, as they build themselves and their brains, the ultimate of complex systems, are the CASY archetype; and we can learn a lot about how to treat our systems from what we have learned about raising and educating our children.

Isaiah describes a future condition where the lamb will lie down with the lion, swords are made into plowshares, and men will make war no more. He says a little child will lead them. Heinz Pagels in his book, *The Dreams of Reason*, says that the nation that masters the science of complexity will become the next superpower. Ideas are powerful, and mastering complex systems would augment that power, but rather than increasing our material, military, and economic power we hope that seeing living agents and their systems in our world as the CASYs they are will better allow us all to be led by a little child.

INTRODUCTION

It is difficult for a group to accept the fact that the way they see the world is faulty or incomplete, but we believe that many Americans are at this point. Change was at the base of both presidential campaigns in 2008, but it was change in the abstract, change only because we were dissatisfied with where we were and where we saw us heading. We don't seem to have an understanding of how to effect healthy changes. We are confronted with problems in all of our systems but they only seem to get worse with everything we do—unintended consequences seem the rule. Our pharmaceutical industry makes new drugs that are supposed to help in one area, but they result in more deaths from their effects in another. We depose a middle-eastern tyrant because of a promoted but mistaken fear that he has weapons of mass destruction and played a role in 9/11, and foment an insurgency and regional instability that sucks financial and human resources from our society to the point of it contributing to an economic crisis at home. And we are stuck in the middle-east because of our responsibility to provide some security and order for the system that we broke.

We try to improve the education of our children by standardizing and regulating our schools, but our efforts seem only to dumb them down; we lose out consistently when testing compares our children with those in other developed nations. And our poorly educated misfits seem increasingly to wind up in jail; at latest count one in a hundred of our adult population are in jail, the highest of any developed country in the world.

On a different level we use antibiotics to kill infecting bacteria. At the same time we promote, with every prescription, antibiotic resistance that ends up killing more of us.

Unintended consequences come from using the wrong model. Like the analytical approach that doesn't help ailing ecosystems our conventional model of medicine sees bothersome symptoms, such as a fever and a runny nose, as indications of illness, as an imbalance in the body's systems. We analyze these symptoms and strive to correct the imbalance in a mechanical way by using drugs to counter them. We use acetaminophen, aspirin, and ibuprofen for fevers, and antihistamines and decongestants to block the runny nose. We do this even though experimentally infected animals die more often when their fever is prevented with these drugs; and now the FDA has announced that the same risks may be present when we block a runny nose with antihistamines and decongestants as they are when we treat a fever. But few look at it this way. When I related this commonsense idea to the FDA as the reason behind the increased mortality associated with the use of antihistamines and decongestants in children, they saw it as an interesting and novel idea. We do not see things in this light when we use a mechanical analytical approach to the body, so we are more likely to blame parental overdosing as the source of the problem.

Every warm blooded animal has the ability to develop a fever, and cold blooded animals commonly move into the sun when they need to elevate their body temperature. And every animal with an airway and a nose has the ability to increase the mucus and water there that hold on to and wash out the irritants and infecting agents that so often enter the body as we breathe, or rub our nose or eyes. These particular symptoms are successful adaptations that help us better deal with the insults and challenges we encounter in our environments. Like all good defenses they come with survival benefits—and those benefits are lost when the symptoms are blocked.

When you support and help these defenses you actually help prevent many of the problems that these defenses are protecting against. When it became clear that the spray helped my granddaughter I began using it in my practice. The incidence of ear infections in ten children with this problem was reduced by more than 92% when they used it regularly. In others it also reduced the vast majority of problems such as sinus infections, allergies, and asthma that begin with either infecting agents or irritants in the nose.

The effectiveness of this spray could not be explained using the conventional model because it didn't balance or turn off this bothersome symptom, it actually promoted it. It soon became apparent that the spray worked to clean the nose and prevent harmful bacteria from holding on there. Cleaning the nose is the major function of the runny nose itself; rhinorrhea is an adaptation that cleans the nose—it's not just a bothersome symptom to be turned off with drugs. Our success consolidated and gave direction to our already firm conviction from the Osteopathic tradition that we need to honor and support our body's defenses.

Because there was no way to explain the success of this spray using the conventional model our problem became the stumbling block that made a new model imperative. We need a model that understands the importance of our successful adaptations, and finds ways to honor, strengthen, and support them, rather than one that treats them with drugs and hobbles them. Hobbling the defense of your favorite football team will make them lose the game, and it's the same with us as we continue our game with the irritants and infecting agents in our own environments.

But it doesn't stop with just the wrongheaded way we treat our bodies. This analytical approach that looks at our systems as if they were machines is the one we use in dealing with most of our problems in all areas of our lives; it's the way we see the world. We have used this approach to analyze and try to fix our ailing ecosystems long enough that we know it doesn't work. If it doesn't work with our ailing ecosystems why should we expect it to work for our profoundly more complex bodies, or our complex economy, or raising and educating our complex children?

We and the systems we join to create are alive and living agents all share the ability to read and adapt to their environments. The mechanical analytical model that dominates in our world can't deal with adaptation. In drug research we try to shut it out by using placebos, pills with no effects, but as many have pointed out the placebo effect is extremely powerful with effects that often come close to matching those of the active drug. And as we point out it is powerful because it represents our ability to adapt; the beneficial action of an inactive pill used in these studies can only be explained by the agent's ability to adapt.

In most of the biological world adaptation is limited to the physical world and it is done at the level of DNA. It is slow, except in the bacterial experts. In the world of human beings and some higher animals, adaptation is also done at the social level as the agents adapt to their differing social environments, and children adapt to their differing cultures. Adaptation at this level is in our neurons and much faster. We can promote adaptation at this level by changing our environments, by changing our school, our job, our church, or by immigrating. On the mental level we adapt even faster as we learn what works and what doesn't, and most importantly, and most rapidly, by changing our paradigm, the way we see the world. This book is about the things that we can do to encourage healthier adaptations at all levels of our systems.

An ecosystem and our bodies are but two examples of CASYs. Adaptive systems resist analysis. They are not well treated by focusing on their parts; such a focus more often leads to unintended consequences. They are far better treated by focusing on their contexts—on their physical, relational and mental environments. We know this is true on the physical level with ecosystems; it is just as true in looking at our bodies.

As we began to use this model in looking at the way we treat our bodies it soon expanded. It led to seeing the importance of adaptations in a variety of areas, to looking at the processes behind the symptoms in our ailing institutions, to looking at the decisions we made that got us there, to looking at adaptation itself, and to the realization that adaptation has no place in our currently dominant mechanical model. Adaptation is real. It happens; it's the key element making the difference between the mechanical viewpoint and the new way of thinking many are examining that is based on establishing networks and the complexity that goes along with it. And mostly we have followed the mechanical model and ignored it.

Adaptation is not a factor in mechanical systems; indeed mechanical systems try to eliminate any adaptation. We are uncomfortable with new ideas or the new problems that confront us when agents adapt; we don't like the unpredictability that comes with CASYs. We would rather have the degree of control that we have over machines that can't adapt beyond our ability to program them. But we all can read our respective environments and adapt to changes in them; and we share this ability with every other living organism, from bacteria, to cellular organisms, to organ systems, and to individual organisms such as us—it's a characteristic of life. And this ability extends beyond individuals to the systems they create, from bacterial biofilm, to insect colonies, to our corporation and to the global economy. All these systems have the ability to adapt to changes in their various environments. They are all CASYs; and they all resist being treated mechanically.

Unintended consequences surface because when we analyze the CASY in question our analysis cuts through many networked interactions that are ignored as we look for the ones we are interested in. These severed relations are important, however, and ignoring them is not in our best interest. Besides arising from these ignored relationships unintended consequences also come because when we manipulate a CASY, agents in that system play with the regulations to improve their survival. Agents in our financial system gamed mortgages for their own benefit to the point that it led to the meltdown of the financial marketplace; and no set of regulations can be complete enough to eliminate the gaming. Unintended consequences are problems that challenge us, but even more they point to anomalies in our understanding that cry out for a new way of seeing. Einstein said that our problems can not be solved on the same level of thinking on which they were created. We need to think differently; we need to reframe our problems, we need a different level of thinking.

Paradigms are the models we build in our brains to represent the world outside us. We use them to explain and explore this outside world, so when one's eyes are pried open to see differently the whole world is often changed. Thomas Kuhn described it well in his marvelous book, *The Structure of Scientific Revolutions,* when he said that a new paradigm doesn't modify the previous way of seeing, "it destroys it by making it meaningless." This is what happened to us as we began to see differently.

In his description of how paradigms change Kuhn points out that after a while problems arise that are not easily explained by the current model; he calls them anomalies. As they continue to build up someone eventually comes up with an idea that explains them better and simpler. This is where we are today and we can learn more about the process by looking at Kuhn's description.

His primary example of such a shift was that accompanying the Newtonian revolution in physics. Kuhn was an historian of science so he looked mostly at this revolution in that arena; he did not follow its effect in other areas. But the new way of thinking about and seeing the world that followed Newton's application of mechanical principles of analysis and measurement to the physical world was appealing because it allowed for prediction. It worked so well in the physical world that it was applied to more and more of the elements and systems in our world—even to those that dealt with living agents. With time anomalies arose in our understanding of the fundamental nature of the world and Newton's paradigm had to be refined with that of quantum physics. But this revision has not yet changed our use of the mechanical analytical model in our coping with other ailing CASYs; Newton still rules our thinking.

We believe that a fundamental error in the Newtonian model was its extension to living agents. Newton likely did not see living agents as machines, but he did lead the way to seeing the physical world in that way. And his view worked so well in the physical world that metaphors were introduced into the language—clockworks, balance of powers, action and reaction, stimulus and response, connect the dots—that affect the way we all think. The mechanical metaphor that Newton used so well to describe the orbiting of the Earth and planets expanded to describe just about everything, even us. This model is linear rather than networked; things are connected in line rather than in networks. We like it because it allows us to predict the results of an action. It has been the way we have looked at the world since we began thinking and making models to explain the events we observed; Newton just gave it a firmer foundation. The analytical, mechanical paradigm is the model that we use overwhelmingly to analyze and fix the problems that we encounter; but it doesn't have a place for adaptation so it's not the best way to treat a CASY.

While it continues to explain much of the physical world, especially on a large scale, our love affair with the precise, predictable world of physics has blinded us to the presence of other types of systems that are more complex, less predictable, and less knowable, but more workable. It has also blinded us to the fact that we are not machines. On some level we all know this and we all can easily recognize the feeling of being manipulated by some higher authority as if we didn't count—we don't like being treated like a machine. But while we see and feel this we don't have many tools or metaphors to explain it; these still come from the mechanical system.

The concept of *systems* and CASYs has been around for the past fifty years, but most of those working in this field have not yet realized it is a way of seeing. Aided by larger and faster computers the goal of these systems analysts remains modeling the world by analytical means, by breaking it down into its numerous elements, as far as the limits of their computers allow. They have created complex simulation programs that attempt to model our complex systems. But this is still the analytical approach and the problems they are trying to solve analytically are really anomalies in Kuhn's sense; they demand that we see differently.

The world of physics has provided the model for how we see and deal with the world around us. Following the rules of science we break everything down into its parts; we analyze them and we fix the faulty parts to make the machine work better. Mechanics do this with cars, doctors do it with people, CEOs do it with corporations, and political leaders do it with states and nations. But the living agents making up the animate part of the world are not machines that can be analyzed; and treating them in this way commonly results in unintended consequences that are often worse than what was treated.

We and our fellow human beings, all forms of life, and the social and cultural systems that we and they join to create cannot be properly understood by these mechanical rules and metaphors because the rules of classical physics don't allow for adaptation. Robert Nadeau points this out for economics in his book *The Wealth of Nature*: the 'laws' of economics are based on the now recognized as incomplete laws of classical physics laid down in the 19th Century. This misapplication of physical principles is present not just in economics; it's true in all areas where living agents play a role. All living things and the systems they join to form have the ability to read their environments and adapt to them, and adaptation often leads to the emergence of novelty that is not understood and ignored, or resisted by those using the mechanical model; living agents are better modeled and understood as the CASYs that they are.

Besides increasing unintended consequences the misapplication of the mechanical model has other harmful effects. At the beginning of the Industrial Revolution the Prussian philosopher Immanuel Kant had the foresight to see where that revolution was leading; he defined abuse as treating another person as an object. In his book, *The Lucifer Effect*, describing the abuses at his Stanford Prison Experiment and Abu Ghraib, Philip Zimbardo defines evil in much the same way: as anything that attempts to dehumanize another. One of our primary messages agrees with but expands on this concept; it applies not just to people but to all CASYs. All living agents are abused when they are seen, analyzed, and treated as objects, and to do so detracts from their identity as living adaptable agents and is evil. Seeing living agents as complex adaptive systems constitutes a paradigm shift that opens up a new way of seeing them in the world.

There are rules for understanding and working with CASYs that will be elaborated later but need to be set out at the beginning. The 'boids' in our title is a term used by Craig Reynolds to describe his simple and successful modeling of the complex behavior of birds flocking. From Reynolds' model we learn that CASYs have: some separation, balanced by cohesion, and a direction or alignment. While we may not like being compared to a flock of birds these rules become clearly appropriate for all CASYs and several corollaries also appear when one thinks about them for a moment. Adequate personal space, *separation*, allows us to function independently and decreases hostility. *Cohesion* is a defensive adaptation; agents join together to increase their efficiency and better deal with danger— "to form a more perfect union . . . and provide for the common defense." Cohesion also provides the secure base that is the home for the increased networking and complexity that is in turn the seed-bed for the emergence of novelty.

Alignment can be, and often is, on something as simple as the next meal, but a few billion years of evolution reveals nature's alignment to be centered both on survival, of which eating is just a part, and increased complexity or diversity. Darwin did a good job explaining how natural selection promotes the expression of characteristics that aid species survival. This is the defensive aspect of evolution; the particular adapting agent gets the benefit and with time and natural selection it spreads to the species. There are also pressures from natural selection that promote diversity with its resultant increases in niches, networks, and complexity, but the benefits of diversity go to the larger system and are often at the expense of the individual. Adaptations in both areas are tested by natural selection and those with survival benefits persist.

Species survival is the defensive pole of adaptation. Defensive adaptations give the agent a survival advantage most often seen as efficiency, or an increase in power such as size or speed. Mostly these are refined by inbreeding, a process that combines agents with the desired characteristic and increases the likelihood that their offspring will express it better. In defensively aligned corporate social CASYs survival is most commonly associated with the profit margin and inbreeding is often used to increase the margin. Defensive adaptations are more the rule in regulated and threatened systems on all levels. A fever and a runny nose are both defensive adaptations which help the agent survive the environmental threats of irritants and infecting agents. Antibiotic resistance in bacteria, the enculturation of a child into a family and culture, the gaming of our systems that all engage in, the emphasis on profits we see in capitalism, and many other current processes are all cut from the same cloth—they are all, on their differing levels, defensive adaptations. The individual agent and its progeny are the beneficiaries of these adaptations and the larger system only gets the benefit as they breed with those having the trait, are able to adopt it on their own, or as the benefits are shared or otherwise trickle down.

Diversity is the creative pole of adaptation. It is also the *sine qua non* of a healthy system. The increased complexity we see in novelty, diversity, and emergence more often requires the cooperation of a number of agents working together—cross-pollinating each other in what is essentially a leaderless organization. The system is the beneficiary of these adaptations since they increase the diversity, the number of niches available to its agents, and the complexity that allows for more networking and even more novelty. To our great benefit the United States continues to lead the world in the development of novelty, but our mechanical way of seeing, the defensive alignment it promotes, and the regulatory tools we use dampen this creative drive.

In order to promote this creative novelty CASYs need to be treated, not by regulation or manipulation, the way we treat machines, but by addressing their contexts—physical, social, and mental—by informing them of their options, increasing the elements available to them on each of these levels, and promoting a safe place where they can play with those elements, become familiar with them, and eventually adapt to their environment in as creative a way as possible. This is the optimal way to raise a child, the CASY archetype, and it works well with all CASYs. Promoting this creative alignment is a primary focus of this book; it is not just about the problems associated with a defensive alignment.

A safe place is a fundamental requirement and the primary rule to keep the system safe is that no other adapting agent be treated as an object. The mechanical approach of analyzing and regulating to maintain control is resisted by CASYs; all outside interference is seen as a threat by any CASY. It prompts excessive cohesion and the defensive alignment that goes along with it. This alignment promotes defenses, foments hostility, and dampens creativity.

Such a defensive alignment commonly follows our standard practice in the mechanical model where control always comes from outside or above. Novel solutions to problems that benefit the whole system rarely come from a defensive alignment, or from outside the system, or from top down leadership. They are much more likely to come from a community of agents in the system, working in a safe place that enables a creative alignment; such an environment encourages diverse and novel adaptations.

In the following we discuss in more detail our use of mental models or paradigms and the nature of complex adaptive systems, and then apply this understanding to several areas. In Part 1 we focus on living agents. Beginning with bacteria, since they are the simplest CASY, we show how our war with the microbial world is not one we can win, and that a better option is treating bacteria as the CASYs they are. We have applied pressure on bacteria to adapt in healthier ways, and they have, but few have seen it, and even fewer have harnessed it. We then look at our bodies, seeing them as adaptive rather than mechanical. Many of our symptoms, as we have seen, are the result of adaptations that are expressed in us because of their survival benefit; and when we realize this we see that treating them in the traditional manner by balancing them, blocks not only the symptoms, but their survival benefits as well. Analyzing and treating symptoms doesn't work to help ailing ecosystems and we argue that it doesn't help any CASY including us.

Notable among our beneficial adaptations are a fever and the bodies washing defenses of diarrhea and its nasal counterpart, rhinorrhea. It took two weeks after the September, 2007 FDA announcement of the increased mortality associated with the use of antihistamines and decongestants for the pharmaceutical industry to voluntarily remove them from the market for children. Hobbling our defensive nasal cleaning robs us of its survival value and is *likely* a major reason why we get sicker and the children died after using drugs that blocked the cleaning. "Likely" is as strong a word as we can use here because no one has ever asked the question.

Questions arise only when we see a problem; and often problems are made visible only after our eyes are pried open to see differently; and then we have a whole set of new questions. Such questions are also not in the financial interests of those paying for the research that guides our healthcare system. Vested interests, historically, are always the largest roadblocks to progress. But if you hobble the defense of your favorite football team they are more than likely to lose the game, and in the game of survival that we are playing with all of the bacteria and other toxins in our environment our defenses play a crucial role and hobbling them is not in our best interest. Conversely there are treatments, like the nasal spray that helped open our eyes, which honor and support our defenses and help prevent more serious illness. While the benefits of a clean nose are clear to the increasing number of people using this spray regularly, it is not used in our healthcare system because of regulation, because it doesn't bring any profits to the system, and because of the simple fact that we don't see things this way.

This book is about us as CASYs and our adaptations; it's about living agents and their systems. Everything alive is a CASY, but so are the groups that they join together to make, from ant and bee colonies to families, teams, corporations and states. And there is enough information from all of these systems to enable us to find some common patterns in how they adapt, both defensively and creatively. And we can see that adaptations of creatively aligned CASYs often bring the greatest value to the broader system. We desperately need to know how to promote this kind of adaptation on a wider scale.

In Part 2 we expand our perspective to look at the systems we have created in our societies. We begin with healthcare. Physicians too are CASY agents working within the higher level CASY of a healthcare system. We have chosen to put this system in the marketplace, which is essentially the playground for the agents, but also functions as a CASY on its own level. When we look at this interplay of CASYs we can see the errors behind treating them mechanically and why more regulation has not been, and continues not to be, a workable option in treating our healthcare system. Seeing these systems as CASYs also makes clear how they should be treated to make them more equitable and effective, and provides abundant examples for how to, and how not to, promote healthier adaptations.

Then we look at the developing child—the CASY archetype with their ability to adapt to a wide variety of cultures and families and build themselves in these differing environments. We look at the child in the context of our educational system. Again we can see that the problems in our current system stem from treating our children more as objects than agents. Our primary tools in education are learned in the laboratory where we train lab rats to go through mazes. And again we can see that with the CASY model solutions to our educational problems become clear.

Besides our healthcare and educational systems other social CASYs are: our societies, that have concentrated on accumulating power and scale rather than the more long lasting diversity of niches found in healthy ecosystems; the military-industrial complex that permeates our society, but that, as a tool of the executive, creates hostility and a defensive alignment that blocks creative and novel solutions wherever it is used; and finally religions, the cores of our differing cultures, which arise from the spiritual experiences of our many religious leaders, but all too often evolve defensively into controlling priesthoods, dogma, and orthodoxy.

At the outset we would like to make clear that the problems we see and discuss are not with individuals but with the mechanical way most of us have of seeing the world. We show how the mechanical treatment of the many CASYs in our world is leading us in a direction most of us do not want, and how recognizing them as CASYs is more helpful.

CHAPTER 1
Seeing with New Eyes

The real voyage of discovery consists not in seeking new landscapes,
but in having new eyes.

Marcel Proust

I graduated from a high school named after Benjamin Franklin. I thought then that he was pretty smart and had lots of good ideas—and still do. But that earlier view was tempered when I went to college and read D. H. Lawrence's criticism of Franklin in his *Studies in Classic American Literature.* Lawrence didn't like him. He particularly did not like the trend that Franklin epitomized and supported of seeing man in a simple mechanical way. In this way of seeing things the object (in Franklin's case, a man) is broken down into its parts—it's analyzed—and the parts are treated, repaired, or adjusted to make the machine, or the man, work better.

Franklin broke us down into several of our human characteristics, and showed how we could be perfected by focusing on and improving those characteristics one by one. Franklin came to see things in this way honestly; he lived in the early days of the Industrial Revolution when machines, like clocks, were becoming more common, and after scientists like Galileo and Newton had destroyed the ideas of Greek science, where things were more fixed in their places by a natural order, and replaced them with analysis, the interplay of forces, the laws of motion, and the powerful idea of progress, where the agent is not limited by birth position or any other natural or social constraint. Analysis and the potential for perfection thus gradually replaced the natural order of things. By Franklin's time the mechanical way of seeing things fostered by these ideas had become accepted as the way things were. The Age of the Machine and the mechanical paradigm it introduced had begun and Franklin fit right in. But more than a century later, seeing where this path led, Lawrence rebelled. He talked of the strange gods who would occasionally come into the clearing of his known self to disrupt his analytical plans and countered: "I am not a mechanical contrivance."

The differing ways that Franklin and Lawrence saw the world is due to what Kuhn explained as their differing paradigms. Paradigms refer to the mental models or schema that we build in our brains to represent the world outside of us. The schema change as we grow in our understanding of the world. A child's mental world is limited to parents and family; it grows as they grow to include more and more of the world until it reaches that of Albert Einstein or the Dalai Lama. Sometimes the ideas we have are so successful they enter into the metaphors of speech that we hear as children so we apply them unconsciously to other areas as we create the neuronal connections in our brains that build our models of the world. Franklin lived at such a time, a century after Newton explained the laws of motion, when the mechanical analytical way of seeing the world was just the way things were. It worked so well explaining the mechanical world that we applied it to everything.

Later I went to medical school and saw how much further we have traveled down this mechanical analytical pathway. Newton helped us see the universe better by analyzing the motion of heavenly bodies; Franklin thought he could do the same with our character by breaking it down into our habits; medicine does it with our body, breaking it down into its functioning systems and biochemical reactions; and others followed suit in other disciplines. Adam Smith described capitalism in mechanical terms with supply balancing demand, price being the force maintaining the balance; he even had an invisible hand pushing the whole system toward greater progress. The checks and balances in our Constitution are based on the mechanical way of seeing, the most advanced model available to its authors. The 'science' of economics, as referenced earlier is based on the mechanical laws of physics. It's the way these leaders saw the world, and it continues today to be how most of us see it We use the mechanical-analytical approach today in dealing with our bodies when we try to restore the balance of blood pressure, cholesterol, glucose, or any other element that is out of balance. We use it with our children when we focus on elements of their behavior that we try to modify with rewards and punishment; our schools use it when they use conditioned learning to teach our children; and even our governments use it when they try to maintain a balance of power or coerce wayward nations with sanctions. Much of the time it seems to work, but, as Lawrence saw, it's flawed.

It works well when dealing with the physical world, but it doesn't work nearly as well when dealing with living adaptable agents because our analysis destroys their networks as we cut down into the system to look for the linear relationships that we can understand and manipulate. These cut connections are then responsible for most of the unintended consequences. It is also incomplete because the agents keep adapting to the imposed regulations and finding ways around them—they game their systems. Kuhn points out that as we continue learning we will eventually uncover problems that are not easily explained by our existing model. We can try to explain them in the old framework but, like the epicycles the Ptolemaic astronomers used to explain the apparent backward motion of the planets, the solutions more often add to the unwieldy hierarchy of the old paradigm and make it more unstable. These problems are more properly seen as anomalies in Kuhn's sense of the word; they tend to collect until someone comes up with a simpler explanation for them that involves seeing differently or changing ones frame of reference. This is what Kuhn calls a paradigm shift. Often such a shift involves a radical change in how we see the world and is very uncomfortable for the people experiencing it.

Social paradigms as adaptations

The ancients who watched the skies at night came up with an almost endless number of cycles and epicycles to explain the transits of the moon and the apparent backward movement of the planets among the fixed stars that was all made meaningless by the simplicity of Copernicus's solar centered system. While the shift in seeing a solar centered system seems relatively easy for us today, the shift in the frame of reference for people experiencing this process has been termed the most unsettling shift in perspective ever to occur in the western world. The place of mankind had been at the center of the universe; we, or at least our rulers and kings, were just below the angels on the ladder of creation; and Copernicus's solar centered system unceremoniously dumped us all from that honored place. Just as our mechanical model leads us to see linear cause and effect and social mobility based on individual effort the people then saw themselves as the center of God's creation in a social setting of His determination. It was a safe and wonderful place, especially for those who liked the order it imposed and kings who could rule by divine right. It was this mental construct that provided the context to which they adapted, but it was undercut by Copernicus.

While the physical world is a part of all agents' context, adaptations to it are likely to have happened long ago: gravity shaped our bodies, bacteria shaped our metabolism, and the environment shaped our defenses. Adaptations to our physical environment continue, but they are slow. Faster is adaptation to ones culture, the social context of our relationships. Children born into our various cultures rapidly mold themselves into their local cultures; the adaptations are in their neurons. The most rapid adaptations are potentially in our mental constructs, like those shaken, destroyed, and remolded by Copernicus.

These are our paradigms. Like all mental structures they can change rapidly, but change here is constrained by society, by conventional wisdom. Like the operating systems of our computers which control their input and output, our paradigm controls how we see and change is often very difficult. Galileo could see with his telescope the orbiting of the moons of Jupiter, which confirmed for him the correctness of Copernicus's model, but, on pain of his death before the church fathers, he had to deny it.

And not just us as individuals are limited by their paradigms, but higher order CASYs as well. Our pharmaceutical companies develop drugs based on their analytical model and are blinded by either their model or the desire for profits to ignore contrary information, so Vioxx resulted in more heart attacks. In much the same way President George W. Bush's analysis of the Middle East saw Iraq as a problem. Whether he lied outright about Iraq having "Weapons of Mass Destruction" and links to Al Qaeda, or was blinded by his paradigm to just not seeing the conflicting evidence that was there, despite testimony that it was indeed presented to him, is a question that will likely not be answered in our generation due to the heightened secrecy of the records. But while the pharmaceutical companies were punished by litigation, the politicians will likely get off with no penalty even though the cost in lives, disabilities, and souls (if the CBS report of veteran suicides is correct) is inestimably higher. These examples vividly portray both the power and the problem of paradigms; they control what and how we see; and systemic problems are not usually seen as anomalies until one can see with new eyes.

In this way problems are collecting in our current mechanical paradigm. Like the epicycles of the Ptolemaic astronomers, we are accumulating an unmanageable amount of regulatory hierarchy as we attempt to control the CASYs in our societies, and we remain blind to seeing them as other than mechanical systems where cause and effect are clear and we have someone to blame. We have not yet come to see the problems with new eyes that see them on a different level.

According to Kant and Zimbardo the mechanical model leads to abuse or evil when used on people. It's just as inadequate and inappropriate when dealing with systems that represent the extensions of people—globalization, economics, politics, education, and healthcare. It doesn't help us deal with anything that is alive or made up of living agents because the mechanical model has no way to deal with a living agent's ability to adapt. We need a new paradigm when it comes to dealing with individuals or their systems that adapt.

Changing a paradigm

The practice of medicine in America is delivered by independent agents embedded in the healthcare system, and problems on both levels provide ready examples of systems in distress and the value of a different paradigm. Skyrocketing healthcare costs demand our attention today as much or more than does the decreasing access that is mostly due to those costs. Critics of our system point to a drop of almost 70% since 1930 in what is called the productivity index. Productivity is measured by the ratio of goods divided by the cost of producing them. Healthcare productivity is measured by life expectancy divided by the cost of healthcare as a percentage of Gross Domestic Product. In 1930 this index was 16.5 while in 2004 it was just over 5, and it continues to sink. Those defending the system analyzed the factors making up this index and claim they are not representative of the real problems. Our homicide rate, for example, is a social problem that brings down our life expectancy by killing mostly the young, but it is not considered a medical problem. They also argue, erroneously, that all of the easy cures have already happened. It's not that all the easy cures have already been found, it's that the system is rewarded for the expensive ones; the easy and inexpensive cures can't fund the research required to get into the system.

While this argument continues, both sides ignore the time period before 1930 which saw dramatic increases in this index, and is the point in bringing it up here. Life expectancy went from 49.2 in 1900 to 59.2 in 1930 without significant increases in healthcare spending. There are cycles of progress in healthcare just as there are in science and other areas of human endeavor—and we need to understand why, and how to stimulate them. This particular cycle followed the understanding that came with the germ theory and the social and technological changes it made sensible, like clean water supplies, better sanitation, hand-washing, immunization, and pasteurization, which made the transmission of infection less likely. Lives were saved by prevention as the paradigm shifted to include the germ theory.

Kuhn listed two criteria in order to be a paradigm: it must be attractive enough to gain adherents, and it must be open ended enough to give them something to do with it. He talked about paradigms in the world of the physical sciences because that was his field, but they occur just as well in other areas. Our understanding of germs and their role in disease was a new paradigm that allowed for the progress in health care as people applied the understanding to clean up water supplies, protect food by better washing, preserving and preparing, and even simple things like hand washing. It was the application of this paradigm that led to the increases in life expectancy. New paradigms are the pathways to progress.

A word of caution

But lest we get overly enthusiastic we must always remember that these are paradigms or mental constructs that can also be taken too far. Once their metaphors enter into our language and the patterns of our thoughts paradigms tend to become not only our model for the world but for how we think in general and this is where we get into trouble.

The ancients saw the world as the center of the universe, but the thinking that went with it saw them as the center of God's attention. Newton showed the value of a mechanical view of the universe, but the thinking that went with it saw everything as a machine. In the metaphor of Alford Korzybski, a leading expert on the use of words and their meaning, we mistake the map we have drawn in our brains, our paradigm, for the territory outside us; we replace the real world with the abstract one we have created in our heads as we are raised in our various familial, cultural and intellectual environments. If we do not recognize this then we do indeed live in a virtual reality. These constructed maps can blind us to the benefits of seeing differently as problems continue to be framed in our various cultural paradigms, just like adding more epicycles.

In this way Franklin saw differently than Lawrence, and Ann Coulter has a different paradigm for seeing the world than Al Franken. People who share the paradigm of either of these polar examples of current American political commentary see the others as blind and stupid. But of course they are not, they just have a different paradigm—they see with different eyes. On an international scale, we see the Iranian leader Mahmoud Ahmadinejad as a radical Islamic leader and a major threat to world peace, while the average Arab sees George Bush as a radical Christian leader and a major threat to world peace. We each see with different eyes and the root of the threat to world peace is not so much the individuals involved, but our collective inability to share our views.

This intercultural blindness is particularly a problem when we have not progressed beyond Piaget's stage of concrete operational to formal operational thinking. Children go through a stage of concrete thinking, usually from age seven to twelve, where the map is more likely to be mistaken for the territory; and often we tend to linger there. In formal thinking we are more able to see a role for the mind and its models, and we are less likely to get stuck in our cultural views.

Once we understand the use of these mental models we can play with them and see how the results of our play fit with the world. Good models help us learn more about the world. Kuhn looked at the use of metaphors in our differing paradigms and pointed out that we are often blind to elements in the world until we have the right metaphor, or mental construct, that allows us to register it in our brains; Copernicus's solar centered system was an almost impossible leap for those seeing mankind at the center of the universe, just as was our seeing George W. Bush as a major threat to world peace in 2003.

Once we have the new metaphor we have new eyes that allow us to see many other things differently. William Harvey, the 16th and 17th Century English physician who first described the circulation of the blood, was exposed to Copernican thought when he went to school in Padua. I have often wondered if he would have had the insight that led to his discovery without Copernicus' model and influence; the blood circulates in the body just like the planets circulate around the sun and, like the planets when they are behind the sun, blood in the capillaries is even invisible. Once we see with new eyes many new applications become apparent.

Paradigms are acquired as we grow and are altered with time and experience, by the uncomfortable means of bringing them to the level of consciousness and being open to seeing anomalies in them; and best, according to Ken Wilbur and many others who have studied the process, with the introspection and meditation that is also the most effective way to strengthen and train our cerebral cortex. Differences cannot be resolved by arguing or debate because it's as if the individuals are speaking different languages; Kuhn calls reconciliation or mutual understanding a problem of translation.

In this way a paradigm is a critical part of every agent's context, the context to which they are continually adapting. One's context is not only the physical environment in which the agent lives and its network of relations, interactions, and interdependencies with others, but the paradigm with which the agent perceives and interprets his or her world, so one's context has a physical component, a social component, and a mental component.

It is in this mental aspect that effective change for our problematic institutions is found. When our application of a model no longer works in the world, when the anomalies become stumbling blocks or millstones, we need a new one—we need a paradigm shift.

We argue here, not for the need of new and more powerful tools to analyze these complex systems, nor for new and better regulations, but for a paradigm shift in the way we see and treat the CASYs in our world. Our traditional mechanical model uses measuring, analyzing, and regulating; it treats CASYs as objects and ignores their ability to adapt. While this model has led to much progress in our understanding of the physical world, expanding it to cope with the complexity of life and CASYs is misguided—and treating CASYs mechanically, as if they were objects, by analyzing, regulating, and manipulating them, is abusive and evil. In the CASY paradigm we see the power that resides in an agent's adaptability, and that by enriching or modifying their context's we can apply pressure for them to adapt in creative ways that are more likely to benefit the system. Such treatment honors the agent rather than abuses them.

CASYs appear too complicated for most of us and we give up before we even start. Many of us have a vested interest in the conventional wisdom that goes along with the old way of seeing. This is why new paradigms are often such a hard sell, with new thinking progressing only with the demise of those with the older view. Often, however, the field is ripe for a new way of seeing.

Paradigm shift in colonial America

Colonial America in 1776 was ripe. Tom Paine's remarkable work, *Common Sense*, changed how colonists in America saw themselves over a few months. Prior to *Common Sense* most Americans saw themselves as English; they were loyal to England, but they had some gripes. After *Common Sense* they saw themselves in a new way—as 'Separatists' with colonial loyalty replacing that to England. Paine's short book opened up a new paradigm for the colonists; it was attractive, sensible, and it challenged them to dream.

His title was appropriate as well for common sense is involved in all paradigm shifts. The new answers are generally simpler than the old way—it's just that they don't fit the conventional wisdom and we don't see them until they are unfolded in front of us.

The choice was not without risk. Had our forefathers lost the Revolutionary War our leaders would have been hung because their vision was strong enough it led to revolt. People who see differently today are not usually executed, but they are likely to be labeled with any number of antisocial epithets. Our forefathers in Colonial America did not like the way things were going with their governance just as the vast majority of Americans today feel that we are on the wrong path. Like our forefathers in Colonial America we too need a different way of looking at our problems and the guts and fortitude to persist in the face of opposition.

The acceptance of a new paradigm depends, just as it did in Colonial America, on the people. Too often we look to government for solutions to our problems, but government listens most often to the power structures and corporate financing that gets the politician elected—power structures embedded in and profiting from the conventional wisdom. It's the same with our media. Designed to inform the public, the media also takes its cues from the power structures and forms rather than informs our way of thinking. In this and in other ways government and our information systems look to the money. As long as our government allows the energy industry to write the energy bill and the pharmaceutical industry to write the drug bill it's not likely that effective change will come from this direction without a great deal of public pressure.

Nor is this kind of change likely to come from the experts. Newton was a student running from the plague when he saw the apple fall; and Einstein was a patent clerk when he realized that time was not a constant but related to velocity—the 'A Ha!' behind his revolutionary 1905 treatises. It is the function of our educational institutions and their experts to fill out and teach the existing paradigms, not come up with new ones. The Institute of Medicine, the group of experts drawn from the National Academy of Sciences and established by Congress to lead the way to healthcare reform, has recommended only increased use of information technology and universal insurance. While these are certainly efficiencies they are not the kind of meaningful, effective, or creative change that our system needs. Those come only with different eyes.

It's the same in other areas; recommendations for repairing all of our ailing systems center on regulations designed to make the working of the system more efficient and in line with our mechanical model. We do not see the fallacies: that regulation continues the mechanical approach; that it leads to inbred defensive adaptations; and that treating a CASY objectively as a machine is abuse.

Education is the most time tested way of coping with the increased complexity we find in our long human history. As people learn about the elements in their environment giving them a safe space to play with them has always led to the greatest progress. Such play is a stimulus to entrepreneurship and encouraging entrepreneurs is generally seen as the most successful way to help an economy progress. This represents the creative pole of adaptation. Educating a people about the unconscious role of paradigms and the way they influence thought patterns is also the first step in opening Kuhn's translation process that enables a better understanding of others who see differently.

CHAPTER 2
Elementary my Dear Watson— NOT!

I am convinced that the nations and people who master the new sciences of complexity will become the economic, cultural, and political superpowers of the next century.
Heinz Pagels. *The Dreams of Reason.* 1988

The significant problems we face cannot be solved at the same level of thinking we were at when we created them.
Albert Einstein

Fifty years ago a group of anthropologists, mathematicians, biologists, and engineers met to try to find a better way to deal with some of the problems of the mechanical reductionist model. Society had become more complex as the number of elements in our systems increased, and especially as the elements shifted increasingly from mechanically oriented ones to those involving people. The old analytical model lost its ability to predict. Even Sherlock Holmes' renowned ability to connect the dots couldn't keep up with the task. Top down hierarchical controls no longer worked, and when complicated global financial investments were on the line the need for better models became critical. Funded by the Macy Foundation, which had ties to international business and felt these needs, the group was formed to find a better way to deal with these unpredictable situations. The concept of systems, and especially complex systems, grew from their work. They defined a *system* as a configuration of parts connected and joined together and functioning as a unit. They described a continuum of systems extending from the simple and mechanical at one end to chaotic systems at the other.

Simple mechanical systems have linear related elements, like the gears in an old clock that allow for accurate prediction and control from the top or outside. At the other extreme the elements in chaotic systems are unrelated, they are unpredictable, and, like the turbulence of class 6 rapids, there is no control. Unlike the orderly motion of the planets the elements of chaotic systems have no order and there is little or no discernible relationship among their elements.

Complex adaptive systems—CASYs

In between these two extremes, but closer to the chaotic, there is a class of systems that relate in complex ways with many interacting elements. The elements here are more stable than in chaotic systems; they interact with each other and form networks of interrelationships. This place of relative stability is called the zone of complexity. In a particular region of this zone of complexity there are also found systems having the ability to read and adapt to their environment—these systems are alive. Living systems have many interrelated elements that are stable enough that they can relate in novel ways, as do complex systems in nature, but these differ from those in the physical world, like weather systems, because of the qualities of being alive: they reproduce, use food to grow and maintain an inner environment; living things are organized; and they have the ability to read, learn from, and adapt to their environment. This ability to sense and adapt to one's environment is a characteristic of life that doesn't make it on to all such lists because of the persistence of our mechanical way of seeing, but it is a critical part of being alive from the CASY point of view.

Mechanical systems can't adapt; their responses can only be programmed. Living agents adapt, they are CASYs and so are the systems that they create, from the biofilm of bacteria, to ant and bee colonies, to flocks, herds, primate groups, and the ecosystem as a whole. And so too are the social systems we make as humans, from the tribe to the team and from the family to the corporation. And when these systems become stable enough they join in forming industry wide CASYs like our healthcare, education, and defense systems. Each of these emergent CASYs is made up of agents, and the agents are CASYs at their own levels. Nested like Russian dolls inside of ever larger systems these CASYs have different elements, functions, and contexts, but they all have some common characteristics.

Those studying CASYs point out that: first of all they adapt; they are emergent in that they can create something new; they are unpredictable; and they are sensitive to changes in their contexts, especially to their initial conditions. These early conditions are important because as the systems grow in layers and are integrated into networks to become more complex their influence is multiplied exponentially.

But as stated earlier, the approach of these first systems theorists was not to find a different way of seeing; it was primarily analytical and mechanical. Like the ancient astronomers they saw their task as dealing with and explaining the problems. The systems they proposed were only a tool that helped them to better understand the problems. They were deeply into the analytical way of seeing; they tried, and continue trying, to get a handle on the increased complexity by using ever more powerful computers to build ever more complex models that incorporate ever more networked variables. They saw solutions in trying to match the complexity of nature. They did not see the problems as anomalies needing a new paradigm and could not see another way of dealing with systems than the analytical.

There are complex systems in nature like weather patterns and saturated solutions that come close to fitting the CASY description because the number and interrelationship of their elements is large enough that they are nearly impossible to predict, but weather patterns are largely predictable, especially with the new and powerful computer models that incorporate more of the known variables. These natural systems come close to qualifying as CASYs, but they fail in that they have not led to any novelty. Large simulation programs can give us good ideas of the complex interplay of why and how storms form, and the analysts' hope is to be able to do the same thing with all complex systems, even CASYs. We wish them luck. While systems in nature are affected by changes in their environments, like storms being influenced by the temperature of the oceans under them, living agents are much more complex and less predictable than the inanimate complex systems found in nature—their adaptation can produce novelty.

In the mechanical model a system is broken down into its parts and the parts are analyzed. With the understanding gained we feed our systems, maintain them, and regulate them, and adjust their many elements in order to optimize output. We put gas in our cars, change the oil regularly, and regulate them with the steering wheel, brake and accelerator; and NASCAR teams endlessly fine tune the many elements in their vehicles to win their races. In the same way scientists working on anti-inflammatory drugs analyzed the body and tried to find ways to fine tune a particular reaction. But the parts in a CASY are interrelated with networked connections that are cut and forgotten in the process of analysis, so treating one part often has unintended consequences elsewhere; a very good anti-inflammatory drug also resulted in more heart attacks.

Our multibillion dollar biotech industry is based on the analytical idea of one gene coding for one protein, and the hope of this vast industry is to profit from altering faulty genes that cause disease. But geneticists are now realizing that genes too are complex in their relationships and that focusing on one is just as risky as analyzing one part of the inflammatory chain.

In the mechanical model the 'machine' is an object with simple linear relationships that can be controlled, modified, adjusted, and played with, by an outside agent to improve its performance. When this model is applied to living agents, however, we enter into the situation that Kant called abusive and Zimbardo called evil. The object of the adjustment in this case is a living agent who is objectified and depersonalized in the process. If they are a child we use behavior modification techniques to change their behavior; if they are adults we similarly modify their behavior overtly with rewards and punishments, or covertly with advertising that threatens their self-image, or their acceptance or membership in a group; if they oppose such treatment we persuade, coerce, ostracize, imprison, or kill them, like we did with the American Indians.

The psychological prelude to such treatment is the necessity of making the other agent into something less than us, less than human, Zimbardo's step toward evil: the Indians were savages, the Jews were vermin, the Tutsi were cockroaches, the states opposing us are the Axis of Evil. On the simplest level we use antibiotics to kill bacteria, and both good and bad bacteria are killed, and the survivors develop resistance. On a higher level we use sanctions or war to coerce countries like Iraq and Cuba, but sanctions hurt both leaders and the people, and lead to hostile relations and more determined enemies. If our view is limited to the mechanical we see such action as the only way to bring about the desired results; it applies force where needed to maintain the balance or insure compliance. But as we should be able to see from antibiotic resistant bacteria, our own failed social experiment with imprisonment to change behavior, or the morass in Iraq, the approach doesn't work well.

CASYs are best treated, not by analysis and regulation directed at them, but by understanding the nature of these systems and how they adapt, and altering their context in ways that promote healthy adaptations; and not by defining them as less than a living adapting agent. This latter task is the fundamental rule for behavior in living with and working with complex adaptive systems. Seeing these agents or systems differently is a critical first step in resolving the problems we have with them.

The evolution of systems

Complexity comes with choices. The more options one has the greater the difficulty or complexity of choosing between them. The fewer options or elements the simpler is the choice. Life was simple a few hundred thousand years ago. People lived in small groups that hunted and gathered what food was available, and moved around when it wasn't. The simplest form of language was sufficient for sharing labor and specifying tasks. There were no classes or other forms of social inequality. This was the life described in the Biblical "Garden of Eden" or the mythical 'golden age' of many cultures, and mostly it was simple enough that we didn't even need a mental model.

Many psychological theorists, from Freud, Erickson, Piaget, Vygotsky, to Bandura, have looked at the stages that we all grow through to some degree or another as individuals, and more recently Ken Wilbur has suggested that we went through similar stages in our social and cultural development as human societies. The earliest stage is *survival* and is centered on eating: infants put everything in their mouths and early hunter-gatherer people ate whatever was available. Families are necessary for mammalian infants to survive and early mankind formed tribal groups for the same purpose. Held together by outside threats they learned to sacrifice to the higher powers to mitigate the threats as they entered what some have called the stage of *magic*. Children too go through a stage, well demonstrated by the success of Harry Potter, where anything is possible.

But we also have brains that soon enough show us the weaknesses of magic. We can see the regularities of nature and our early ancestors, and all of us, make models of nature that allows us to manipulate it; we cultivate crops and domesticate animals, and as infants we learn how to manipulate our families. As we grow socially we learn the fundamental necessities of life: which plants are OK to eat, which help when we were sick, the rudiments of first aid and the social taboos. Much of this learning is unconscious or preconscious and learned by copying behavior, by what is called mirror learning, and by seeing which behaviors work—like how a baby learns to smile at the camera by seeing how happy it makes its parents. This preconscious learning is called informal education and it is how we all learned the values and behaviors that make up our respective cultures.

The number of choices increased and ancient societies became more complex when they gave up wandering. Planting and herding allowed them to stay in one area and accommodate larger numbers. Builders and potters and brick-makers were needed as towns and cities were built. Being in one place allowed for the development of fermentation skills and spurred the arts. These and other institutions emerged from the creative adaptations of the agents at the time. Society became more complex. And the process continues today as children grow and interact with others outside the immediate family, and expand the patterns they have learned in family interactions.

An important emergent concept that arose from stationary society was that of private property. It had a survival value for the industrious individual that changed the orientation from the family group or tribe to the industrious or charismatic individual; and it introduced social classes and the hostility between the propertied aristocratic farmer and the wandering herder or peasant that has carried on from Cain and Abel to our own west. The number of elements in society increased along with its complexity; and it became more structured. The stage of *power* began as individuals rose to the top in this social structure and began to concentrate authority. On an individual level this is reflected by the shift in orientation of growing children from the family to the peer group with their inherent social hierarchy, and sometimes to the gang.

Larger communities also spurred communication. While hunter-gatherers could communicate with simple sounds, like the clicking sounds common in the African San community, communicating more complex ideas required a more precise language. Property needed to be marked and laborers needed to be told how to better work it—and a warrior class was needed to protect it. Plato called them the guardians and also pointed out the need for a worker class, and of course a governing class he called the philosopher kings. He neglected to mention the slaves that his society was built on, just as those in India didn't talk about the "Untouchables" who cleaned their cities of their daily sewage and waste.

Everyone had their place in these early societies; it was determined by the social order of the family and there was little mobility. As we have seen, it reflected the hierarchy seen in God's ordering of the heavens. Aristotelian science expanded on this social order to the point that everything in nature was also secured in its own proper place. It was the way they saw things—it was their paradigm. These early class structures introduced authorities and the necessity of obedience. This was the stage of *power*.

The arbitrary use of power by these authorities, however, needs restraint. In family life this balance is most often provided by the power of the parents as they interact with the outside world in protecting the child. Long ago leaders like Hammurabi, Moses, and Confucius, parents to our differing cultures, came up with rules for living that limited the powers, introduced some degree of fairness and balance, and promoted the value of the community. These inspired leaders introduced a stage that centered on *law and order*.

Mental models and the real world

These stages of development are paradigms for the people in them; they are ways of seeing and relating to one's outside world. But all models or paradigms have weaknesses in that there are always things from the real world that don't fit into them; that's why we move from one to the other as we grow. Industrious individuals from the dike building Netherlands and independent thinkers from the Italian city-states who capitalized on the cross pollination introduced from the Arab world, broke through the class structure that dominated the stages of authority or power, and law and order, to begin the fragmentation of the whole system. The crack created by these economic and philosophical adventurers eventually led to the greater questioning seen in the Renaissance, the Reformation, and the Industrial Revolution; and it empowered the stage of *autonomy* that had been introduced earlier by Augustine but overwhelmed by the church.

The Copernican Revolution and the Renaissance prompted a rethinking about the Aristotelian world view. The Reformation turned this rethinking to the world of religion and introduced the ability of the agent to choose his form of religious observance, an autonomous idea that continued spreading to the area of governance. Religious ideas became something people could discuss, rather than being dictated by the gods and their priests. Political leaders also lost the sanctity and power that had been theirs with the 'divine right of kings.' In this and in the Industrial Revolution that followed, people were expected to think for themselves. Life and society became more mobile and much more complex. Specialized workers and tradesmen, who formed the early guilds and organizations like the Masons, were able to offset some of the power of the propertied upper class. Trained in their protestant revolts they had tasted autonomy and wanted more of it; they formed a middle class and fostered democratic ideas. The parallel with our own individual development continues as young adults today are introduced into a complex world and expected to make their way on their own.

With the questioning of Aristotelian science the world with all of its interacting and related systems was added to the elements with which mankind could play, even to the point, according to Francis Bacon, of torturing it to get at its secrets. Technological advances like the printing press added to the complexity by making more information available to more people. Formal education was needed to help deal with these tasks and provided then, as it still does, the foundations of social mobility.

All of this tumult that western societies have experienced over the last five hundred years came from changes in how we saw the world. They were not primarily changes in the physical world, nor the social world, though they had effects in these areas. They were changes in the paradigms of the people as they adapted to these new and unsettling ideas.

People living in each of these stages built a model of their world in their heads, and it defined their world and what was possible in it. In the early models there was little or no sense of discrimination among the different classes because that was just the way things were. God ordered the Universe in that all heavenly bodies had their place around the earth; nature was ordered with everything in its place below mankind; and people were in their place as determined by their family's social position. Their model was congruent with their reality, but their reality, as is ours, is first of all a mental construct—it's a paradigm.

There was little of what today's psychologists call cognitive dissonance in these early cultures. Cognitive dissonance occurs when we consciously recognize that something doesn't fit in our mental model. When this happens we can either ignore it, modify it to fit our paradigm, or modify our paradigm to make it more congruent with reality—and the choice is largely framed by one's orientation or alignment. A defensive alignment tends to concentrate resources on dealing with the threat and to ignoring new data, or manipulating to make it useful in ones defense, while a creative alignment leads to modifying ones own paradigm to make it more congruent with the real world. This is the goal in either case, but it is relatively easy in most societies to manipulate how we see the world instead of disturbing the way we think. That choice generally does not lead to a workable solution. The ancient Mediterranean Phocaeans knew the Earth was round and had data showing its accurate size, but it was ignored, or not seen, because it did not fit with the dominant model. This is an ever-present problem, especially when trust is in short supply and the alignment defensive.

Education and complexity

Informal education is the part that comes from parental and community activities in which the child is immersed; it perpetuates the culture and its paradigm and in most cases it is preconscious. In early cultures informal education was sufficient, but as more elements were added to society education needed a broader base that often introduced different ways of seeing the world.

Formal education, with teachers, was introduced when the elements became too numerous for informal education to handle, but it brought both new paradigms and the conflict that so often comes with them. Socrates, one of the more notable of these ancient teachers, was criticized and condemned to death for corrupting the young by teaching doctrines foreign to those held by his community. Albeit without such drastic consequences, reactionary school boards continue the problem today. In the best formal education, models are questioned and expanded to look beyond one's immediate culture; and it is best done in a safe place that supports a creative alignment as the student integrates the information into his or her paradigm. Seldom, in any CASY, does the diversity that benefits the larger system come from a defensive alignment. If the information comes gently, or from within the local system, it is more likely that the agents will play with it, incorporate it into their own model, and find more novel ways to use it in a peaceful evolution. But the school system that goes against its normally conservative and defensively aligned school board by teaching about the cultural models we all build is rare indeed.

Informal education, modeled by the family and culture and absorbed by the child, builds the first models or paradigms that we have of our world and perpetuates our various cultures; but it also handicaps our understanding of other cultures. We adapt by playing with elements in our environments and when those elements are limited so is our development. On a simpler level of CASY than culture, children whose informal education does not expose them to a wide variety of the elements in our world have a harder time adapting to that world. Those, for example, with little exposure to books have a harder time learning to read.

Socrates tried to expand the world of his students by adding more elements and critical ways of looking at them so that their future decisions would have a broader base in the real world rather than just being reliant on Athenian custom. But that was uncomfortable for those with a more limited paradigm and Socrates lost. Informal education with its local and limited paradigms, based on culture and custom, continues to have a strong influence on what is taught in all of our schools, and too often Socrates is sacrificed; and we sacrifice with him and his counterparts in our schools today an understanding of the important nature these mental models have in our lives. These models make up the mental part of our context and they are critical from the CASY perspective because they are the easiest part of the context to modify.

The goal of formal education is to provide the tools that help us deal better with our environment, like skills in reading, math, and science. In most formal education the operating cultural paradigm is unquestioned and education is limited to explaining the elements of the local environment within the constraints of the dominant paradigm. This limited view is the foundation of most of our differing cultures, our differing views of the world, and the reason behind most of our wars.

The mechanical model

In this unconscious way we learned to see and treat the world and those in it mechanically. Beginning about 300 years ago as mankind entered into the stage of autonomy our ancestors began playing with their world more fully. They made machines to do their bidding; ornate clocks became the center of every town. Newton's laws of motion explained how the forces of gravitation maintain planetary orbits and the gravitational effect on the pendulum controlled the working of a clock; more machines, the Industrial Revolution, and the mechanical paradigm followed. In this paradigm, as pointed out earlier, the system is taken apart down to its more predictable physical elements. As technology increased the parts became ever smaller and their numbers increased. Newton and his contemporary Leibniz independently came up with the tool of calculus that made the elements infinitesimal and their number infinite—at least in mathematics.

The best example of this mechanical paradigm is the early clock with all of its interrelated gears, each getting its input from one side and giving its output to the other. Adam Smith used this model to analyze the manufacture of a pin and Henry Ford used it to develop the assembly line, and it continues today to be the basis of most top-down organizations. Order is imposed from the top, or from outside, in mechanical systems. God wound up the universe in the Deistic Newtonian mechanical paradigm, and it's been running like a clock ever since.

If we can take things apart enough, says this model, we will be able to know the end from the beginning—everything will be predictable. This kind of analysis is the fundamental goal of mechanical systems and the idea permeates our world. When Adam Smith showed how financial forces and self-interest led to a marketplace of commodities he was applying the mechanical paradigm to the economy. When Darwin showed how the forces of natural selection led to evolution he applied it to biology. Marx applied it to history with his concept of historical determinism; and when America's founding fathers incorporated checks and balances and separation of powers into the Constitution they applied it to politics. We have witnessed the failure of Marx's analytical interpretation of history and are experiencing today the shortcomings of relying on self-interest in our economy, but we have not seen the common denominator in the mechanical interpretation of our various systems.

Limits to the mechanical model

Cause and effect has been the foundation of our mental models since the world began and the mechanical paradigm has been its latest refinement over the last five hundred years. But models need to be as accurate as possible. The mechanical paradigm works well when dealing with the physical world, but there are problems even here as the systems get more refined and complex and we have to introduce the quantum world and indeterminacy. It works best with linear relations where, like the cogs in a gear box, influence is direct and limited. When the number of elements increases and they are networked rather than linear in their relationships we rapidly lose the ability to predict outcome. Philip Anderson, a physicist dealing with complex problems, points out that the difficulty in his work is rooted in the fact that "combinatorial numbers are bigger than cosmic numbers;" complex systems in nature are networks. Our biggest computer networks now deal with 'terabytes' of information. That's a trillion bytes, enough to hold about a million books such as this, one with twelve following zeros. In contrast the possible combinations in the ordering of a deck of cards is on the order of eight with sixty-seven zeros; and that doesn't include the possibilities of the combinations using less than the whole deck. Combinatorial numbers are bigger than cosmic numbers. When one is dealing with complex living adapting agents that have had time to play with and integrate their networked relationships the chance of reliable prediction approaches zero.

Networking and unpredictability introduce uncertainty where action on one element can introduce unintended consequences elsewhere. NAFTA, for example, was intended to increase trade between the U.S. and Mexico, an increase that was proposed to benefit the economy of both nations. But it had the consequence, seen by a few, but either not seen or ignored by those benefiting and their patrons making the policy, of displacing many small Mexican farmers who could not compete with mass produced and subsidized American corn. Instead of benefiting Mexico the displaced farmers forced the cost of labor down in both countries as impoverished citizens entered the labor force in Mexico without the benefit of labor laws and, mostly illegally, crossed the border into the US in order to find work. This migration of workers will then have other effects on the divided families, where the children will wind up getting their support from local gangs instead of parents. Few see effects that are down the chain from an initial act because few see the many interrelated connections in these networks and even fewer see in terms of an agent's adaptation. Most are blind to this, choosing, in NAFTA's case, to focus on the single aspect of increasing markets for subsidized American produce—and it is the large industrialized producers that both framed the policy and reap the benefits.

Vioxx, similarly, performed well at its planned function of reducing inflammation and pain, but it also came back to bite us in the rear by increasing heart attacks. The more interacting elements there are in a system the more likely there will be problems with unintended consequences when, as with Vioxx or NAFTA, one or two elements are taken out of context to become the focus of play while all of their networked connections are severed and ignored. Maps model the territory, but the mechanical model cannot accurately represent this territory—the elements of CASYs and their network of interrelationships have expanded to the point where we cannot keep track of all the connections; the combinatorial numbers that

Anderson talks about have overwhelmed our computational capacities. And even if we were able to control the numbers we still have no way to handle the emergence of novelty that is a potential in all CASYs. Top down control is no longer possible. People are in the equation now far more than they were in the past and people are not mechanical—they adapt.

The goal of the mechanical paradigm, of understanding the whole from the working of the parts, would be much more attainable if relationships were always linear, where agents interact with just their neighbors, and if all the relationships had equal weight, but they aren't, and they don't; at least not when the agents are CASYs in their own right. All CASYs come with Anderson's combinatorial capabilities—the combinatorial numbers that overwhelm the cosmic numbers—and applying mechanical analysis to their control, with managers maintaining a top to bottom order in corporations, government, the military, education, and in virtually all aspects of society, is an exercise in frustration for all involved. The Soviet Union tried and failed to manage an economy in that way.

People in these organizations are often treated more as objects than individuals, but as Kant pointed out, that's abuse, and as Zimbardo points out, it's evil. Not just people, but all CASY agents respond defensively to such treatment.

In a friendly environment a defensive alignment leads to gaming the system; in an unfriendly one it leads to an arms race. Either way society, or the larger system, loses. More and more we are seeing that analytical and mechanical controls don't work well when we are dealing with complex systems like ecosystems. We need to realize that they work even less well with other people—they use the wrong model.

Leaders in international business began to recognize this many years ago because it was costing them. They sponsored the meetings that fifty years ago gave birth to "systems thinking." Many books in the business field now deal with networking rather than hierarchical organization. Networking is the foundation of novelty; novelty is what the entrepreneur takes to the marketplace; novelty is what makes poor nations wealthy. We now realize this. The failure of the mechanical model in business and finance is accepted, but proposed new business models often do little more than apply mechanically based computer models to business. Even the 'organismic' model promoted by Peter Senge of the MIT Sloan School of Management and the Society for Organizational Learning, does not seem to realize the central importance of the agent's/organism's adaptability. The failure of the mechanical model in the business community is a glaring anomaly, but we have no clear alternative with which to replace it.

Larger institutions, like governments and societies, have similar problems. Long ago Aristotle described government and other institutions using metaphors from life, probably because his father was a physician, but they are described today in analytical terms. We measure their parts, like percent unemployed, or their output, like Gross Domestic Product, that are more appropriate for the mechanical analytical paradigm. These measures are good at showing how well the system is working mechanically, but do little to tell how healthy it is. The 15% of our GDP that we spend on health care and the significant recent increases in the costs of health care and pharmaceuticals make these measures appear even better, but the system is hardly healthy; it's like taking pride in the growth of our cancer. We leave it to small poor nations like Bhutan to rebel against these measures and replace them with their Gross Domestic Happiness index.

Despite these drawbacks we continue seeing these issues as problems. They are not only problems! They're anomalies! And they cry out for a new way of seeing.

Dealing with CASYs

The operative word in the CASY phrase is *adaptive*. Mechanical systems can't adapt; there is no choice, no learning, and no adaptation. But all living things can read their environment, learn from it, and adapt to it—it's a characteristic of life. And adaptation occurs both defensively and creatively on many different levels as CASY agents play with the elements of their own peculiar systems.

"Agent" is the term used to describe the acting participant in a CASY. It may be easier to substitute "person" in its place, but one of our major points is that all life forms, even bacteria, are CASYs in their own particular spheres. So too are our immune systems, our brains, and on to the social structures that CASYs create. While our courts may identify corporations as persons and thereby grant them immortality (which eliminates a part of their nature as CASYs), they are in fact CASY agents on a higher level of complexity. And the different levels go on when human institutions, like corporations, form groups like our banking, healthcare, and educational systems. These too are CASYs as our systems analysts have discovered. Anything alive or made up of living agents can be seen as a CASY.

Biological metaphors are more useful than mechanical ones in our increasingly complex world because our interactions with the physical world are decreasing while those with other CASYS are increasing—and they all adapt. Darwinian evolution looks mostly at the defensive adaptations that helped the agent to survive. But there is another pole of adaptation in CASYs, toward diversity, that is less understood.

Creative adaptation

Just as natural selection promotes the defensive adaptations that aid survival it also promotes the creative adaptations that lead to workable novelty and diversity. What is commonly called emergence occurs most often when CASYs on their many levels join together with other agents in their respective systems and have time to play with the various elements available to them to create something more diverse and complex; and the processes behind this appear overwhelmingly cooperative. Peter Senge takes the extreme position: "People as individuals don't create anything. Creation, or bringing something new into being[,] is always a product of human communities." Natural selection results in the survival and expansion of both these processes, defensive and creative, if they work. But while the survival benefit goes to the individual and its progeny in the case of defensive adaptations, it is more often the larger system that benefits from the increased complexity associated with the creative adaptation. The evolutionary drive appears equally strong in both dimensions.

When the ancient bacteria that had adapted to use light energy to form carbohydrates, and others that had adapted to use those carbohydrates for energy, gave up their independent life to be engulfed in a much larger cell, they became the chloroplasts that distinguish the cells in the plant kingdom, and the mitochondria that are the centers for energy production in all cells—they cooperated and nature benefited. It became more complex as cellular life emerged and diverged into plants and animals. Perhaps the same forces behind this step are represented in the atom, with its quantum rules, giving up its independent existence and those quantum rules to create a larger molecule with a different set of rules. This is the process of emergence and it helps the system, often at the expense of the individual agent. Nature is characterized by defensive adaptations on the one hand that enhance the individual's success, and creative diversity on the other that enhance the system's success. Both are tested in nature by natural selection and those with a survival advantage are promoted.

Social CASYs, those that lower order CASYs form by cooperation, also reflect the polarities of survival and diversity. All CASYs on all levels like to maintain their own existence or autonomy and become defensively aligned when threatened, like bacteria do in the presence of an antibiotic, or like we American's did after 9/11. Given a safe place in which to live and play CASYs on all levels are more likely to cooperate and adapt toward greater complexity and greater networking, even to the point of sacrificing themselves for a greater good.

While maintaining these polarities CASYs also adapt at their different levels. Bacteria adapt by playing with their DNA. When threatened they respond defensively by speeding their mutation rate by up to 50,000 times to increase the potential of developing a solution to the threat; and when they are not threatened they creatively seek for better ways to recycle the elements in their worlds. Our immune systems work defensively when they recognize a threat and turn on defensive measures like a fever, diarrhea or rhinorrhea to deal with it; or creatively at the level of immune cells which learn to recognize invading toxins, viruses, or bacteria and build specific proteins that help us neutralize these environmental challenges as well as remember them for future reference. The enculturation of children can be seen as a defensive adaptation. Children adapt to their culture in thought patterns and behavior; if they didn't they would be seen as different, as outsiders—as strangers. Older children adopted into a different culture are outsiders and are likely to have problems adjusting since both their social and their mental contexts are changed.

It takes longer to establish the type of community that allows for creative adaptation. Our focus remains on survival so children defensively adapt to their culture, and when corporations adapt they do so defensively by entering into new contracts, restructuring, layoffs, or a variety of other maneuvers aimed at increasing efficiency and profits. This is easier than creating novelty.

On all levels there are significant differences between defensively and creatively aligned adaptations. Defensive adaptations are more often a response to a recognized challenge—bacteria to antibiotics, the immune system to an infection, or a corporation to competition. Emergence, on the other hand, "the creation of something new", as Carl Jung put it, "is not accomplished by the intellect but by the play instinct acting from inner necessity. The creative mind plays with the objects it loves." We would substitute 'agent' for Jung's use of 'intellect' because this is not, as he says, a cognitive intellectual process. The creative agent is at work here, playing with the elements of their environment. Bacteria have no brain as we know it, but they can sense a threat and mount defenses when they are in a colony. The immune system has no brain, but it learns. Creative play is something done in a safe place, "from inner necessity," and as Senge points out it's done in a cooperative community of agents, whether they be bacteria, immune cells, or a group at work. This is not our normal state of mind; that is one of vigilance, of paying attention to our environment for any threats—and one has a hard time playing when threatened. Creative play requires a safe environment.

Mechanical systems are evaluated by how efficiently they produce the desired output. CASYs are evaluated, not by measuring their output, nor by taking them apart and analyzing the components, but by the processes of natural selection—by seeing if they work. And they are most successfully treated, not by regulation, which threatens the CASY's autonomy, but by making small changes in their contexts in a non threatening way that preserves and supports the agent's creative alignment, and allowing time for them to adapt. Nobel Prize winner Muhammed Yunus did this when he started the Grameen Bank that centers on small loans to entrepreneurs in developing countries. He added the significant element of capital to these peoples' context and allowed them to adapt. When CASYs are allowed to adapt to non-threatening changes in their environments the results are more likely to be the emergence of novelty that benefits the whole system.

We easily accept the fact that people are complex, but complexity theory has not been particularly friendly in showing us how to deal with them. The group that came up with the systems approach to our organizations was sponsored by the Macy Foundation, with mostly business interests; they saw how businesses were increasingly networked, but they continued the analytical method of connecting the dots even though it is an impossible task to trace causality when the dots are networked—it takes time to see differently. Once we began looking at systems we soon saw those that were CASYs—the systems that were emergent, adaptable, and, even with large computer models, unpredictable—they are alive or made up of living agents, but we still tried to analyze and deal with them mechanically.

Treating CASYs as machines

Analysts looking at our systems, especially our ecosystems, have concluded that many of our problems with them are due to our mechanical model. In ecosystems many compensatory systems have become unbalanced before the system crashes and we recognize a problem. The same holds true for our economy. Restoring the system is not done by addressing the immediate precipitate to the crash, something else is needed—often something that doesn't seem to fit, like getting rid of the fish in phosphate polluted lakes.

In human systems the mechanical treatment of conscious agents—which breaks the system down into its parts, which sees and treats CASY agents as objects, which tries to regulate their behavior, limit their options, and control their output—is seen as a threat to their autonomy. It is easy to see this on a personal level. We don't like it when we are objectified and treated as if our own feelings, wants, and wishes were immaterial. We understand why Kant called it abuse and Zimbardo evil. This is why, as our economists, business leaders, and social scientists are finding out, financial incentives are problematic—insufficient pay leads to hostility, but even rewards can be used in a mechanical manipulative manner that treats the agent as an object. Treating any CASY in this way prompts a defensive alignment.

The unpredictable events that often follow mechanical treatment occur in part because the agents that make up CASYs read these mechanical interventions as threats and resist them by whatever means is possible, so such treatment is seldom as simple as first thought and often leads to unintended consequences. In this way, for example, our intervention in Iraq has become a *cause célèbre* for fundamentalist Islamic jihadists that has vastly increased their numbers and the potential for more acts of terrorism, an opinion expressed unanimously by the 16 agencies of our intelligence community in their consensus report, the *National Intelligence Estimate.* But while the new science of complexity helps us to recognize and understand the dynamics of how this happens it has provided little help on how to deal with CASY agents in a healthier way; so we continue treating them mechanically, as objects, and our systems continue getting more distressed.

CASY models

Science is trying to find ways to cope with complexity, but is doing so mostly from a mechanical point of view—by analysis of the elements in the particular system. Helping this approach are larger and faster computers that enable more and more elements to be included in ever more complex computer models. But no one has found out yet how to give computers the ability to love and play with these elements to create something new.

Mathematics has a branch that deals with complex problems. Like the game of chess such problems have so many variables that solving them in the traditional way is not a possibility. Computer programs now enable mathematicians to play with different elements in these problems and to plot their different solutions. What they find is that the solutions plot into wonderful patterns, like the wings of a butterfly, which show the presence of seeming 'centers of interest' for the system. These centers are called *attractors* and they play a large role in the science of complexity. Adding more variables to these systems leads to *strange attractors.* Attractors show stable patterns, but in strange attractors the patterns evolve over time.

The variety of human cultures and religions, and the mostly unconscious limits they place upon their agents, reflect the strength of these attractors in our own CASYs. Our cultures have their own patterns, just like the attractors, but as we become a global society the variables that establish the attractors for our differing cultures are multiplied—they are becoming strange attractors—and, often with a great deal of resistance, our cultures are evolving. These tools from complex mathematics help us to better understand what is happening in our world, but they don't provide much help for planning or purposeful action. It is difficult if not impossible to apply the understanding of attractors to a model that helps us plan global economics because neither the actions nor the results are specific; the same action can lead to different results so accurate prediction of effect remains unlikely. Other tools from mathematics are similarly handicapped.

The branch of mathematics called 'game theory' provided Noble Prize winning John Nash, of "A Beautiful Mind" fame, a better model for economics. Game theory deals with probability and odds, and introduces the flexibility of chance and choice—it deals with *conscious* play. Applying game theory to our CASYs in economics shows how agents in them work by "gaming the system."

Gaming the system

Most often such "gaming" has a bad connotation, as when farmers, or doctors, welfare recipients, and financial agents game their respective regulatory and mechanical systems for their own benefit. Gaming is defensively aligned playing with the elements of ones' system aimed at enhancing the agent's survival. To be fair, some Enron whiz kids may have been moral individuals who were just caught up in gaming California's power grid, but the company recordings monitoring their work show that they had every understanding of the effects of their play on the people of

California. They, just as the guards in the Stanford Prison experiment or at Abu Ghraib, were rapidly polluted by the bad barrel they worked in as they gamed their elements for their own advantage and succumbed to the perceived power of objectifying and being superior to another human.

Gaming, in a mechanical regulatory framework, means cheating. This derogatory label comes from the power structures that have set up the environment and the rules for play, rules that are mostly designed to force behavior in certain directions. Agents, however, adapt to their environments; and they adapt by playing with the elements available to them at their particular level. When that environment is perceived as manipulative but not too hostile the agents will game it to maximize their survival. It's what Enron agents did; it's what welfare recipients do; it's what doctors and hospitals do, it's what lobbyists and politicians do. Gaming is the play in how agents adapt—it's what CASYs do in a friendly regulatory environment and further regulation is not going to stop it; more regulation just enriches the playing field. The task is not to stop the play, but to keep the gaming creatively aligned.

But neither does the understanding of gaming lend itself to building a model for purposive action. While we are continuing to learn more about how human behavior adapts in complex systems using game theory, it's hard to defend a model designed to help one make critical decisions that is based on gaming. Soviet foreign policy during the Cold War was often compared to a chess game. In such games offensive and defensive maneuvers dominate the play so there is little room for creative play. In the Cold War the defensive alignment led to adaptations that increased the size and power of the military on both sides, at the ultimate expense of both sides; and likely the rest of the world as well because we continue to see the peace that came from the threat of mutually assured destruction as successful.

Complex mathematics and game theory try to deal with CASYs by looking at the variables, the elements of the systems. They are a bottom up approach that continues in the framework of the mechanical analytical model by looking at the parts—but the parts are increasingly CASYs in their own right.

There is another way to look at the problem that comes from biology. More accurately it comes from the cross-pollination of biology and computer modeling. Using metaphors from biology is encouraged by people dealing with CASYs because they are more appropriate than mechanical images.

"Boid" rules

When Craig Reynolds used separation, cohesion, and alignment to model a flock of birds (he called them 'boids') for his computer programs he didn't think about their application in the human world, but both we and the birds are CASYs. Separation means keeping enough space between the birds that they can fly; cohesion means that if space is available the bird would move to the center; and alignment means that the flock goes in the same general direction at the same speed. These rules describe the complex behavior we call flocking and enable flocks of birds and schools of fish to be modeled on a computer, but while we may resent being compared to a flock of birds, the rules apply to all CASY behavior. The clear simplicity of these rules belies their significance.

Separation allows agents their own space in which to function, recognizes their autonomy, and dampens hostility. Evolutionary adaptations long ago developed a cell membrane that separated the agent from its environment. A necessary adaptation, it expanded so that all life forms have a skin, or bark, or something separating them from the external environment—it defines the individual. We have homes or shelters that wall our families off from the rest of our communities. China, East Germany, Israel, and now the United States used, and use this approach by building walls to define their borders.

Cohesion is related to external threat because the center of the group is always the safest place when predators are about, and the size of the group is often a deterrent to the predator. European finches form large dense flocks to avoid predatory hawks while those on the Galapagos, where there are fewer predators, group only to better find food. Cohesion is a defensive adaptation because animals at the top of their respective food chains, where there is little outside threat, aren't cohesive and don't have flocking behavior. Some cohesion also enables the group to feed more effectively so lions are more likely to hunt in groups when food is scarce. This rule also helps define the group because without cohesion the members disperse and the group is gone. Jews and Muslims are less group-conscious in America than in many other countries because they are less threatened. Japanese leaders prior to WW II misread American diversity and thought that we could not be pulled together enough to be an effective enemy. The cohesiveness that followed their bombing of Pearl Harbor proved them wrong and led to what we call our greatest generation despite the internment of Asian Americans and the continued segregation of African Americans.

Primitive mammal grouping was an adaptation needed to care for their relatively helpless offspring, but these social units also functioned to provide food in times of scarcity and defense when there was a threat; and they continue today largely to supply these same needs. Social cohesion benefits the members of the group by helping to supply their needs and is directly related to external threat; it's a defensive adaptation that comes with a survival benefit for the members of the group.

Alignment implies a direction and a purpose. On the surface it is usually seen as looking for the next meal and, as we will see later in looking at healthcare, how systems are fed has a great influence on their alignment. But on a deeper level it gets back to the fundamental alignment seen in all of nature: increased complexity on the one hand

and survival on the other—or diversity and defense.

In the natural world there is much more diversity in the tropics than in the temperate zones. The tropics are generally richer in food sources and less challenging environmentally, factors more favorable to creative adaptations that translate to the greater diversity we see there. Conversely there are more environmental challenges and risks in temperate zones so the alignment there tends to defensive adaptations and less novelty. Life emerged in the tropics as creative diversity; society emerged in the temperate zones as a defensive adaptation. The differing alignments result from the differing environments and often appear mutually exclusive. In most cases the perception of threat effectively blocks the cooperative play that is associated with a creative alignment; except for passive defenses like camouflage it is not often that a defensively aligned agent focusing on self preservation finds a defense in diversity.

Defensive adaptations allow the agent to survive better. It can run faster, or longer, or has some other trait that gives it a survival benefit over others in the system. The agent and its offspring are the primary beneficiaries, and such adaptations are also refined and strengthened by their inbreeding. Only as this family expands does the larger system see a benefit. With creative adaptations, which add niches and diversity, the benefit to the system occurs earlier. Both defensive and creative adaptations are tested by natural selection and must have a survival benefit of some sort to be continued.

Reynolds' three rules may be simple, but they provide insight on how to influence all complex adaptive systems because all CASY agents follow these rules. They cannot be analyzed and controlled in a mechanical way, from the top down or from outside, but they can be seen from this boid's eye view to have rules that they follow. While the mechanical paradigm takes apart, analyzes and controls by regulation, this paradigm enables us to better understand the importance of the context; separation and cohesion have to do with the social, relational aspects of the context, and alignment has to do with the social and the mental. This understanding opens a new paradigm that honors, rather than regulates, their complexity, and utilizes common sense and principles of life, rather than mechanical regulations, to guide them.

The "boid" model and CASYs

The 'boid rules' can model complex adaptive behavior—they have been used successfully to route trucks and airplanes—but they also give us insight into the processes of life and nature; and they open the door to simple rules for dealing with CASYs on all levels. There are also other suggestions coming from analysts looking at our systems that are applicable to this way of seeing.

Paul Plsek is an analyst who looks at our healthcare system as a CASY. Writing in the appendix of the Institute of Medicine's *Crossing the Quality Chasm*, he proposes rules for us as we deal with CASYs. His first suggestion is to make sure that our rules for CASYs are simple, and Reynolds' rules are certainly that. Three other conditions for working with CASYs are: use metaphors from life, create an environment in which the system can evolve naturally over time, and set out a vision and create a space so that novelty can "emerge from local actions *within the system*" (emphasis added).

Metaphors from life

His first condition, using metaphors from life, demands that many of us change the way we look at life. Our current view is framed in the mechanical model. Doctors and scientists, for example, look at our own species in the way promoted by Jacques Monod, the Nobel Prize winning biochemist who worked out much of the way that DNA is read and translated into our various proteins. More than anyone else Monod was the father of the one gene-one protein concept that is now being replaced by one of interrelationships and complexity. At the time that he worked with them these basic elements appeared stable and linearly related; he was firmly in the mechanical model when he argued that: "the cell is a machine, the animal is a machine. Man is a machine."

Medicine follows this mechanical model, seeing imbalances in our body's functioning and using drugs to improve the balance. Looking at the body in this way medicine has followed the reductionist trend that analyzes our problems down to their most fundamental level. Today that means we look for genetic reasons for illness.

Of course there are genetic factors in illness, but they are usually complex in their expression. Phenylketonuria is a genetic disease that is routinely identified before newborn babies leave the hospital. If an infant is diagnosed with the problem they can now lead a normal life by avoiding foods having the amino acid phenylalanine; and all foods containing this simple building-block of protein carry a warning label. Sickle cell disease is a genetic disease; we even know the precise location of the faulty nucleic acid in the gene coding for hemoglobin. But sickle cell disease would be less of a problem it if it did not provide a survival benefit for those with malaria.

Our current epidemic of diabetes has a genetic base in our evolutionary history of periodic famines and annual dietary changes. The ability to change sugars into fat and store it was a decided benefit in a famine situation and enabled our ancestors to make it through many winters when the sugars we prefer were not available. We have all inherited to a greater or lesser degree this decreased ability to deal with sugar on a regular basis and would be able to avoid this epidemic if we could convince ourselves—contrary to our millennia of adapting (with the likelihood of genetic changes as well)—that we don't need the extra food that we store as fat for the coming famine. Genetic traits are factors in many conditions, but their expression is most often mediated by other factors.

Our current emphasis on genetic sources for illness is reminiscent of the Islamic story of the man on his hands and knees searching the street under a lamp post for his lost key. A passerby stopped to help and after a period of fruitless searching asked about the circumstances of the loss. The man said he thought he had lost it closer to his doorway. "Then why are you searching here?" questioned the helper. "Because there is more light here." In our case the light is funding and it tends to go with the latest technology. We need to realize that ours are not simple mechanical problems with one solution, but complex, like the rest of life.

We are CASYs with many variables—environmental, emotional, social, and spiritual—that are all factors in our diseases, not genetic machines with only one. This degree of complexity is what we need to remember when we use biological metaphors in describing CASYs.

These examples come from looking at the CASY that is our body, but the principle applies to all CASYs. Those looking at revitalizing local ecosystems are finding that analytical methods which address and try to balance various elements of the ecosystem are less effective than addressing its context, i.e., making sure the environment is safe is more effective than providing food for one of its distressed members. It is as likely that those trying to reboot our financial system will uncover the same problems. Reducing any CASY to its fundamental elements robs it of the richness of its networks and blinds us to its complex adaptive nature. CASYs are alive and adaptable and only when we include these elements in our metaphors will they truthfully reflect life.

Creating an environment for evolution—How to stimulate creative novelty

Mihalyi Csikszentmihalyi, in his books *Creativity* and *Flow,* points to the factors involved in the processes of creativity: engagement, incubation, insight, evaluation, and elaboration. The first of these, engagement, is something more than just being associated with the subject in question—it is a special state of mind that is associated with optimal awareness. Csikszentmihalyi calls it "flow," athletes call it the "Zone," and children call it "play."

Entering into this state has one requirement: there must be no perception of threat. Creative thought is blocked by the perception of danger. When CASY agents perceive a threat they stop processing their world and revert to primitive reflexes. Children become one with the mother or their primary defender. Adults commonly respond with the flight or fight response that is hard-wired in the primitive section of our brains that some call the reptilian brain. Threat shifts alignment to the defense which precludes the child from exploring and adapting to their environment and counters thoughtful processing of the threat in the adult. If the challenge is not seen as a major threat children are more likely to play with it and incorporate it into their world and adults are more likely to game it.

Athletes playing for high stakes are at risk here because as their focus shifts to the reward and the fear of its loss they have a problem getting in the "zone" that enhances their play. It's why coaches encourage the players to just "play the game," and may be part of the reason our high paid players are no longer able to dominate team sports with other countries where the player's egos are less defined by their salaries and teamwork is better developed.

Engagement means that one is immersed in the problem or task at hand. If the solution is not forthcoming then setting the problem aside consciously, or incubation, allows the unconscious to work on it while we enter a state of relaxation or mindless activity such as gardening or bathing. In this state our subconscious can present ideas suddenly to our consciousness as the "A-ha" experience, as dreams, or flashes of insight. A creative idea, says Csikszentmihalyi, needs to "percolate under the level of consciousness in a place where we have no way to make them obey our own desires or our own direction." Consciousness deals with our established models. Creativity often transcends consciousness. Many even think these flashes of insight come from God and ignore their evaluation, the critical fourth step—it's hard to evaluate ideas objectively when they have a divine origin.

Not just our own personal problems are answered in this way but many significant advances in the sciences came similarly. Jacques Hadamard was a prominent mathematician in the early part of the 20th Century. He was interested in the methods used by the great mathematicians of his day to come up with novelty in the cutting edge field of higher mathematics, so he asked his colleagues how they did it. Most of them explained their process as similar to those outlined much later by Csikszentmihalyi and earlier by Graham Wallace: first, spending the time necessary to familiarize themselves with the elements of the problem, of trying to work it out consciously (preparation); secondly, leaving it for a while and letting it 'percolate under the level of consciousness' (incubation), This was frequently followed by a flash of insight while they were distracted with something else, like shaving or relaxing in the bath (insight). The "A-ha", that propelled Archimedes from his bath to run naked shouting "Eureka" through the streets of ancient Syracuse resulted from the same process as that experienced by Hadamard's mathematicians. It is truly a Eureka—an "I found it!"—experience and is almost always accompanied by a feeling of certainty that it is indeed the right answer—even though many of them turn out to be wrong. One of Hadamard's more famous colleagues, Henri Poincaré, even cautioned about relying too much on this method because of the errors introduced by its subconscious play. Conscious and cognitive verification of the "A-ha" (verification) was always an integral, and final, part of this process in Hadamard's mathematicians, as it should well be for all those relying on it, even when it is considered of divine origin.

Advances in the field of mathematics are of interest because mathematicians were at the leading edge of those building the models of the world that we construct in our brains, at least until they started introducing curved space and 13 dimensions. They tried and failed to solve their problems by consciously playing with their elements, but because the solutions were often not in the framework available they had to come from somewhere else.

Einstein's response to Hadamard suggests that he could remain conscious through more of his inner processes. He told about the vagueness of the mental elements of the particular problems on which he was working, but he gave them form—"some of them are even muscular," he wrote. After Einstein died his brain was examined microscopically and the only significant difference between his brain and others was in the size of his parietal lobes which are associated with controlling muscle movement. It has been suggested that this playful use of his muscles may have been at the core of his genius.

Einstein explained to Hadamard that there "is, of course, a certain connection between those elements and relevant logical concepts." Being Einstein the "elements" he was dealing with likely represented the anomalous properties of light, mass, inertia, and energy whose properties and interactions were not adequately explained by the laws and models of physics of his day. And even Einstein had an "A-ha" when he realized that time was not a constant, but varied with velocity. "It is also clear that the desire to arrive finally at logically connected concepts is the emotional basis of this rather vague *play* with the above mentioned elements." The problem to him was like an environmental challenge—and he was adapting. "But taken from a psychological viewpoint, *this combinatory play seem[sic] to be the essential feature in productive thought*—before there is any connection with logical construction in words or other kinds of signs which can be communicated to others." (Emphases added).

Einstein's description of his own creative processes is congruent with Jung's description of creation as coming from the inner necessity of playing with the objects loved. This ability to play with the elements of one's environment, even when they are outside of consciousness, is a hallmark of complex adaptive systems and such play permeates, on its many levels, all of life and all of our CASYs—it's how we adapt. Bacteria play with their DNA, infants play with their neurons, teenagers play with their relationships, Einstein gave his muscles meaning and played with them—we all play with the elements of our world.

Einstein's response to Hadamard gave no mention and no credit to his wife, but those who knew him during this period of his life point to the fact that she was also a brilliant physicist. Many state the belief that his work, like the creative novelty that Senge talks about, was a cooperative venture.

Such cooperative play is particularly the case with the creative pole where the result is diversity and novelty that comes more from insight than cognition. In constrast, in our social CASYs where the elements are more visible and easier to manipulate the defensive pole is more often cognitive; we can identify the elements and how to use them for our advantage. Follow, for example, any lobbyist for a day as they use their elements—money, favors, influence, and power—to play with and manipulate their legislative environments. Such play panders to the defensive side of the politicians as they seek for more power, prestige, wealth, and re-election. A creative alignment relies on play just as much as the defensive; it too is based on this same type of playful, at times not even cognitive, manipulation of the elements of the system, but the play is more often by cooperating agents working in the system with no fear aspect that promotes the defenses.

In biology the conventional wisdom is that novelty comes from random mutation that is selected and expressed in future generations because of a survival benefit. But we know now that bacteria have some control over their rate of mutation and that there are particular areas of the DNA where mutation is more likely—it is not just random. We also know that people using lots of antibiotics have more of these rapidly mutating bacteria in their own GI tracts as they adapt to the threats in their own environment that are posed by the antibiotics. Seeing random mutation as the primary source of genetic novelty also ignores the significant part played by cooperation.

Cooperation and the plasmid model

Mutating bacteria commonly share their genetic novelty in packets called "plasmids" with others of their strain and even with other types of bacteria. They cooperate! This allows all the others to further refine the novelty to make it even more effective. And when our computer programmers use this plasmid model in projects like Linux and the Wikipedia they confirm its unparalleled efficacy and efficiency at propagating and improving novel diversity.

Lockheed Martin's legendary "Skunk Works," that came up with aircraft novelty from the U-2 to the Stealth, is a safe place that facilitates playing with ideas and cross-pollinating them with others. This kind of play applies the plasmid model to human situations.

Enron also provided a safe place where capable agents played with the elements of their environment. But the creative accounting and trading practices they developed helped a few and hurt many. The critical difference was in alignment. Lockheed Martin's was creative and on product novelty. Enron's was equally creative, but defensively aligned on profit. A similar alignment has plagued our healthcare system as agents in it have adapted to its regulatory environment by gaming it for their own benefit until it has become our current system—the best health care that money can buy. Regulatory environments, like that in which Enron was born, and in which our healthcare system exists, stimulate a defensive, profit oriented, alignment.

The problems associated with a defensive alignment show the folly of leaving systems to manage themselves, but also the folly of regulatory solutions. We tried that approach a century ago with Social Darwinism, the idea that survival of the fittest should be allowed in society; we thought that competition would allow for more winners and improve the economy. *Laissez faire* capitalism was allowed free reign; powerful and successful people and companies were allowed to grow because they were the 'fittest'. When we realized that these companies were the equivalent of tumors in society we took a mechanical approach and passed legislation designed to block the formation of large trusts, and tried to balance these strong corporations by empowering labor. We saw and still mistakenly see the counterbalance to *laissez faire* capitalism as being managed capitalism.

We also unknowingly helped out in ways consistent with the CASY model by promoting secondary education, by giving our children more ability to cope with the increased complexity and enabling more social mobility. Social Darwinism had a needed demise. Unfortunately we are seeing many of the same ideas today with the "ownership society" where those that are able to be owners are given the benefits, with little effort to lift those who are not "owners" into the group—other than picking their pockets with sub-prime interest rates. What we are seeing in these periods is the shadow side of capitalism—the time when Darwin's principle of defensive adaptation is unrestrained and agents are allowed the freedom to insure as best as possible their own survival without consideration for the larger system. What is forgotten or not seen is that such an alignment in social CASYs ignores the agents of which the larger system is made and for whom it exists. Also not seen is that this alignment handicaps any creativity for finding better solutions—it enables and promotes a defensive alignment over a creative one.

One of the most common defensive adaptations is increased size; the bigger you are the less others are going to bother you. We saw this played out in evolution in the age of the dinosaurs, on a societal scale we saw it in Social Darwinism, and we see it today in corporate mergers that allow for greater efficiency and larger profits. But in these defensive maneuvers it is altogether too easy for the larger higher level CASYs to ignore and forget the lower level agents who are then the collateral damage.

Another problem that comes with increased size is decreased efficiency of the agents in the system. Workers in small companies commonly spend more than 75% of their time in productive work, while those in larger companies spend closer to 25% so occupied, and a son working for a large international corporation says that's being generous. The larger and more impersonal the company the more its employees will fail to receive recognition for their part in making it work and the more they will invest time elsewhere to get such recognition.

At its best a society that maximizes its creative potential will educate their population to the point that they are comfortable and competent as they play with the elements in their environments, and it will provide a safe place for them to do so. At the same time it will educate them about alignment and how objectifying other agents promotes hostility and a defensive alignment. This will make more transparent the defensive adaptations that now focus on size, power, and profits—and counter the frequent bullying, profiteering, and abuse with which it is associated. Children are very concerned about gaining the respect of others and rapidly and easily learn that the key to this is in their own respecting of others. The real solution to the shadow defensive side of capitalism and other of our misaligned systems is not to manage or to regulate them, but to counter the defensive adaptations by encouraging a creative one.

Creating a space and a vision

Alignment is critical when dealing with CASYs because a perceived threat that leads to a defensive alignment also shifts the system toward the chaotic end of the systems continuum. When a CASY is threatened it focuses on dealing with the threat and may pick any method close at hand. Bacteria speed up their mutation rate, mammalian mothers become vicious, corporate accounting becomes self-serving, and systems break down because of the shift toward self preservation and away from trust and cooperation. A creative alignment with its resultant increase in diversity is almost always more beneficial for the agents in the related systems because it increases complexity, which by itself opens doors for more networks and opportunities.

This is not to say that a creative alignment is beneficial for all. Enron, Al Qaeda, and our drug dealers were and are very creative in the alignment of agents in their systems. Their agents had and have the opportunity to progress faster than in traditional mechanical top-down systems; they were and are more excited and challenged than agents working in mechanical systems. These are examples of organizations built with a space and a vision, but vision can be self serving and defensive as well as altruistic and noble. While we may not like its purpose, fundamentalist Moslems, adapting to combat western interference to their rigid Islamic social codes, created a very effective CASY that is self organizing, rapidly adapting, and increasingly wide spread. Such organizations are difficult to counter with conventional forces as our failed "War on Drugs" confirms. Ori Brafman and Rod Beckstrom describe such organizations as Al Qaeda and our illegal drug distribution system as starfish; you can try to kill a starfish by cutting it up, but each of the parts makes a new starfish. As with all CASYs the most effective way to deal with them is not outside force, but addressing the context of the system and allowing for adaptation. In the particular case of Al Qaeda it means that we will likely be more successful at defeating it by addressing the factors of discouraged Muslims dealing with their oil rich corrupt states seemingly supported by American power, the introduction of different moral views via imported Western television, and the Palestinian Israeli conflict, than by military conquest.

The problem before us in providing an environment for complexity to evolve is not how to control the play, or the gaming, but how to alter the agent's context in a way that will stimulate more friendly adaptations, and to make the area safe and the environment respectful in order to increase the likelihood of the adaptation being creative. A good example of this process, both defensive and creative alignments, comes from our own experience with health care.

If there is any single characteristic that defines American health care it must be expense. Its size and profit margin are both defensive adaptations that have come from its regulated environment. For the past half century our health care system has consistently outpaced the growth of the rest of the economy. More than anything else this adaptation has resulted from the defensively aligned agents in this system gaming it for their own survival. These agents now spread over $300 million of their financial semen annually into government lobbying and other alliances in order to guarantee their continued growth; and supported by the deep pocket of government that is opened in this process, its growth is mostly unrestrained.

On the other hand treating our healthcare or any other dysfunctional system as a CASY and tickling the proper elements in its context can affect its alignment and have major results. A well known characteristic of CASYs is the non-linear relationship of input and output. Like the 'butterfly effect,' where a butterfly flapping its wings in China initiates changes in wind patterns that eventually lead to a tornado in Oklahoma, small initial changes can have enormous results later; that is why we use the term tickling. But even the tickling of the context must not be threatening in order to allow the CASY to adapt creatively. To satisfy this requirement Plsek's fourth rule says the adaptation must come from within the system itself.

A vision and space for local actions

Plsek's fourth criterion, providing a vision and a space for local actions, follows simple rules, metaphors from life, and creating the right context. The difficult part here is that change must come from within the system. Outside intervention doesn't work because agents in the system see the intervention either as outright invasion to be defended against, or as just more regulation to be gamed with all the rest. Government regulation is not an option. Regulation from the top in hierarchical organizations is not an option. Solutions to our various problems must come from within the systems—from the agents that form them. And here too we need to see differently.

We all have our own particular way of seeing things that often includes being blind to what others clearly see as our own social problems. Romania has a problem with orphans that it can't seem to fix so the orphans are abandoned, psychologically maimed, relabeled as retarded, institutionalized, and die sooner. South Africa has a problem recognizing the connection between HIV and AIDS so preventive measures are less effective and more die. The U. S. has a problem with the one adult out of every hundred who is in jail learning mostly how to be a better criminal, and with the military power that we feel gives us rights of domination over lesser powered countries that produce substances critical to our system. Yet while these problems have been pointed out by outsiders—the European Union and Romania, the World Health Organization and South Africa, European nations and the U.N. and the United States—each of these high level CASYs remains blind to their problem. Recognition and eventual solutions must come from within the systems themselves. But how do we do that if we can't even see them?

Machiavelli taught that a ruler should keep his friends close, but his enemies closer. Most have considered the reason for this to be that keeping enemies closer would prevent their plotting an overthrow. But there was another reason as well. One's enemies are much more likely than one's friends to point out the weaknesses in the programs to which the ruler may be blind.

Staying close to your enemies in our polarized mechanically oriented society, however, is collaboration and contrary to the way we do things; it disturbs the balance. The mechanical paradigm sees opposing forces rather than information.

Historically mankind has more often taken the mechanical and defensive approach of marshaling allies and battling it out, but there is another way. Recognizing our systems as CASYs persuades us to play with their context and let the systems adapt. Developmental psychologists studying the growth and development of children, the archetype of CASYs, suggest the same thing. Children thrive when raised in an environment similar to that described by Plsek for CASYs: simple rules, a safe and nurturing place to play, a rich environment that promotes discovery, and time to use it. But this way promotes novelty with which many are uncomfortable. We would rather have predictability than adaptability so we continue with the mechanical model.

When we see through mechanical eyes we see the value of power, but when the use of power, or any other concept that leads to social ranking, is institutionalized in a society it plants the seeds of its own destruction; it leads to a social hierarchy that sooner or later becomes top heavy and too expensive to maintain. But while the growth of a power hierarchy leads eventually to its instability and fall the primary cause is often found in the ideas that gave it birth. These early ideas provide the initial context to which CASYs are particularly sensitive; they are the initial variables that become raised to very high powers as the system grows in size and complexity by repeated integrations. The power of early ideas is again demonstrated by the "butterfly effect."

Defensively aligned CASYs are not likely able to adapt creatively, but there may be elements in the system with more favorable alignments. Following the fourth rule we need to find such elements. We can get a hint of how to stimulate them by looking at an example of what worked in healthcare from our own history. And applying the principle in other areas is not that difficult.

A hundred years ago Dr. Sara "Jo" Baker was working in the New York City Health Department, a part of the

Public Health Service. Her area of the city, Hell's Kitchen, was the center of epidemics of cholera and typhoid that were killing hundreds of the city's children every year. It was Dr. Baker who was twice instrumental in apprehending "Typhoid Mary," the immigrant Irish cook who earned her name by infecting so many people with typhoid. Typhoid and cholera are caused by bacteria that live in the digestive tracts of some people, like Mary, and are passed to others because of poor hygiene. Dr. Baker addressed the epidemic not only by removing the cause as best she could, as she did with Mary, but by training mothers and their older daughters, who often cared for the children while the mother worked, better hygiene—primarily more and better hand washing—when caring for the children. Lives were saved as the severity of the epidemic decreased.

This kind of intervention from the Public Health sector was an application of the understanding that came from the germ theory and it helped control the epidemic. In Public Health success is measured by the absence or prevention of problems. Its function is on providing information that will help us to live healthier lives. Public Health, albeit small and neglected, is already a part of our healthcare system so changes here satisfy Plsek's fourth criteria of coming from within the system; and it is already oriented on maintaining the public's health and the education needed to support it. In order to help our healthcare system become healthier we need to feed the Dr. Baker's and try to stimulate a creative alignment in this sector—without forgetting that we are dealing with a CASY; the same holds as we shall see with our other distressed systems.

More help comes from an understanding of the biological processes behind defensive and creative alignments. It is to this that we turn next.

CHAPTER 3
Incest in the System

Incest: sexual intercourse between persons so closely related that their marriage is prohibited by law or custom.

Metaphors from biology are useful in understanding CASYs because both include adaptation as a fundamental part of the system. Adaptation in bacteria is necessarily by mutation and is hampered by an element of randomness and the unknown. When sex evolved it raised the level of the playing field. Bacterial adaptation relied on random mutation in the DNA; sex enabled the couple, or the biologist, to focus on desirable characteristics. Adaptation blossomed. One of the most fruitful metaphors from biology is in comparing breeding practices and seeing how they apply in the world of social CASYs.

Purposeful breeding in the animal and plant world extends from inbreeding, where close relatives, either plant or animal, are bred together, to cross-pollination, where different strains are combined. The purpose of inbreeding is to refine particular characteristics that are shared by both parents; anything from a finer pelt, faster growth, more milk, or disease resistance can be improved by inbreeding. Cross-pollination is used to introduce other strengths into the strain or to promote novelty—or to correct inbred problems.

Of course most breeding is not controlled by an animal or plant scientist. In the natural world the adaptations that result from random mutation, inbreeding, or cross-pollination, rely on time and natural selection to judge their success. On all levels CASY agents adapt by playing with the elements available to them to come up with something different that may work a little better, either for themselves or their systems. Stress appears to speed up the 'themselves' side of this process and humans have the distinct advantage of being able, at least to some degree, to plan their adaptation.

A critical part of being alive is the ability to sense ones environment. All CASYs engage in interactive play with other agents in their environment and have some means of communication. Bacteria communicate with others by elaborating chemicals that trigger an action when the voices get loud enough ,i.e., when the concentration reaches a critical point. It's called quorum sensing and it leads to biofilm construction with one chemical or increased mutation with another. Acacia trees use chemicals to communicate with giraffes, allowing just so much browsing before a chemical is released into the leaves that eliminates the taste appeal. Eventually, in successful ecosystems, the agents reach a measure of harmony—the balance seen as the state of health in the mechanical model.

Adaptation in nature is based on the elements available to the agent and is stimulated by their context. In the natural world an agent's context is mostly limited to the physical environment and the relationships they have with other agents, but even in simple agents like bacteria there is the ability to recognize threat, a mental component which affects alignment. In humans the mental level is represented in the paradigm where adaptation is fastest.

Social CASYs rise to another level. The context here is made up of the agents in the system, their relationship with each other, and the mental aspect of the purpose of the system (athletic, business, religious, etc.). Just as with living agents, desirable characteristics for social CASYs can be enhanced by inbreeding, by entering into contracts with other CASYs. But it is good to remember the importance of biological metaphors because this process also has its down side.

The potential problem with inbred relationships between agents in the same family is that they commonly lead to inbred weaknesses. When animals and plants are intentionally bred to close relatives it's done to enhance desirable traits. The goal of the plant or animal scientist is on strengthening a genetic novelty, like a nicer pelt, faster growth, or resistance to disease. But all inbreeding risks introducing weaknesses and our social CASYs are just as prone to this problem as those in nature.

Breeders know the risks and are prepared to deal with them. Quarter horses are bred for speed running a quarter of a mile, but the inbreeding used to optimize their speed often results in horses that give out before the race is finished—endurance is sacrificed for speed. Bulldogs are bred for their wide and powerful stance, but most now are delivered surgically because their shoulders are too wide for the mother's birth canal. But while we can see the problematic results of inbreeding in horse racing, dog breeding, and biology in general we remain blind to the presence of inbred and incestuous business relationships—to say nothing of those in government—and the problems that result from them within the complex adaptive systems in our society. The CASY paradigm allows us to see these relationships and their results for what they are: incest and inbred weaknesses.

Nature has shown us that relationships between agents in the same family are incestuous; the CASY paradigm shows us that social CASYs have the same problem. On some level we all know this; we've talked around it for years—Washington being the most inbred city in the world, and how different but related governmental agencies are 'married.' We need to bring this out into the open: this is incest and most of the problems we have can be seen as inbred weaknesses.

When natural selection operates in nature it selects traits that add survival benefits; the process is random and it takes a long time for natural selection to promote the desirable traits. When breeders and horticulturists inbreed to refine and strengthen desirable characteristics it is purposive and the results are relatively rapid, as we can easily see by looking at the great variety of dogs we have today after the relatively brief 15,000 years we have been breeding them. When social agents compete defensively in this way it is also rapid; they know what they are doing and it is not random, but all such inbreeding risks opening the system to inbred weaknesses.

Defensively aligned agents entering into mergers and contracts with other agents in the same family, as we see happening in healthcare, are those most at risk. They have a purpose similar to that of the animal scientist in trying to enhance a desirable characteristic. But when corporate alignment is defensive, contractual relations, as we saw with Enron, mostly aim at getting larger, more powerful, and more profitable.

The alignment of a system is critical in social CASYs because their ability to adapt is so much faster. While such contracts may be beneficial when the alignment is on creative novelty, e.g., when introducing a new product or increasing diversity, they are both more common and more problematic when the alignment is defensive and the contracts tend to focus on survival—and even more so when they are made with closely related institutions in the same family.

The most common inbred weakness in people is some type of mental retardation. The hemophilia that spread through the inbred royal houses of Europe in the 18th and 19th centuries is another example of what can happen. Incest taboos were the way our ancestors prevented those problems from becoming common in humanity—they are our oldest and most wide spread taboos.

Big Pharma and healthcare

Marcia Angell and Jerome Kassirer, both past editors of the prestigious *New England Journal of Medicine*, have recently written excellent books detailing the problematic relationships between the medical profession and "big Pharma," the coalition of the major pharmaceutical companies. Seen with CASY eyes the relationship between these two siblings in the healthcare system amounts to incest; it increases profits for both, but it has also introduced many inbred weaknesses, with the major one being our reliance on pills. How this works is exemplified in big Pharma's role in the education of doctors.

Physicians are required to attend a number of hours of continuing education to maintain their licenses and membership in their professional societies. The doctors presenting the programs at these conferences are usually from major medical schools where, as well as teaching, they have contracts (incestuous) with major pharmaceutical companies that supplement their teacher's pay. They are paid to do research on new and promising drugs and this is what they generally talk about at the conferences. So the attending physicians leave with a bit more understanding of the analysis of human physiology—which tries to simplify a complex system—but mostly how new, patented and expensive drugs affect a segment of that physiology. The resultant overuse of new expensive drugs is an inbred weakness.

Dr.'s Angell and Kassirer also relate several examples where such monetary relations distorted the findings of the research—accentuating inbred weakness. If you watch the news, read the papers, or recent books like Thomas Campbell's *The China Study*, you will see many more and learn how the system fosters them. Even the movies have picked up the theme in films like "The Constant Gardener" and "The Fugitive."

These stories show how financial interests and contractual relations between these interested parties distort the truth to increase the profits. But few if any have seen this problem from the CASY viewpoint: it's an inbred weakness due to incest. In the CASY that is our economic system, family is determined by focus, so physicians and the drug companies are members of the same healthcare family, and their incestuous relations are bringing both expense and weakness into a system aligned defensively on profit. Inbred weaknesses are a large reason why we are paying more but getting less with our healthcare dollars.

The problem is not only in the system itself, but has spread to its interaction with government. The Food and Drug Administration was established to improve the quality of our food supply and to assure the public that drugs were safe. Its growth paralleled that of the pharmaceutical industry until Congress in 1992, under the spell of Reaganomics, felt that it should be privatized to decrease its reliance on government. Funding for the FDA was altered so that a significant portion now comes from the pharmaceutical companies. Big pharma and the FDA were essentially put to bed together and the alignment of the FDA shifted significantly from protecting the public to promoting the interests of big Pharma. According to David Graham, the FDA research physician that blew the whistle on the increased cardiac risks associated with Vioxx, this incestuous relationship was a major factor in delaying the FDA's action that resulted in the projected deaths of as many as 55,000 Americans.

There is, however, a sense that these inbred relationships are not healthy. Responding to government pressures Big Pharma agreed on regulations that mandated disclosure of all financial relationships for authors of medical studies and presenters at medical conventions. But while this increased transparency takes the doors off the bedrooms and helps us see more of the incest it will not stop it—that's just how we do business. Until we recognize that incestuous relations are as potentially damaging to social CASYs as they are to our own families the incest will continue. Only when we realize that these relationships are incestuous will the absent bedroom doors be helpful. When that realization occurs further regulation will likely not be necessary because such relationships will be seen for what they are and their prohibition will become a cultural taboo.

The need for balance

In nature the presence of food and predators, nature's supply and demand, limits growth and eventually results in a balanced ecosystem. When animals are introduced into different ecological systems, where there are no natural predators, they grow unchecked, like the rabbits did in Australia. Similarly, plants relocated to different environments where they have no natural controls often spread rapidly and are called weeds.

Uncontrolled growth in nature usually destroys the local system, and it's the same in all CASYs. Cancer grows when it is able to avoid triggering the body's immune responses. Cells like our 'natural killer' cells are a critical part of our immune systems; they act as the predator in our bodies, killing off invaders and cancer cells whenever they recognize them. In our own mechanical model we've let the government regulators do the work of the predator. But government is ill suited to the task because it is often in an incestuous relationship with the CASY agents that warrant the most concern.

There is in the United States an open door between industry and government policy makers that promotes such incest. Those calling Washington D.C. the most inbred city on earth miss the more appropriate definition. Maintaining a separation between the regulator and the system regulated and not becoming confused in our attempts to privatize government, as we did with the FDA, allows the regulators to function best.

At the same time we need to remember how easy it is to just game regulations and the defensive alignment they promote. Effective means of coping with these problems requires that we see and treat the systems, not in a mechanical way, but as the CASYs they are; the absent bedroom doors need to be combined with the CASY understanding that such practices are incest.

Regulation may be necessary to control this social incest, but mostly it just increases the gaming. Regulatory power is coercive so CASYs respond defensively. Persuasion, a less threatening use of power, also increases gaming. Both stimulate defensive adaptations that find ways around the regulators. Creative adaptations are stimulated when the context is changed to less threatening and regulations removed—the main argument behind *laissez faire* capitalism. What we are prone to forget in this is the critical place of the system's alignment—defensive helps the agent survive better, sometimes at the expense of the larger system, and creative helps the larger system, sometimes at the expense of the agent.

When adaptation is rapid, as it is in our social CASYs, alignment determines whether the system responds defensively, adapting to increase the agents survival, or creatively, searching for new and novel niches. Inbreeding in defensively aligned systems will select for traits—size or increased efficiency—that increase survival; they are almost always in the agent's interest rather than that of the larger system. If a social CASY is defensively aligned toward profits and scale then agents will game their system to discover ways to improve their survival: by manipulation, as Enron did with California's power grid; by increased efficiency and larger scale, as Wal-Mart does with volume purchasing, undercutting competition, and reduced employee compensation; or by finding a deeper pocket, as healthcare has done with third-party payers and government support. Maintaining a creative environment also has requirements: it must be a safe place where no one is treated as an object, and there a delegated leader, observer, or manager to insure this. A variety of creatively aligned systems from child centered play therapy to Lockeed-Martin's Skunk Works bear this out.

Rarely if ever does novelty come from inbreeding. Inbreeding refines traits and makes them stronger, as well as doing the same for inherited weaknesses. Cross-pollination is the source of novelty. If a system is oriented to creative novelty then it will develop or create new ways to overcome the problems in its path. The hand washing introduced by Dr. Baker and our nasal wash are just two of the many successes that came from such creative play with the elements of their respective environments. The demonstration that the lethal dehydration of cholera could be lessened by a specific type of oral rehydration was another. These are examples that show what can be done with an alignment on creative novelty. Dr. Baker's work saved thousands of children's lives in New York; and the Bangladeshi NGO, BRAC, which took the information about oral rehydration to the people, reduced the death toll from cholera by more than 60% and saved millions. The point here is not the particular success, but what is possible with creative play.

Addressing incest in complex systems

Inbred weaknesses in nature are eventually eliminated by natural selection and those in society eventually fall, as did Enron and our housing market, from their own inbred weaknesses. In our planned breeding programs, where they are a recognized and common problem, they are addressed by cross breeding with stock having traits that counter the weakness. In the case of the quarter horses that have lost out on endurance, Arabians or Mustangs, known for this particular trait, are cross-bred into the stock to counter that inbred weakness.

In the same way we will see in later chapters how the practice of medicine could be improved by crossbreeding with its root stock in biology, where it would learn to honor and support defenses rather than turn them off. Even our profit oriented healthcare system could be helped in this way by cross-breeding with Public Health, which, at least potentially, has strengths that counter our current weaknesses: it is aligned on health and the prevention of illness, and focused on education. And it complies with Plsek's rule that solutions have to come from within the system. Under our current budget, however, more than 97% of government healthcare spending goes directly to feed the profit oriented system.

Not only the budget, but leadership positions continue supporting the profit orientation. Appointments to positions of authority, like the heads of the FDA or the Department of Health and Human Services, have uniformly come from the private, profit oriented sector of the industry. Reversing both these budgetary and leadership trends would be a large step in the right direction. These changes would cross-pollinate the system and make it much more effective, but diversity also needs stimulus at the level of the practice.

Diversity and cross-pollination

The need for diversity in a marketplace is critical to its success, as is the value of the margins in producing that diversity. The margins can do this because that is where cross-pollination takes place. Insects carrying pollen from one plant to another in the center of a planted field are not likely to introduce anything wild or different, but on the margins the chance for this increases.

Those in the center of the healthcare field, in our temples of healing, have a limited view of medicine that is based on a mechanical model of drugs and procedures. This viewpoint is the primary reason the experts at the Institute of Medicine can only see solutions for our ailing system in efficiencies like universal insurance and information technology. Those on the margins see evidence of healing in everything from herbs and diet (Ayurveda), to non-ordinary states of consciousness (shamanism and dream healing), and from acupuncture and massage (Oriental, energy based), to prayer, forgiveness, and reconciliation. The wealth of diversity that can come from cross-pollination with all of these elements is enormous and the role they can all play in enhancing our health is robbed from us by limiting our view to only seeing the body as a machine.

Encouraging cross-pollination

The cohesion rule of aiming for the center identifies the group. Were it not for this rule the group would scatter and lose its identity as a system—and agents would be more open to cross-pollination. The strength of this rule is directly related to the number and strength of predators; the greater the threat the more cohesive the group.

We can see examples of this rule not only in the animal world, but in the cohesiveness of those groups, like the Jewish people and the Mormons, that have a history of persecution and are still highly group conscious. The current rise of Arab nationalism and Islamic fundamentalism can also be seen in this light, to say nothing of our own increased nationalism post 9/11.

Understanding this relationship suggests that one can modify cohesion by reducing threat. The Jewish population in America is far less cohesive than in countries where they are perceived as a threat or different. Reducing the threat is the basis for the great spiritual teachings of our human heritage on how to get along with each other. Rather than seeing the stranger as a threat Moses, Jesus, and Mohammed all taught us to see them as our neighbor and as someone who should be honored and respected. Reducing threat and cohesion should open all CASYs to the benefits of increased cross-pollination.

The threat is a critical part of the mental context; more than any other factor fear has the ability to affect alignment. In order to have a more creatively aligned society we need to look at and try to reduce the elements that make up this threat.

Threats to healthcare practitioners

The primary threats to social CASYs come from regulation or competition, but anything perceived as a block to our self actualization is a threat. Applying this to healthcare practitioners a major stimulus that is pressuring for adaptation is third party payer hassles, which encourages agents to leave private practice and leave the hassle to someone else. But the two major threats come from state licensing agencies and from the patients in the form of malpractice.

Malpractice

The response of the agent to the malpractice threat is defensive medicine: there are more tests, more referrals to specialists, and more expense—to make sure there is nothing left out of consideration that could come back to haunt them later. There is also more cohesion. Medicine is practiced by the book with few exceptions—even when the book isn't working as we have seen in particular with ear infections.

When what we are doing is not working, says "Reality Therapy," we need to do something else. But our defensive alignment keeps us focused on the standard nonworking treatment. Doctors are much less likely to try a different approach when the threat of its failure may mean a lawsuit or being reported to the state licensing agency. This aspect of the system would not likely be a problem had not the patient been excluded from the relationship by the third party payers; if the patients were the ones paying for their services there would be a closer relationship with the physician, who would thereby tend to be more creatively aligned on the patient and less defensively aligned on cohesion with the system.

The closer the patient physician relationship the less likely those untoward events which are always possible will lead to legal recourse. Patients are far less likely to sue when they are treated as a person than when seen and treated mechanically, as an object, an illness, or a condition. Malpractice reform would likely be unnecessary, but would be an effective way to reduce the threat that prevents us from having a more open and dispersed system.

Licensing agencies

State licensing agencies, given the mandate to insure good medical practice, are often seen as a threat by those practicing alternative medicine. A common alternative treatment for hardening of the arteries, for example, is chelation therapy. Many physicians, and patients for that matter, believe in the value of this treatment. Chelating molecules, given intravenously, bind to heavy metals and to the molecular complexes making up the matrix of arterial plaque (the stuff that makes the arteries hard) and carry them out of the body through the kidneys. This is acceptable treatment for heavy metal poisoning. Some are even using it, and reporting success, in children with autism to address presumed toxic amounts of mercury. But when used for hardening of the arteries and symptoms related to it, it has resulted in many physicians being questioned by their state agencies. While such questioning seldom arises without someone complaining, few therapies work on everyone and this one is safe.

If we want a more open and diverse system we should look at reducing these threats. There is discussion of reforming the FDA so that it concentrates on safety more than efficacy, and the same reforms could be applied to state licensing boards.

This isn't as bad as it sounds. We all want things that work and efficacy matters. The problem is that the limited mechanical view of efficacy that dominates this system may not be all that is important; it may not be the right kind of efficacy. In our current model drug efficacy is determined by the gold standard of randomized and blinded clinical trials. Such studies take the elements in the system apart as much as possible to find out what the drug does. 'Evidence based medicine' finds the best drug for the particular problem, but ignores human variety, as well as our ability to adapt that is reflected in the placebo that works. The body is a CASY that is networked; taking it apart and watching symptoms doesn't tell us what will happen. The unexpected side effects and after market recalls we have seen with promising new drugs over the last two decades should show us that. The only way to test for efficacy in a CASY is to tickle the context and watch; but you watch, not for symptom relief, but for survival advantage. This takes a long time and is not practical under our profit oriented system. It took 60 years to finally see that the miracle drugs of the 1940s and 50s reduced survival. Healing efficacy, however, is a far more important measure than symptom efficacy, and the many networked factors involved in regaining health defy analytical mechanical modeling. Using a plasmid model within the Public Health Service before a drug is released for general use would remove the blinders of profit and determine the true benefit, or lack thereof, much sooner and with less damage.

Conventional wisdom also limits our choice of drugs to those the pharmaceutical industry advertises—and profits from. The World Health Organization must deal with the varieties of healthcare systems all over the world so their recommendations cover more of the bases. In those for treating malaria, for example, the standard western medications are listed along with *artemisinin*, an oriental herb that has been shown to be an effective anti-malarial. Herbs can be defined as drugs in our system but are less profitable and not generally promoted so few know about *artemisinin*. Education along these lines will not likely be done by the pharmaceutical and healthcare industry because given a choice many people would opt for the herb over the more expensive and profitable drugs. Again there is a balance between diversity and threat, between risk and regulation.

Health care over the last 50 years has been heavily regulated and standardized; and it has also become more expensive. Over the last 20 years there has been a reactionary shift by the people to more diversity. Whether we want to support that shift further by decreasing the threats and supporting individual choice are decisions we will make in the future. But again, those decisions should be based on an understanding of complex adaptive systems rather than seeing either the body or the larger system in limited mechanical terms.

The role of the Public Health Service

Empowering Public Health introduces a health oriented alignment into our present system that would work to better inform our public on healthy living choices. The Public Health Service now provides immunizations and preventive services, like condoms. Expanding it to include other preventive services that maintain the individual's health would be of great benefit. These would likely focus on education, screening tests and exams, and some specific services.

The recent release of the "morning after pill" for contraception was delayed for over two years because of political squabbling about it causing abortions. Pharmacists did not want the responsibility. Safety is not a major factor with this pill *if it is used as directed.* Making it available without restriction, however, is associated with the risks of its incorrect use. Making it available through Public Health resolves this problem by enabling more education on proper use as well as assurance against improper use.

The most important service provided by Public Health has always been education. This was true in the time of Dr. Baker and through the work of the Center for Disease Control and Prevention it remains true today. But it needs expansion.

Another benefit of supporting Public Health and the education it can provide is the potential of implementing the plasmid model into healthcare. We know that groups of people sharing a particular problem provide one of the best ways of managing that problem because the group provides social, moral and spiritual support for those in it. They also provide the best environment in which to practice the plasmid model. Coordination through the Public Health Service is the most effective way to set up, inform, and guide such groups. Groups of mutating bacteria sharing their work in plasmids are likely the most effective model for creative adaptation known, and groups supported and informed by public health would be able to apply this model to improving our health.

Part I
Living Agents as Complex Adaptive Systems

While the earliest use of complex systems dealt with living agents that application has been forgotten as leaders in a variety of other fields have applied it to their own areas. But everything alive can adapt; all living organisms are CASYs.

In the following three chapters we look first at the simplest of living organisms, bacteria, and then at some of the defensive adaptations that we have inherited because they survived the test of natural selection. Again, these helpful adaptations are much better honored and supported than blocked with drugs.

CHAPTER 4
OF GERMS AND MEN

By using evolutionary tactics, we should be able to change the pathogens so that they will not be the terrible enemies that they once were, so that we will not need to invest so heavily in the "arms races" to deter them just before they attack us or to destroy them just after they have attacked. We shall, in a sense, domesticate them so that they can live with us in a less damaging way than they have throughout our history.

(Paul W. Ewald, *Evolution of Infectious Disease*)

Bacteria are the simplest CASY and we have been at war with them since we learned of their existence as the agents responsible for many of our illnesses. It was not until many years later that we learned of the many benefits that come from the bacteria that live in and with us. Our experiences in this war can help us to understand how to deal more effectively with them, as well as with CASYs on all levels.

Antibiotics, our armament in this war, have saved countless lives since Fleming first noted the effect of bread mold on growing bacteria, but they have a down side. Every time we use an antibiotic to treat an infection we are stimulating defensive adaptations in the infecting bacteria; it results in stronger and more resistant bacteria. Antibiotics are a real *catch 22*—the more lives that are saved by their use the more we promote strains of bacteria that are not killed by them. Every time we use an antibiotic there are some bacteria that survive—they are resistant. Nietzsche said, "What doesn't kill me makes me stronger," and it's the same with bacteria. Not only are they stronger because of their resistance, but they can multiply easier because the antibiotic has killed off the other bacteria that were competing for the same food and space.

Multiple drug resistant bacteria are now a fact of life that doctors have to deal with. For many years they were limited to hospitals where the heavy and prolonged doses of antibiotics, that promote the development of resistance, are more common, but they are now out in our communities and around the world. Across the country healthy people, even healthy young people, are getting infections from bacteria that are resistant to our antibiotics.

So far we have relied on pharmaceutical companies to deal with this problem because conventional wisdom says we need to kill these infecting bacteria. But this way of seeing things is what has gotten us into our current dilemma where the problem is made worse with every new antibiotic prescription. While conventional wisdom says killing this enemy is the best solution, we know now that this is neither possible nor practical.

Warfare with bacteria

We have essentially the same problem in our war with bacteria that Moshe Yaalon, the Israeli Defense Minister, recognized as being present in Israel's Palestinian problem: "In our tactical decisions," he said, "we are operating contrary to our strategic interests." Every time Israel used military force, a tactical decision, they promoted a violent reaction from the other side that was not in their strategic interest, which is to live in peace with their Palestinian and Arab neighbors. Every time we use an antibiotic we are making a tactical decision, and we are likely to win a battle, but at the same time we are shooting ourselves in the foot by promoting antibiotic resistance that is not in our strategic interest. In both situations one is dealing with a CASY and the tactical decision to use violence, whether an antibiotic, or a mortar attack, or even a road block, stimulates defensive adaptations in the "enemy" that make them stronger, or more resistant, a result opposite to the intended strategy. All CASYs, bacteria as well as nations, treated mechanically as objects, will adapt defensively and will likely turn out to be stronger and more determined foes. Remember Reality Therapy: If what you are doing is not working, try something else.

We rely on the pharmaceutical industry to solve this problem by making better antibiotics; the focus remains on killing the bacteria. The process of developing a new drug takes lots of time, involves lots of people, expensive clinical testing, and requires a patent so the company can make a profit. The process of developing resistance, on the other hand, is much faster. With over three billion years of experience bacteria are the experts at playing with their DNA—they likely developed it. While bacteria have no brains or central nervous system, or even ganglia or neurons, that lets them learn as we commonly think of the term, they are capable of both recognizing a threat and playing with the elements in their environments to deal with it, and those elements are primarily their DNA. When threatened they increase their mutation rate, pick on areas of their DNA that are more open to manipulation, and share the changes in plasmids, allowing other bacteria to refine and improve the changes. Resistance involves an adaptation, or mutation in one out of a billion or so bacteria, which can then multiply unimpeded because the other competing bacteria have been killed off. The resistant bacterium thus passes the resistance on to its own progeny, as well as sharing it with others in the plasmids—with no concern at all for intellectual property rights or profit. They are a formidable foe and we have little chance of winning this war.

A different view of our chances comes from a realistic look at history. People studying the beginnings of bacteria find the earliest evidence of their existence about three and a half billion years ago. For two billion years they were the only living things on the earth. They shaped our environment, created our atmosphere, and recycled themselves when they died. And they adapted to use DNA to store information about useful proteins. Of the many types of bacteria that were present on the earth a billion and a half years ago, when the first nucleated cell emerged, 95% are still around. Of the higher organisms that have developed since that time 99% are now extinct. Those are not very good odds when one is choosing sides in a war. We need another option, another way of looking at the problem, another paradigm—one that allows for Ewald's hope that these enemies can be "domesticated." Seeing even simple bacteria as complex adaptive systems has significant advantages, allows for this domestication, shows a few cases where some bacteria have already been tamed, and shows how we can all help in the process.

A single bacterium seems like a very simple organism and individually they may not even qualify as CASYs, but there is no doubt that the colonies they form are. When they are threatened with antibiotics or starvation these colonies have enough of a sense of self to first of all recognize the threat and then to have some members of the colony deal with it by increasing their rate of mutation—some, but not all. For all bacteria to join in this rampant mutation would be suicidal.

We usually consider self identification in evolution as associated with the Hydra which is the first organism in evolutionary history showing both a rudimentary central nervous system and an immune system; it is also the first to have tumors and cancer. The immune system working in plants and animals has the responsibility to identify self and protect against foreign agents and has developed a means of both identifying self and communicating the difference between self and other.

One of the first things CASYs do at every level is learn to communicate with other agents at their level. Bacteria have neither a central nervous nor an immune system, but they are able to communicate among themselves because not all speed up their rate of mutation. We know a bit more about how this communication takes place in the process of biofilm formation.

Biofilm is like a house for bacteria that protects them from environmental dangers, including the antibiotics we use to kill them. When bacteria adhere to a host and start to multiply they talk to each other using chemicals. When a particular chemical 'voice' gets loud enough it triggers the process called "quorum sensing" and some of the bacteria start changing their bodies into walls and making a biofilm. We can feel this as the slime on a wet dishcloth; the plaque on our teeth is another example. When we take pictures of biofilm through an electron microscope we see futuristic type structures that look like a city from "Star Wars."

Those looking at infectious diseases are concluding now that many infections are resistant because the bacteria have established a biofilm somewhere in the body that protects them from our antibiotics. Chronic ear infections are thought to be an example of resistance caused by bacteria protected by biofilm. Artificial prostheses are particularly susceptible to biofilm formation and the chronic infections they bring.

Bees seem to have a form of quorum sensing as well. When a swarm is looking for a new hive the first prospect to collect 15 bees on its doorstep is invariably the winner.

Bacterial alignment

Like all CASYs and nature herself, bacteria are aligned either defensively on survival or creatively on diversity. The creative pole leads to the variety of recycling techniques bacteria use—recycling the world is what bacteria are all about. The defensive pole, as usual, is focused on staying alive, so bacterial adaptations to antibiotics result from defensive adaptations. The threatened bacteria are oriented to saving their lives which, at least temporarily, shifts their interest away from recycling us. Early studies looking at resistant bacteria confirmed this shift by showing them to be less virulent—they did not cause as many infections.

But enough time has passed that these antibiotic resistant bacteria have now realigned themselves creatively and have found new ways to hold on and to avoid early triggering of our immune system. Gonorrhea is now resistant to penicillin and also causes far fewer symptoms, but it still makes many women sterile by the inflammation it causes. These and other similar problem bacteria are the kinds that are causing our current problems. They are complex adaptive systems and we need to treat them as such. There is no chance of changing their underlying alignment on trying to recycle us because that's what they've done for over two billion years and if they didn't do it life on earth would be impossible. We need other ways to deal with them instead of the direct frontal assault of trying to kill them.

One way to do this is by controlling the use of antibiotics. Some resistant adaptations are genetically expensive and are given up when the bacteria are not threatened. This has actually happened in some areas of Europe where the proper use of antibiotics is taught and promoted; the decreased use of the antibiotics led to many bacteria dropping their antibiotic resistance. Other avenues such as immunization have been even more useful.

Antibiotic alternatives—Immunization

The best track record in dealing with infections, both viral and bacterial, has been educating our immune system to recognize them before they infect us. That way when they do get in, our immune system identifies them promptly, deals with them effectively, and most of the time we don't even know it. This educating is usually done chemically, with parts of the infecting agent that our immune systems can recognize, or weaker strains that are less of a threat than the real thing. These substances are recognized by our immune system as being intruders and they establish a chemical memory for the foreign agent that enables the body to deal effectively with future invasions. This education is called immunization and we've done it with smallpox for over three hundred years—and now we don't have smallpox anymore. We've done it with polio for almost 50, and are almost as successful.

Often our immunizations are not aimed at recognizing and helping us kill the infecting agent, but at the particular bacterial adaptation that makes them a problem—and of the immunizations that we have these are the most effective and durable. This is the case with the immunizations we use for tetanus and diphtheria where we don't target the bacteria, but the toxins these bacteria produce that makes them dangerous to us. Targeting the bacteria, just like using an antibiotic, stimulates a defensive response that speeds up their rate of mutation, and eventually to the bacteria finding a way around the immunization—a problem we are now seeing with our immunization against whooping cough. If we just target their adaptations, like the toxins that make us sick, it doesn't threaten the bacteria, so even though the immunizations for tetanus and diphtheria have been around for many years they are still effective. Addressing manipulative adaptations is a far more successful approach than antibacterial warfare because while they put pressure on the bacteria to change they don't attack them; it's the CASY principle of encouraging a creative alignment.

Other alternatives

Since the more successful immunizations are those that address microbial adaptations that make the bacteria more virulent, but don't present a lethal threat to the bacteria themselves, our search for alternatives ought to look for similar methods. Biologists who teach us about the defensive adaptations that we all have, like a fever and a runny nose, also show that some symptoms we have when we get sick are present because they provide a survival benefit to the infecting agent; they are bacterial adaptations that trigger symptoms in us that help the infecting agent. The profound weakness of a person with a malarial fever provides a safe meal for hungry mosquitoes that makes the spread of the disease much easier just as does the profuse watery diarrhea of the person with cholera. The creative adaptations of the bacteria that lead to these symptoms are called manipulations because they manipulate the host into doing something that benefits not them, but the infecting bacteria. The best way to deal with these manipulations is to block them; change the context of the manipulated system to make it less effective. Mosquito netting over people infected with malaria addresses this manipulation and prevents its spread, clean water addresses the manipulation of bacteria that spread by increasing diarrhea, the new "standard procedures," gowns, gloves and masks when dealing with newly injured people in our emergency rooms, addresses the spread of unknown infections like HIV/AIDS, condoms also address the spread of HIV/AIDS as well as other sexually transmitted diseases, and even good old-fashioned soap and water addresses the spread of bacteria in social contact. All of these different methods block the adaptations that microbes have made that allow them to better get from person to person. They change the physical context of the bacterial environment and eliminate the benefit of the manipulation.

In his book, *The Evolution of Infectious Disease,* Paul Ewald gives several examples where addressing or blocking such adaptive manipulations has resulted in the bacteria adapting in a way that make them less virulent. Many who study infections used to think that the natural course of evolution was toward bacteria becoming less virulent as they learned to live with their host and found ways to benefit each other. Ewald pointed out that infecting agents need a nudge to do this. If bacteria or viruses can get to a new host easily there is no pressure to adapt to the current one. The bacteria causing epidemic cholera, for example, adapted creatively long ago to take advantage of poor sanitation. These bacteria made a toxin that that appeared as a real threat to our immune systems and so triggered the profuse watery diarrhea that is the hallmark of this disease. Coupled with poor sanitation this toxin made it a whole lot easier for the bacteria to get around and infect other people. But when sanitation was improved and these bacteria prevented from easily getting to a new host evolutionary pressure was applied for them to adapt to the new environment. Epidemic cholera is in fact being replaced by the more benign El Tor strain where the mortality rate is almost negligible compared to what it had been. This kind of experience is the basis for Ewald's hope of domesticating bacteria expressed in the chapter's opening. Blocking their transmission limits the context of their physical world and applies evolutionary pressure on bacteria to adapt away from virulence.

Domesticating bacteria by addressing adherence

There is also another way to do this, but it is new, unregulated, and it has not made any money for the pharmaceutical industry, so few people know about it. And it isn't promoted—except by grandmother and those that listen to her. And grandmother doesn't really know why it works. Here again the science came after the success for while grandma's advice to drink cranberry juice to prevent urinary infections does work, few people really know why; and grandma's advice may lead us to ways of defending against many infections, not just those in the urinary tract.

If they are able to get to a new host the next step for the infecting agents is to hold on. This step is necessary because only after they adhere to a new host do they start to multiply. Bacteria that are not attached to a host are called planktonic—they float like plankton in the ocean. If they remain floating in our bodies they are just washed out; they don't cause any infections and they don't cause any symptoms. It's when they adapt and find a way to hold on to the cells in our bodies that they become a problem. So this adaptation that enables them to adhere to our cell surfaces, infect us, and better recycle us is one that can be addressed without directly attacking the agent. Like the immunizations that address bacterial toxins and the mechanical means used to block their transmission this method doesn't threaten the bacteria, but it changes the physical context of their environment by blocking their ability to hold on to a host. Changing their context without threatening them encourages them to adapt—and while studies are limited they appear to adapt in nice ways.

What most bacteria hold on *with* are particularly shaped proteins called lectins which are like molecular sized hands that fit and hold on to particular molecules, called receptors, that are on our cell surfaces. Nathan Sharon, one of the first researchers to look at this process, pointed out that the lectins had a sweet tooth because most often the receptors they hold on to are specific sugar complexes on the protein surfaces of our cells.

Sharon also proposed that putting an appropriate sugar in the bacterium's environment would fill up their empty hands and block their ability to adhere to the body. It's a process called competitive inhibition—and it works!

One of the earliest lectins identified was one on the strain of E. coli that causes most urinary tract infections. Researchers found that the lectins on these bacteria hold on to mannose, a sugar similar to glucose that is plentiful in the body. It is especially common on the cell surfaces in the genitourinary tract, which is why these bacteria cause so many urinary tract infections—there are lots of places for them to hold on. According to Sharon's concept, putting mannose in the bladder would fill up the lectins of any infecting bacteria and prevent them from holding on to the mannose molecules on the wall of the genitourinary tract. These bacteria would remain planktonic and would all get washed out when the person emptied her bladder—preventing a urinary tract infection.

Getting mannose to the bladder is not a problem. When we eat it most of it is taken up into the blood stream and a fair amount is filtered into the urine, so eating mannose can get some into the bladder. But since most urinary tract infections begin with bacteria from one's own GI tract it may not even be necessary to get it in the bladder.

Eating mannose regularly means that the bacteria in the GI tract that hold on to mannose are less likely to hold on to the bowel wall and more likely to get removed, and this change has been demonstrated in people. Fewer bacteria with mannose lectins in the GI tract means there will be fewer to cause urinary tract infections.

But mannose is a naturally occurring sugar that can't be patented. No patent means no profit and no profit means no money for research so few pay attention to this line of dealing with infections and few know about these benefits. While there is a fair amount of research looking for patentable and profitable alternatives to these natural sugars, there is very little looking at mannose itself as a means of decreasing adherence and preventing infections. Sheryl King is an exception. Dr. King is an Animal Science researcher who works with horses. A frequent problem with both natural breeding and artificial insemination is infection introduced into the mare's genital tract. Dr. King wanted to know if mannose would prevent these infections since the major problem bacteria were those having mannose lectins. First she used cell cultures of tissue from the inside of the mare's uterus. Bacteria were able to hold on to these cells just like they do in real life, but when she added mannose the adherence of most of the bacteria was blocked. Seeing that it worked in the lab the next step was including the bacteria and mannose along with artificial insemination. And it worked here too because none of the mares treated this way got infected.

Unfortunately it worked too well because neither did any of the mares get pregnant. When she looked at her mixture under the microscope the sperm were hanging on all over the bacteria so there weren't any left to get the mare pregnant. What she discovered was something that doctors studying fertility have known for some time, the tip of the human (and the horse) spermatozoa—the part that adheres to the egg in the process of fertilization—is a mannose lectin, similar to the lectins on the bacteria. But different in that it holds on to a different part of the mannose, so while the bacteria held on to one side of the mannose the spermatozoa held on to the other. It would not be too successful an adaptation for the spermatozoa to hold on to the parts of the numerous mannose molecules in the GU tract that the bacteria hold on to because they would attach to the walls of the genitourinary tract and never get to the egg.

Since this lectin on the tip of the spermatozoa is what holds on to the female egg in the process of fertilization then it is quite possible that our profit oriented system is not only losing out on a means of preventing urinary infections, but possibly also a non-hormonal means of inexpensive contraception as well. Laboratory studies have shown this lectin is present on many spermatozoa, that the number increases with time, and that those with the lectin have an advantage in fertilization. Putting a few trillion molecules (less than a microgram) of mannose in the vagina before engaging in intercourse could conceivably bind with these lectins and prevent fertilization.

Another study demonstrating the success of this type of prevention was done in Finland using a combination of cranberry and lingonberry juice extracts to prevent urinary infections. In this study grandmother's advice on drinking cranberry juice to prevent these infections was put to a test—and grandma passed.

There have been lots of studies looking at how cranberry juice works, mostly funded by the cranberry juice industry. They show that there are substances in cranberry juice that kill some bacteria and that the nature of the juice acidifies the urine, making it harder for bacteria to live there. But there is more to it than that.

The Finnish study was done on women with recurring urinary infections. They were given the extract twice a day and the time until they got another infection was measured. It was significantly longer with the women on the extract than with women in other branches of the study—they proved grandmother was right.

One of the more interesting and neglected parts of this study, and the part that suggests there is more to cranberry juice than just killing the bacteria or acidifying the urine, comes from the fact that it was designed to last a year, but the supplier of the extract went out of business six months into the study. This is significant because while the women in this treatment group only got six months worth of treatment, there was a benefit that lasted for the whole year!

These women were in this study because their infections were chronic—despite killing the bacteria regularly with antibiotics the infections kept coming back. If the extract's ability to kill bacteria and acidify the urine were the only means of action the women in the group getting the extract would have started getting infected right after the supply ran out—but they didn't. They received a *long-term benefit.*

Long-term benefits

Long-term benefits, when dealing with infections, mean either that the host defenses are stronger or the bacteria are weaker. While there may be something in these extracts that make the host defenses stronger previous studies by Sharon and his group, as well as others, argue strongly for this effect being on the bacteria—they either shape up or they ship out.

E. coli and other bacteria that cause urinary infections are able to infect us because there are lots of mannose molecules on the cells lining the urinary tract. The bacteria hold on to these molecules, multiply, and pretty soon the person has an infection. Cranberry and lingonberry extracts do not have very much mannose, but earlier research showed that another sugar, fructose, blocked adherence about a tenth as well as mannose, and these extracts have lots of fructose.

As pointed out these bacteria mostly come from the person's own gastrointestinal tract—it's their reservoir. They get into the genitourinary tract by moving across the perineum. Sometimes they are helped by poor hygiene, like wiping the wrong direction. Often they migrate in bath water. So dealing with these bacteria in the GI tract is a reasonable approach and researchers have confirmed that the replacement of pathogens in the GI tract actually happens. When people use cranberry juice regularly the E. coli in the bowel with mannose lectins hold on to the fructose in the juice and over time are replaced by other strains without the mannose lectin—they ship out. The new bacteria, that don't hold on to mannose, or fructose, can't cause urinary infections. The patients received the long-term benefit because their reservoir of bacteria changed to types that could not cause urinary infections. Like the much more benign El Tor strain of cholera you might say these bacteria had been tamed.

When CASY agents such as bacteria and their human hosts are in a conflict situation with each other our current mechanical model rests on the use of force to insure control by killing the bacteria; peace is best maintained in this model by the control of the dominant, more powerful agent, so we take antibiotics to kill the presumed less powerful bacteria. This model is applied at all levels, from dealing with bacteria to international statecraft. But with time this approach always leads to periodic violent change as the dominant agent eventually becomes weaker and the weaker agent stronger.

The CASY and evolutionary way of dealing with conflict is to keep the opponent's mental context creatively aligned while looking for elements that can be played with in either their physical or relational context that may relate to the problem. Effort is thus directed at the context and the agent is allowed to adapt to the change. Rudyard Kipling tells the story about the grandmother, 7,000 or so generations ago, who fed the wolf to keep it from eating her children and grandchildren. She was addressing the context of hunger in the wolf that led to conflict when it ate her family. Current thought has the wolf feeding from the community dump, but whether the grandmother or the refuse pile eating in close proximity to humans rapidly selects for shorter distance fear, to wolves that could tolerate being closer to our ancestors, and feeding the wolf for a few generations led to the dog, man's best friend. This evidence suggests that we can do the same kind of thing with bacteria by feeding them the right kind of sugars.

The message delivered by such treatment is not a threat that stimulates resistance, but a friendly 'shape up or ship out.' The wolves that did not adapt to eating close to humans did not change and got left out in this taming relationship. That is the kind of pressure we should be putting on our pathogenic bacteria at all times—or at least often enough that they get the message.

Taming bacteria—shipping out

Paul Ewald, in his discussion of domesticating bacteria, did not address blocking adherence as means of pressuring bacteria toward friendlier adaptations, but looked only at blocking transmission. Blocking the transmission of bacteria from one host to another alters their context and applies evolutionary pressure toward adaptations that make them less damaging or harmful to their current host. When bacteria can't easily get from one host to another killing their current host becomes a dead end for the bacteria as well. Much to his credit, Ewald saw this and correctly predicted that the deadly Ebola epidemic would only cause local outbreaks, not the global pandemic that many feared. This virus killed people so rapidly that there was not enough time for it to get to another host; most of the transmission in the affected communities came from caring for the bodies of the victims. All that is needed to prevent its spread is the use of "standard procedures" (gown, gloves, and mask) when caring for the bodies of the victims. What Ewald didn't see was that blocking adherence changes the context in a similar way, exerts the same pressures to adapt, and is just as effective at doing so as blocking transmission.

This kind of evolutionary pressure is the kind we want to use in guiding all CASYs—bacteria as well as states. It's what happens when we use CASY principles to play with a context rather than mechanical principles to manipulate or kill the oppositional agents. It's what we all learn at church when we are told to love the sinner, but hate the sin. Addressing adaptations, bacterial and otherwise, is like addressing the sin. It does not focus on the agent so it doesn't raise their defenses. In this way changing the physical context of the bacteria by cleaning water led to adaptations in the cholera bacteria to the El Tor strain that kills fewer people, and feeding the wolf changed it into a dog. Changing the physical context of these agents encouraged them to adapt, and maintaining a non-threatening context allowed for creative adaptations that were healthier for us as well. These methods address adaptations made by the agents as they cope with their environments, in their choice of food, the level of their aggression, or other behaviors harmful to us. They don't try to kill the agent. Killing bacteria pressures them toward defensive adaptations. But there is no such threat, as Ewald points out, from decreasing their transmission, or, as we point out, from decreasing their adherence. Both approaches can domesticate bacteria.

In the examples above where mechanical methods blocked the spread of infecting agents or sugars decreased their adherence, the harmful bacteria 'shipped out' and were replaced by other less virulent strains. In another case the bacteria themselves change.

Taming bacteria—shaping up

Xylitol is a naturally occurring sugar substitute that is increasingly used today because it is safe for diabetics and prevents tooth decay. The human body makes about a teaspoon of xylitol every day and the sugar, xylose, is one of those commonly found on our cell surfaces, but the xylose is deep enough among these other sugars that it doesn't usually play a part in any of the known adherence mechanisms.

In this country most sugar alcohols (xylitol, sorbitol, maltitol, etc.) can make the commercial claim of reducing tooth decay, but mostly they do this by replacing the sugar in our foods and stimulating saliva that protects the teeth; and because they are not absorbed as well as regular sugars they can claim fewer calories—and they all share the side effect of diarrhea if used excessively. While they all help prevent tooth decay by replacing the sugar in our diets xylitol does something more as well.

Tooth decay is begun when the bacteria living in the plaque on our teeth make an acid as they digest the sugars we eat. The acid eats through the enamel surfaces of our teeth and a cavity is begun. Reducing the refined sugars in our diets can help, and all sugar alcohols do this. But addressing the bacteria can do more, and that is where xylitol has an exclusive benefit.

One of the more prominent culprits in making the acid that eats our teeth is a strain of bacteria called *Streptococcus mutans*. When these bacteria are exposed to xylitol they eat it, thinking that it's like sugar. Xylitol, however, differs from most other sugars in our diets in that it has five carbon atoms instead of the more usual six, and these bacteria can't digest it.

Xylitol comes from xylose, which is wood sugar. There are many bacteria that recycle plants that can easily handle five carbon sugars, but they don't try to recycle animals where six carbon sugars are the rule, and so are not the pathogens that infect us.

S. mutans, and most other bacteria that are associated with animals, use six carbon sugars for food and don't have the means to digest five carbon sugars—so they get indigestion when they try. And it is a serious type of indigestion that disrupts even the structure of the bacteria, so they adapt to not eat the xylitol any more; they become what are called xylitol resistant. But at the same time they also change so that they don't produce as much acid. Less acid means less tooth decay. The benefit in these cases is due, not to the type of bacteria being changed, but by the nature of the bacteria changing—they shape up.

Xylitol also decreases the adherence of this bacterium so they ship out more often and are replaced by others that don't cause tooth decay. One of the better examples of this process and the long-term benefits associated with xylitol is its use on children in Belize. The initial study was two years long, used several gums with varying amounts of differing sugar alcohols, and was done on children in Kindergarten and first grade. There were no surprises, with the xylitol-only sweetened gum doing significantly better than all others. But five years later, with no exposure to xylitol during this interval, the researchers returned to look at the teeth again. They found that the permanent teeth that had erupted during the earlier two year long study had 95% less tooth decay than the child's other teeth. Again, long-term benefits such as these are explained either by the bacteria shaping up or shipping out. In this particular case the most reasonable explanation is that the xylitol helped determine the bacteria that makes up the plaque, or biofilm, on the erupting teeth; the xylitol reduced the cariogenic, or cavity forming, bacteria to the point that they were not there at the time the biofilm was formed. Less cariogenic bacteria made up the stable biofilm on these kid's teeth and they got the long-term benefit.

While this is a significant benefit in dealing with *Streptococcus mutans*, the cause of most tooth decay, it may have even more benefit as we try to deal with their cousins, *Streptococcus pneumoniae*, living in the nose, that are a major cause of respiratory infections. These cousins share the same genetic inability to handle xylitol, and their adherence is decreased as well.

Other bacteria appear similarly affected. The adherence of Clostridium difficile, a serious problem causing bacteria that often colonizes the GI tract when people are on heavy doses of antibiotics, is also significantly decreased by xylitol. How it decreases this adherence has not been studied in enough detail yet, but we know that many bacteria are affected. Researchers at the Center for Biofilm

Engineering at the University of Montana point out that xylitol has "broad spectrum" ability to block bacterial as well as biofilm adhesion, and dental researchers are finding the same broad spectrum ability to block oral bacteria from adhering to tooth surfaces.

Xylitol is the ingredient that makes our nasal spray so effective and the power and importance of this concept is best demonstrated by our early experience with two patients using this spray. One patient had persistent fluid in his middle ear that interfered with his hearing. The other had serious problems with asthma for which she was taking six different medications, including steroids with their growth slowing effects. After several days of regular use both of these children had episodes where they got rid of significant amounts of material from their noses, not outward where you can wipe it, but backward into the throat where it choked them. In the process they gagged and vomited, and one of the mothers expressed the fear that her child was losing her brains. Both mothers described the material as being thicker and more structured than mucus. Not being there and witnessing these events I cannot say the material was biofilm or not, but it sounds suspicious, and their conditions disappeared after the cleansing episodes. The volume immediately went down on the TV for the child with the ear problems, and six months later the asthmatic child was playing basketball and doing gymnastics without any of her prior medications. Both children had a recurrence of their problems when they stopped using the spray.

One possible explanation for the broad spectrum effect that xylitol has on these different bacteria may be related to xylitol's flexibility. Most of the sugar complexes that bacteria hang on to are fixed in their structure so the bacterial lectins can identify them easily. Xylitol, on the other hand has the same kind and conformation of atoms, but is not fixed. It is able to bend and twist and rotate so that it can conform itself to look like a lot of these other sugars; it might not fit the lectin exactly, but it comes close enough to confuse the issue. It's like the fructose that confuses bacteria with mannose lectins. Such 'look-a-like' molecules are called mimetic. Frequent exposure to large amounts of xylitol, the most effective way to prevent tooth decay that has been demonstrated in thirty years of clinical studies, is also the best way to flood the bacterial lectins with these mimetic molecules and interfere with their adherence. But the 'large amount' referred to here is in molecular terms. There are billions of bacteria in the mouth; it is one of the dirtiest parts of the body in bacterial terms, but the bottom line of thirty years of clinical studies show that only a gram of xylitol in gum five times a day reduces tooth decay by about 80%.

Changing the nature and the type of bacteria in the mouth, we gain, as did the women with the urinary infections, long term benefits. One Finnish researcher, where the benefits of xylitol in preventing tooth decay were first discovered, even found that women who regularly used xylitol chewing gum obtained a benefit, in reduced tooth decay, not only for themselves, but for their newborn children up to age five, who were never themselves exposed to xylitol. We will talk more about the dental and other benefits of xylitol later, but these long-term benefits are what we see when bacteria are tamed.

Conclusion

Specific sugars that interfere with bacterial adherence block the adaptive manipulation that bacteria made long ago when they first started infecting animals. That early adaptation allowed the bacteria to adhere—the first step in any infection. Blocking this adaptation has been shown to change the type and the nature of the bacteria that we are surrounded by and live with, to types that cause us less harm. The future that Ewald envisioned in 1994 is here. Decreasing a bacterium's ability to both get to and to hold on to a new host changes its context and puts evolutionary pressure on it to adapt in ways that have proven more friendly to us. It is a means of negotiating a settlement to our current antibiotic warfare, and of taming, or domesticating, bacteria.

In order to promote this friendly type of adaptation bacterial CASYs cannot be threatened. A threat promotes a defensive alignment that results eventually in our enemy becoming more powerful. Using much the same methods that domesticated the dog we can address the context in the bacterial environment that makes them our enemies. The wolf needed to eat, and the bacteria to hold on somewhere so they can eat. By supplying those needs in a different fashion and allowing time for adaptation we encourage our potential enemies to adapt in ways that may be friendlier. The potential is here to tame bacteria just as our remote ancestors did the wolf. But since war is more profitable than peace the utilization of this method will take a realignment of our system to one that is health rather than profit oriented.

Not just health care is oriented on profits, but its research arm as well. One researcher was looking at the adherence of the bacteria that causes whooping cough and found that another sugar complex, galactose, was involved. Galactose is one of the simple sugars that make up the more complex sugar, lactose, which is in milk. This is important because the current immunization for whooping cough is one that teaches us to recognize and kill the agent, so many of these bacteria have come up with new adaptations making our immunization less effective. Does this mean that gargling with milk might prevent or be a treatment for whooping cough? Proteins and sugar complexes in milk are already known to inhibit the adherence of 12 major pathogens even before they looked at it with whooping cough—and human breast milk, that contains more galactose, is even better. Would it really work? We'll never know in the case of whooping cough because the funding was cut. In our current system there is little interest in treatments that don't make a lot of profit and there is no profitable return using non-patentable sugars or foods in such ways. The money is in patentable treatments, not natural sugars. Testing and promoting these concepts is another great opportunity for our Public Health Service since the private, profit oriented, sector has shown little interest.

This problem is not in the practice of medicine, but in the system and how it has been set up. We have seen in this chapter how viewing and treating bacteria mechanically has ended up creating stronger and more resistant bacteria. Bacteria are CASYs with the ability to adapt to changes in their contexts. Addressing their context and promoting creative adaptation is the best way to deal with any CASY, including bacteria.

Moving up the scale we look now at the CASYs that are our bodies, at some of our more helpful adaptations, and the models that we have used to view and treat them in the past—and continue to use even now.

CHAPTER 5
SYMPTOMS, SYMPTOMS, AND MORE SYMPTOMS

Most of what we do is reflexive and there is no intelligence in a reflex.

Michael Mendizza

Michael Mendizza heads the organization "Touch the Future" that suggests ways to optimize learning in children. We learn best when we are in the state that athletes call the "Zone," that Csikszentmihalyi calls "Flow," and that children call "play." This is the mental state where the ability to creatively play with the elements of one's environment is optimized; and it requires a non-threatening and safe environment. It is in this state that we all as children played with our neurons and adapted and organized ourselves to fit into our differing familial and cultural environments; and our decisions as adults often do little more than reflect this enculturation in mindless reflex actions. It is the same in the culture of healthcare where most physicians accept and stay within the paradigm they learned at medical school. As such their decisions and actions as physicians are often little more than reflexes—and there is no intelligence in a reflex. Reflexes are based on mental models and neural pathways made long ago that often have little association with current reality.

Culture and healthcare

Healthcare is culturally specific. A western person generally does better with a pill than with Ayurvedic or energy based medicine, while an indigenous person often does better with treatment based on relationships, spirits, and herbs, than with pills. All medical systems deal with restoring balance to the body—illness is defined by symptoms reflecting loss of that balance. But the *balance* in oriental medicine is in the body's energy systems; in Ayurveda it is the body's *doshas*; in indigenous cultures it is more often an imbalance in relationship with others or with nature. All of these traditions go back thousands of years—it's as if this information is in our DNA.

Our own model goes back to ancient Greece where the concept of humoral medicine originated. Illness, according to the Greeks, was an imbalance in the body's *humors*, and treatment was aimed at restoring the balance—and whether we realize it or not we have retained this orientation in our healthcare culture today. In humoral medicine particular symptoms indicated an imbalance in the humors and the symptoms were treated by inducing the opposite condition. So if the patient had a fever they were cooled, if a sore was wet they used herbs to dry it, and if it was dry they used poultices to wet it. And if a person had symptoms indicating they had too much blood they were cut and allowed to bleed.

If you ask most doctors today about the humoral system they will likely tell you it is dead and gone and that today we practice scientific medicine. What killed it, they will say, were the studies done in the 19th century on blood-letting. This death sentence is a bit premature because the *culture* of humoral medicine continues to play a central role in how we think about illness. "Scientific" medicine has been very successful at multiplying our humors and making them correlate better with our physiology, but the focus remains on balancing them. Beginning in the last century we have added things like vitamin deficiencies, blood pressure, acid levels in our stomachs, and even levels of chemicals in our blood like cholesterol; and when unbalanced we generally try to restore the balance with drugs.

This approach makes sense if we limit ourselves to the analytical mechanical model where the particular element is taken out of its networked context and analyzed to find ways of controlling it, and there are many successes, just as there are limited successes in balancing elements in an ecosystem. But the method comes up short in the long term; and if it doesn't work with ecosystems why should we expect it to work on an equally, if not more, complex and adaptive human? We need to go beyond the mechanical linear thinking of our current paradigm to realize that we are profoundly networked and to recognize our ability to adapt. We need to realize that many of the symptoms we have, that have been labeled imbalances needing correction are helpful defenses. We need to ask, "Why are the imbalances there?" and "Why do we have the symptoms that we have?" And we need to learn from our treatment of ailing ecosystems that addressing their context is a more fruitful treatment than is trying to balance the elements. The networked and interacting balances of a functioning ecosystem allows it to adapt to environmental stresses in ways that we cannot predict and attempting to balance one element is not helpful. Phosphate polluted lakes crash suddenly from clear blue to cloudy and green, but reducing the phosphate levels doesn't help correct this because other compensatory systems have been involved. The same methods don't work with people and they are not likely to work on our economy.

Networks rather than cogs

The processes of adaptation are complex and networked and they are not well understood, which makes risky the analytical practice where many links in the network are cut and discarded as we search for those we can understand and manipulate. This process is comparable to the mathematical process of differentiation. When a complex equation is differentiated the power of the variable is reduced by one and the constants are dropped. Doing this repeatedly one can arrive finally at something that is simple to understand; and this is what we do in the process of analysis. But even complex equations can't adequately model the networked relationships in our systems which gives the systems life and adaptability—and ignoring this complexity is what leads to the unintended consequences. This is how we analyzed the ailing ecosystem, but the treatment didn't help because these systems are networked; they are not cogs in a machine, or even variables in a complex equation.

Adaptation is like a game that agents play with their contexts and they have both an offensive and a defensive team. While the offense plays with the elements and finds ways to expand the agent's niche in the system, the defense plays with them to find ways to deal with the challenges presented by other agents. As we have seen earlier the benefits of defensive adaptations usually go to the agent, and take time to spread into the whole group. Over time defensive adaptations have been passed down to all of us because the survival value associated with them led to its becoming wide spread—and we have inherited the best of them. Because they have passed the test of time our defensive adaptations need first to be recognized as such; then they need to be supported.

Creative adaptations come from play with the elements of our systems. For humans a large part of these elements, which we can actually play with, is what we eat. T. Colin Campbell is one of America's leading nutritional researchers and scholars. As the director of the China study he led the largest epidemiologic study ever done on the role of nutrition in disease. In his book, *The China Study*, he explains the results of that study and gives us what is most likely the best advice available today for maintaining a healthy context in this area. Unfortunately, as he points out, our system is not open to preventive ways of seeing, but continues in the analytical mechanical paradigm of treating or balancing symptoms only after they have become a problem. And as he also confirms it maintains these blinders because the system is profitable to powerful interests that control the information.

Nor, as pointed out earlier, does our model recognize that many of our bothersome symptoms are defensive adaptations; it sees them only as symptoms to be balanced with drugs. But again, hobbling your defense means you will likely lose the game. If symptoms are defenses they need to be honored.

Hypertension, for example, is a critical part of the flight or fight response; it insures optimal blood supply to the muscles needed for this task, whichever one is chosen. It's a defense! While it was very useful to us when we lived in the jungle and had to deal with predators, we don't often have to deal with threats on this level today. But the reaction is still there; it's just that the predators have moved into our social environment. While they are not likely to eat us, there are many that take advantage, and the reflex is the same. Is there a connection here, where black people, with their long history of slavery, abuse, and discrimination, have higher blood pressure because of the chronic nature of their apprehension and anxiety? And would there be a better way to address this than a pill?

Hypertension and cholesterol are more than humors yet we treat these conditions just like our ancestors treated any humoral imbalance. Such treatment remains the focus of our system which reaps billions of dollars every year from drugs we all consider safe, that are designed to reverse uncomfortable symptoms from a fever to acid indigestion, and from diarrhea to a runny nose. But when we see the body as a CASY we understand that such treatment, using drugs to restore a mechanically defined balance, is often abuse.

Symptoms and adaptation

Seeing the body as a machine blinds us to its adaptations. Machines can't adapt and without a metaphor in our language and thought processes describing adaptation we don't see it—it remains invisible. But symptoms, that in the mechanical model define an illness or a condition to be balanced, are expressed for a reason. When one looks more closely at the symptoms we have we see that most of them are expressed in us because somewhere they provide a survival advantage—like hypertension they are present because of natural selection.

Living agents all sense and interact with the context of their environments—and adapt to it. Defensive adaptations help the agent survive and natural selection spreads these beneficial adaptations throughout future generations. This is what Darwinian evolution, as explained in his *The Origin of the Species*, is mostly about. What Darwin does not talk much about is the creative play that results in the diversity of nature. The novel adaptations that lead to diversity more often come from cooperation and cross-pollination among the members of the system; they are tested by natural selection as well, but it is the larger system that gets the survival advantage.

In their book *Why We Get Sick,* George Williams and Randolph Nesse speak for most biologists in elaborating on this way of looking at our symptoms. They point out that many of the symptoms we have when we get "sick" are actually adaptive defenses that give us a survival benefit. A fever, for example, makes it harder for infecting agents, either viruses or bacteria, to multiply—it's a defensive adaptation that helps us deal more effectively with an infection. This particular adaptation occurred a long time ago because every warm blooded animal has the ability to develop a fever. And cold blooded reptiles commonly move to the sun and warm up when they have an infection and need a fever. Such adaptations are expressed in us much later in time because they work—they have a survival benefit. Experimentally infected snakes that are allowed to move into the sun and warm up survive better than those who can't, and experimentally infected rabbits given the drugs we use in us to treat fevers die more often. But we have been taught to fear a fever, and our current humoral based model says we need to balance it, so we ignore the harm it does to infected rabbits and continue to treat a fever with any of the variety of drugs promoted and sold for that purpose. *Defensive symptoms may be bothersome, but they should not be feared because they actual help us deal better with a threat; they come with a survival advantage and should be honored and supported.*

Another class of symptoms are the *manipulations* we discussed in the prior chapter. We used as examples the prostration of malaria and the profuse diarrhea of cholera. Other examples mentioned earlier are the toxins produced by the bacteria causing tetanus and diphtheria. Again, manipulations are symptoms that our bodies are tricked into doing that help not us, but the bacteria or other infecting agents. Both a fever and diarrhea show the sometimes confusing nature of this differentiation of symptoms since both are initially defenses. But even defenses can be manipulated in the processes of adaptation and it should not stop us from honoring the defenses. Such manipulations are creative adaptations made by infecting agents that enable them to spread easier to other hosts. And they are best addressed, not by treating them to eliminate them, but by blocking their efficacy; in the examples given using mosquito nets and clean water to block the manipulation, by changing the physical context so the manipulation doesn't work any more.

Conventional wisdom again takes another direction here, for when a person is sick they are usually expected to take a cold pill and go to work. If we are to properly deal with all of the manipulations of infecting agents this is the wrong thing to do. Sick people should stay home and not share their germs—isolation works; and the mosquito nets, the clean water, the condoms, the universal precautions and all the other methods used to prevent bacteria and viruses from spreading, work by isolating the infecting agent. Going to work when one is sick is the wrong thing to do.

There are also some symptoms that are just *side effects*, where neither the host nor the infecting agent benefits. The dry eyes associated with many auto-immune diseases are a side effect. These can be treated without consideration for why they are there.

Cross pollinating from biology

This is a different way of looking at our symptoms than that common in the practice of medicine. It is not being taught in most medical schools where the analytical, mechanical model continues to dominate. It comes mostly from biology where they are asking questions about the expression of symptoms. Many of the problems in our way of seeing come from the incestuous relationship between agents in our various systems, in this case the physicians and the drug companies. These are inbred problems that can best be treated by cross-pollinating with the healthy root stock—and for the practice of medicine that root stock is biology. It is critical today that health care professionals look to their roots in biology where this model is being developed—only then will the humoral concept be put to rest. And only then will we have the enhanced level of health that has historically accompanied a change in perspective.

Creative adaptations have produced the diversity of life that we see around us; defensive adaptations protect us from environmental predators. While we argue more for the social benefits associated with the creative pole, both are vital to life. When one sees on an evolutionary time scale we understand better the necessity of and benefits accompanying our defensive adaptations—even those that are bothersome. Natural selection has had the time to refine these adaptations to where they are the best that are available. Our tendency, as encouraged by the mechanical model, is to see these bothersome symptoms as indications of imbalance, to focus on them as the problem, and to balance them with a variety of readily available drugs—and it is misguided and more harmful than we realize. If you want the other team to win, then just hobble your defense; and our increasing rates of many illnesses strongly suggests that this is what is happening with many of our current medical treatments.

As an Osteopathic Physician I have been more interested in helping our defenses work better. In the flu pandemic that followed the First World War the mortality rate in the United States for those who were sick with the flu and treated with standard medical care was around 5%. In those treated by Osteopathic Physicians it was closer to 0.25%. In other words, around one out of twenty of those treated in a conventional manner died, while in those treated by Osteopathic Physicians it was closer to one out of four hundred. The Osteopathic Physicians originally reporting this difference credited it only to the physical manipulation of the body that is characteristic of early Osteopaths. Others looking later have raised some questions as to the presence of other factors. Manipulation has been shown to improve ones immune functioning but likely more important than the manipulation is the different way Osteopathic Physicians saw and dealt with their patient's illness. In the days before antibiotics standard medical treatment for the flu was cough suppressants for the cough and aspirin for the fever. Osteopathic Physicians, however, recognized that these symptoms were actually part of the body's defenses brought into play to deal with the virus, and that blocking such defenses compromised the patient's ability to cope with the illness. Hobbling these defenses with cough suppressants and aspirin gave an edge to the flu and one out of twenty died. Osteopathic Physicians honored and supported them, and helped them along with gentle manipulation, giving an edge to the patient, and one out of four hundred died.

When we experimentally infect animals and give them the same drugs we use to treat a fever, or prevent the cold blooded ones from moving into the sunlight, more of them die. Those with a higher temperature are more likely to live and reproduce. That's how natural selection works. It is our position that there are many current medical treatments that deal with bothersome symptoms mechanically, that we do not stop to consider that those symptoms may be defenses, *and that using drugs to block such defen-*

sive symptoms robs us of their survival benefit and is in itself a major reason why we get sick. Applying the CASY paradigm to this situation we can easily see these symptoms as the defensive adaptations they are, and hobbling your defense means the other team scores—something we all want to avoid when the other team is made up of infecting agents.

This analytical and mechanical treatment is based on our western medical culture, is inbred, is more harmful than we realize, and contributes significantly to our nations declining health. A runny nose is another example.

Just about everyone has had an episode where their nose runs. In the 1930s we found that histamine was the major trigger for this condition and developed antihistamines in the 1940s. They and decongestants sanitized the runny nose. They were the miracle drugs of the post war era and soon became standard treatment. But we now know that the runny nose is our body's attempt to remove irritants. It's a major defense that washes the airway. The fact that this washing is a successful adaptation is witnessed by its expression in all air breathing animals with lungs and an airway leading to them. What happens to the irritants and infecting agents in the nose if we turn it off?

Common sense, biological, and medical studies all confirm that the runny nose is but one of our many evolutionary defenses. In September, 2007 the FDA paid service to this point by reporting the deaths of children that were associated with the use of antihistamines and decongestants. But they missed the point of the washing being a defense in stating that the deaths were due to parental overdoses or drug effects. Within a month, and without an argument, the pharmaceutical companies withdrew these drugs from use in children. Such defenses are adaptations, made long ago and refined ever since, that help the agents live more successfully in their challenging environments. In the language of evolution and CASYs these adaptations were successful because they provided the survival advantage that is at the foundation of all natural selection.

When we see symptoms like the runny nose from the humoral viewpoint, where they are treated by inducing the opposite condition, it is easy to justify blocking them—especially when they are such a nuisance. But when we realize that we are CASYs we see that these are adaptations and that blocking them robs us of the survival benefit associated with the defense because it decreases our ability to cope with the irritant. Again, if you hobble the defense of your favorite team, the other side is more likely to score and it's the same with our bodies—and more children die.

Living agents are able to adapt and a runny nose is just one example of the kind of beneficial adaptations that our predecessors made in our evolutionary history. Reptiles blow their noses and birds get runny noses; every animal with lungs and airway leading to them has some ability to clean that airway. We are all endowed with many such defenses, not just those in the airway. Many of them work without any outward sign; those that are noticeable, like the runny nose, fever, or diarrhea, are usually secondary defenses. The irritation of the symptom is in itself useful because there may be something the person can do to help. But in the mechanical and humoral model the symptom itself is seen as the problem and treatment balances the body by turning it off.

This way of seeing has been with us for centuries and is firmly established as the "conventional wisdom." According to John Kenneth Galbraith who coined the phrase, conventional wisdom is blinded by profit so there is little interest in questioning these practices that make billions annually for the pharmaceutical and healthcare industries, and definitely no financial support for questioning their value.

Our roots in humoral medicine: blood-letting

Blood-letting is the practice that "killed" humoral medicine and it provides an example of the perils of a mechanical model as well as an idea for how long such errors can persist. It was done by cutting the patient's arm and letting them bleed. The first instance of blood-letting is lost in antiquity, but by the 5th Century BC it was common practice. The symbol of medicine, what is today the stethoscope, was for centuries the knife and the bleeding pan. The humoral diagnosis that led to the blood-letting was an excess of the sanguine humor—the patient had too much blood. It was a reasonable treatment for the diagnosis, but in the mid 19th century, when we began asking the right questions, we found that it was not very good for the patients—more of them died. So physicians stopped blood-letting and switched to scientific medicine. But changing a practice is much easier than changing a paradigm and we really did not learn the lesson of why blood-letting was harmful, nor use that understanding to question the larger model. But we are making progress; blood-letting persisted for close to three thousand years before we noticed more people dying, while it only took just over sixty to see the same problem with cold pills. But again, as long as we blame the deaths on parental overdosing we haven't really seen the true nature of the problem.

Most people, even most doctors, think that it's the misuse or overuse of these drugs that is the problem, just as we thought that blood-letting caused more people to die because of the loss of blood. Regularly giving blood today is actually associated with better health because it lowers the normally excessive amount of iron in the body with all of its associated free-radicals. It was not the loss of blood that increased the mortality of those bled; it was more subtle than that.

When someone was diagnosed with too much blood it was usually because certain signs and symptoms—redness, pain, fever, and swelling—were present. These signs represented to them an excess of the sanguine humor—the patient had too much blood. But today they represent a complex that every medical student learns as the *rubor, dolor, calor, and tumor* of the inflammatory reaction. The practice of blood-letting ended around the turn of the last century, but the inflammatory reaction was not understood until about a generation later, so they remain unconnected; even today few understand that blood-letting was in fact a very effective treatment for the inflammatory reaction.

When the body detects an injury or an invasion the inflammatory reaction is its first line of defense. When someone, for example, injures an ankle the inflammatory reaction opens the small blood vessels in the area so that they leak. This results in the pain, redness, and swelling that led, as recently as 100 years ago, to the diagnosis of too much blood and the treatment of blood-letting. But the swelling also splints the injured joint from the inside and causes enough pain for the person to stay off it until it's had a chance to heal a little. It's a *defense* that helps the person deal more effectively with the injury.

When a person is bled, or loses blood for any other reason, the body compensates with another defense: it closes down the circulation to the skin and the extremities in order to save blood for the vital organs in the center of the body—what we recognize today as shock. When the person with an ankle injury was bled, and enough blood lost to trigger this altered circulation, you could literally watch the swelling lessen, the redness disappear, and the pain diminish as less blood went to the injured area. It was a very effective way to resolve those inflammatory symptoms, but wrong for the patient.

Blood-letting probably did no great harm when used to reverse the symptoms of an injury, especially if we paid attention to the warning light these symptoms provided and honored them by splinting and supporting the injury from the outside. But with infection causing the inflammatory reaction it was a different story.

When the immune system triggers the inflammatory reaction it's usually because of an infection. Just as with an injury the small blood vessels are opened, but in this case the purpose is not to splint, but to bring a whole host of the body's blood borne natural defenses to the area of infection. But the symptoms, like with an injury, are the redness, swelling, pain, with the likelihood now of a fever as well. And just as with an injury, the diagnosis 150 years ago was too much blood, and the treatment was blood-letting; and just as with an injury you could literally watch your patient get better—blood loss is a more critical condition and it always trumps inflammation. But when the defensive adaptation of the inflammatory response is blocked it means that our natural blood borne defenses don't get to the site of infection. The infection has time to grow and spread. And when we finally got around to asking the right questions, mostly in people with pneumonia, we found that more of them died after being bled; so we stopped blood-letting, we pronounced the humoral system dead, and we now practice scientific medicine. But we didn't learn the lesson.

The increased mortality that followed the practice of blood-letting was an anomaly that should have brought the whole system into question, but it didn't. We have just expanded the number of humors and given them a firmer base in physiology—but our emphasis is still balancing them. The question they asked about blood-letting addressed mortality rather than symptom relief, but we didn't learn this lesson either as we continue to look at symptom relief rather than mortality in our drug studies. Treating ailing ecosystems by balancing their symptoms is not effective and neither is treating the body by balancing its. Yet we still follow this mechanical model of balancing symptoms, and most of the time we do it without even asking *why* the symptoms are there in the first place. It's a reflex; and there is no intelligence in a reflex. We do it because balancing symptoms in this way is bred into the system—and it's an inbred weakness.

Compensating for inbred weaknesses

A practice is easier to change than a paradigm as our experience with blood-letting demonstrates. When a particular way of thinking persists long enough it gets embedded in the economy of the society and becomes conventional wisdom—it gets inbred. Our view of other options and ideas in such systems is handicapped by our way of seeing. If we can't see them, the questions aren't there so we don't even bother looking, and even if we did see them the vested interests, the most powerful roadblock to any progress, would be a potent obstacle.

Livestock are commonly inbred to improve desirable characteristics such as speed, pelt, milk, more meat, or whatever. Inbreeding, as we have seen, is not done to produce novelty, but to improve the quality of something already present; as such it shares many characteristics with a defensive alignment with its focus on improving survival qualities. A common problem with the practice, however, is that along with the efficiencies one gets inbred weaknesses; and this is a potential problem in all CASYs. When this happens to the breeder or horticulturist they go back to the healthy root stock for a strain with strengths that compensates for the weakness. The solution for all inbred weaknesses lies not in the system itself, but in its healthier root stock.

In the practice of medicine this root stock is biology. Congress, when they established the Institute of Medicine, took experts from health care and gave them the task of reforming our system. So far their major recommendations have been universal health insurance and increased use of information technology. These are certainly efficiencies that will help our system work better, but they are hardly solutions to our problems. They are the kind of defensively aligned changes one finds with inbreeding where particular characteristics are focused on and improved. Inbreeding leads to efficiencies rather than novelties, but the inbred weaknesses that come with them need to be recognized as such or they will overwhelm the system. Washington D.C. has been called the most inbred city in our country and it provides a good example of the down side of inbreeding and why we have taboos against incest.

Had the Institute of Medicine included a few more biologists they may have arrived at a few more substantive changes. One such change is what we have been presenting in seeing the body as adaptive rather than as a machine. Biologists have looked at the problem of treating our defensive symptoms and proposed alternatives. But while they have been written about in both the biological and medical literature they have not penetrated the culture of American healthcare so we continue reflexively making the same error our ancestors did when they bled their patients, the error of mechanically addressing the body, of not seeing the adaptations and natural selection behind its symptoms, and of often hobbling its defenses. And there is no intelligence in a reflex.

Biologists ask *why* the symptoms are there. They found that the inflammatory reaction, which for almost three thousand years we routinely blocked in western medicine by blood-letting, is one of the body's major defenses against injury and infection. Biologists point out that defensive adaptations, which help us survive, need to be honored and supported rather than blocked. But our primary treatment of fever, diarrhea, rhinorrhea, and a host of other symptoms that also happen to be defenses, similar to the inflammatory reaction, remains blocking them or turning them off. While our history of blood-letting vividly portrays the problems of this approach, few have made the connection that it hurt us because it blocked a helpful defense. Mostly we think it was harmful because of the loss of blood, not the disabling of the inflammatory response the loss triggered—so our harmful practices continue.

Today we even have scientific validation showing how effective drugs are at reversing bothersome symptoms. But the studies looking at the side effects of these drugs last only a few weeks and don't even try to address the long-term effects of what happens when the symptom is blocked—the question that our great-grandparents asked about blood-letting.

This is one of the areas where studies in the Public Health sector of our healthcare system would be beneficial. Studies that ask about the long term effects of blocking defenses are not likely to be done by the pharmaceutical industry that makes billions off the drugs that do this, and that would also have some legal liability if inquiries revealed any foreknowledge of the problem. At the same time, while just about every doctor knows that a fever is a defense, the healthcare industry does not seem to be interested in spending the time and effort to educate the public about the potential harm of treating fevers and other bothersome defenses. This educational job is what the Public Health Service has excelled at in the past and they should be empowered to do it again.

Paradigm shifts change the way we see things and are generally associated with increases in understanding; and putting that understanding into practice leads to increased benefits for mankind. The changes accompanying our understanding of the germ theory meant that clean water, sanitation, immunization and Pasteurization made sense; and their adoption was responsible for the significant extension in life expectancy we saw in America and around the world as the changes were implemented a century ago. In the same way seeing the body as a CASY leads to honoring and supporting, rather than blocking, our defenses; and putting this understanding into practice would enable us all to benefit from the survival advantage associated with these defenses and likewise enhance our health and improve our lives. That means we need to look at these particular symptoms in the framework of our larger defenses.

CHAPTER 6
GO! DEFENSE

A good defense squeezes the field so the attack is forced to play in tight areas that are more difficult.
(Professional soccer training)

Just as with soccer, our own defenses limit the field where infecting agents can enter the body. This is what the skin does in our own game with the environment. It's the barrier between us and the outside. But it's a good barrier and a good defense only when it's intact. When it's injured we need to take action to help our defenses prevent the infections to which the injury has opened us. With good cleaning and proper care most wounds will not get infected.

It's different with insect bites that penetrate the skin, often without our awareness. Vector borne infections like Lyme disease and Rocky Mountain Spotted Fever in this country, and malaria and Leishmaniasis, in the tropics, to name but a few, are difficult to deal with because the insect that is the vector for the particular disease penetrates the skin and introduces the infecting agent directly into the body—they bypass our defenses. And we are more vulnerable when the event goes unnoticed and we miss the chance of helping our immune system's defenses earlier.

Normally the skin squeezes the field so that the environmental agents must play in the areas that are open to them. The three open areas, where we get the most infections, are the GI tract, the respiratory tract, and the genitourinary tract; and these areas are where our defenses are the strongest.

Living adapting agents and natural selection have had millions of years to test adaptations that deal with challenges in these necessary openings to the body, and we have inherited the best of them all. Primary defenses in these areas are constant and without associated symptoms. Secondary defenses are often bothersome in order to tell us that something is going on, and that there is perhaps something that we can do to help. Like the wound in the skin that needs our help, bothersome symptoms are also signals. Good things happen when we pay attention and honor them.

Gastrointestinal defenses

Considering the amount of food we put into our mouths it is a tribute to our food inspection programs that we don't have more problems with our GI tracts. While there is a lot that we don't know about food safety and many areas where it could be improved, our food supply is likely the safest anywhere, but we still have our share of problems.

As is typical in the body we have first-line defenses in our GI tracts that don't cause bothersome symptoms. The acid and other enzyme systems in the stomach act to break down the food to make it more digestible, but they also are defenses that kill most of the bacteria and breakdown other harmful substances that we eat, or swallow as drainage from the airway. Another primary defense comes from the good bacteria that live with us cooperatively and create a protective biofilm in our GI tracts which acts as a defense by preventing the adherence and excessive growth of harmful bacteria. These bacteria are often regional and take some getting used to so travelers to different countries need to take more care when eating local foods than the people living there. When these and other GI defenses are challenged and overwhelmed there is always a back-up that most travelers have experienced at one time or another. And the back-up is more than likely to signal to us that something is wrong—it's bothersome.

Gastroenteritis, or nausea, vomiting and diarrhea, is the back-up for the GI tract; it's how it responds to things it doesn't like—it tries to get rid of them. While this is bothersome, *it's a defense!* Despite our food inspection programs gastroenteritis remains one of the most common problems in our Emergency Rooms and most of the treatments include at least some measures that block this defensive cleaning of the irritated GI tract. By the time they get to the ER this is often seen as necessary because of fluid losses, but The World Health Organization cautions us about blocking this defense early in treatment. If the cause is bacterial then blocking, delaying, or slowing the diarrhea by any means increases the chance of the infecting agent adapting to, adhering to, and colonizing the GI tract, like the typhoid bacillus was able to do in "Typhoid Mary." If it is a virus or toxin, delaying the emptying only gives it more chance to irritate us. This is why using drugs to stop this cleaning is associated with increased levels of both irritable and inflammatory bowel disease. Gastroenteritis is bothersome, but it is not something to be turned off without seriously considering the consequences of doing so. At times such emergency treatment is considered necessary because significant fluid loss makes it harder for the body to work right, but fluid replacement is always a better choice. And the dehydration that is the most significant problem with gastroenteritis is far less likely to be a problem when early treatment centers on oral rehydration—a treatment that few in this country know about and even fewer understand.

Supporting this gastrointestinal defense with oral rehydration

Oral rehydration is simply a way to keep the body's tank of fluids full by drinking the right mixture of water, salt, and sugar. In the proper proportions these molecules activate a pump in the stomach and small intestine that pumps water into the body. It's called the sodium-glucose-transport system and it is the most cost effective way in existence of getting water into the body. One molecule of glucose (the sugar) and two molecules of sodium (the salt), turn on this system that then actively pumps 210 molecules of water into the body—and it even works when one is vomiting. That's the science behind why oral rehydration works as well as it does, but like many things in healthcare the science came after the success.

Oral rehydration was developed in the 1960s as a treatment for cholera epidemics. In third world countries, like Bangladesh where the research was done that led to its development, cholera was a major problem because of overcrowding and poor sanitation. Epidemics raged periodically and mortality was high. In more wealthy countries cholera is treated with intravenous fluids and antibiotics and few people die. The most important part of the treatment is the IV fluids, because cholera kills from dehydration, not from the infection. Antibiotics shorten the time when the bacteria are shed by only a few days and people recover just as well without them when they have enough fluid.

This is one case where a defense kills; asthma is another. When it recognizes the cholera toxin, perceiving (erroneously it turns out) this bacterial manipulation to be a deadly threat, the body opens every tap in the effort to remove it. The profuse watery diarrhea that results is the hallmark of cholera and quickly empties the body of its fluids and salts so that functioning of the major organs becomes impossible. While cholera gets the blame, dehydration is the immediate cause of death.

Oral rehydration made it possible to keep the tank full despite the diarrhea. Potassium is added too since it is lost with diarrhea, but it doesn't play a part in the pump that makes oral rehydration so effective a treatment. BRAC is the organization in Bangladesh that took the information from this research to the people. Thousands of people were trained to teach the principle of oral rehydration: a liter of water, a pinch of baking soda, and a fist full of sugar—and millions of lives were saved. In twenty years it saved more lives than penicillin had in 50 and in 1989 the editors of the leading medical journal *Lancet* called it one of the greatest achievements of 20th century medicine. But while the United Nations and World Health Organization promote the use of oral rehydration throughout the world, few here in the United States have heard of it. A conference at Johns Hopkins on oral rehydration concluded it is greatly underused in this country. But while it continues to be underused even here there are successes. In the recent 2007 Salmonella epidemic associated with contaminated peanut butter many people drank oral rehydration fluids and were better by the time of their appointments with the overwhelmed doctors.

Blocks to the use of oral rehydration

Part of the reason for our lack of knowledge about oral rehydration is regulatory and financial, and part is social. The social part comes from both our difficulty accepting that we could learn anything from a particular success in third-world medicine and our mistaken association of efficacy with expense, so an inexpensive treatment is seen as ineffective. Besides we don't have cholera in America. Like our problem moving from blood-letting to seeing the error of treating defenses, we have difficulty learning from particulars, of seeing the broader picture that such a treatment, that honors and supports the defense, may be useful for all gastroenteritis and not just cholera.

The regulatory reasons have to do with government regulations and the fact that salt, sugar and water are impossible to control and patent because they can be mixed up at home. Anything in this country besides soap and water that is claimed to prevent or treat illness comes under the control of the Food and Drug Administration. If a company were to make the claims that are clearly appropriate for oral rehydration they would first have to get approval from the FDA, repeat the studies showing its efficacy, then they would have to make their product following FDA guidelines. Following these guidelines allows them to make medical claims and educate the public about their product. But this would increase the demand and invite others to compete in making a less expensive product.

Competitors would not have to educate the public, would not have to comply with FDA regulations, and could market a much less expensive product and walk away with all the business. The introducing, experimenting, educating, promoting, and FDA complying company would be left holding the bag for all these additional expenses, and all businesses in this sector of the industry understand this dynamic. To their credit Ross Laboratories has done extensive research on oral rehydration in making their product *Pedialyte®*, and packets like those distributed by the World Health Organization are available from a company in Kansas City at far less expense, but neither company makes any claims for health benefits—so few learn the lesson of why oral rehydration was such a significant advance.

Finally the financial reasons have to do with the way the system is set up, and this will be discussed in much greater detail in a later chapter. Basically they boil down to the fact that the system is rewarded for expensive care. If you present to an Emergency Room with gastroenteritis and mild to moderate dehydration you will be treated with intravenous solutions and charged a minimum of $200. Those running the system are there to make a profit and substituting a quart of oral rehydration solution costing 40 cents (its cost at Egyptian pharmacies), or even $10.00 for a bottle of Pedialyte®, has far less profit margin than an IV. Such a change is not likely to happen without restructuring the system.

Far easier than restructuring as a means of dealing with this type of problem, however, would be empowering and allowing our Public Health Departments to provide this education. That is the kind of education that the Public Health Service excels at. Even better is having them supply the readily available packets, which are available at little expense at pharmacies throughout the world, or information, like that provided by the BRAC trainees, on how to make it at home.

Oral rehydration is also a very good way to deal with fever. Whenever the body is infected it tries to wash out the bacteria or get blood to the area of inflammation. Optimizing fluid volume is one of the best ways to help. It also facilitates the body's fever control systems by supporting its ability to perspire, where evaporation cools the body.

Genitourinary tract defenses

Primary defenses here are provided by regular washing and friendly bacteria. We mentioned earlier the defense that is provided by friendly bacteria living in our GI tracts, which prevent colonization by others that may not be as friendly. Friendly bacteria living throughout our bodies compete for the same food and space and prevent many pathogens from getting a start. Nowhere in the human is this type of defense refined as much as in the female vagina; and, because it is more open and the urethra shorter in the female, genitourinary infections are much more common in females. Good bacteria here maintain an acid environment that bad germs don't like, and their biofilm prevents pathogenic bacteria from adhering. These friendly bacteria even make a *bacteriocin* that attacks some of the more common vaginal pathogens and keeps them from adhering there.

Many fish and animals living in wetlands are similarly covered with a protective biofilm made up of good bacteria, and removing it, even by touching these animals, can open them to infection. Divers at the Great Barrier Reef in Australia are warned not to touch the wildlife for this reason—and not just the fish because even the reef is alive, protected by its own biofilm, and vulnerable. It's similar with the human genitourinary tract where this biofilm is a first-line defense. It is the primary defense of the female genital tract.

Washing also plays a role in genitourinary defenses. The process of emptying the bladder washes the urethra regularly removing non-adherent bacteria. Regular menses, though less frequent, do the same for the vagina. Women who don't drink enough water, or are in positions where they cannot urinate regularly, increase their frequency of urinary infections. And, similarly, women who interrupt their menses by taking hormones risk more vaginal infections.

The healthcare industry has also made too much of a good thing with washing here. Copious washing in all areas—respiratory, GI, as well as genitourinary—risks removing the protective biofilm and eliminating its benefit, and douching in particular can be excessive. It tends to wash out the normal bacteria with its biofilm, thus eliminating this major defense and opening the area to infection. Just as with the wetland animals that are similarly protected, removing the biofilm in the vagina opens the door to infection.

Most of the time problems in this area bring women to the doctor where they are treated with antibiotics. Here again we are finding more bacteria that are resistant to our antibiotics, as well as more that have creatively adapted to acting quietly, without significant outward symptoms. Gonorrhea now causes few bothersome symptoms, and neither do the chlamydial infections that are currently epidemic. But infections with these bacteria are rapidly becoming the greatest cause of female sterility because the inflammation they cause blocks the Fallopian tubes that carry both the sperm to the egg and then the fertilized egg back to the uterus. The best available means of preventing such infections is that recommended by Ewald in a previous chapter: blocking transmission, either by abstinence or the use of condoms.

Honoring and promoting these defenses is also beneficial here just as it is in the other areas. As one of my professors in medical school explained, a treatment as simple as boric acid restores the acid balance in the genitourinary tract, stimulates the growth of the good bacteria, and is sufficient treatment for most vaginal yeast infections; but it doesn't make any money for the system because you can buy boric acid, put it in large gelatin capsules, and make this treatment in your kitchen, so few know about it.

Sexually transmitted diseases (STDs)

Many, if not most, infections of the genitourinary system are sexually transmitted and in a real sense vector borne where the partner plays the part of the transmitting insect; and just as those with an insect vector, they tend to bypass our defenses. Just as screens block insects and reduce malaria, common sense says that using a condom to block the transmission of these bacteria would be useful, but humans seem altogether too willing to share their body fluids along with all of their known and unknown bacterial and viral contents.

For our religiously oriented youth who are taught that premarital sex is a sin, using a condom indicates that sex was premeditated. Premeditation is the factor differentiating first-degree murder from the lesser crime of manslaughter. Likewise premeditated sex, where a condom is available and used, gets the greater condemnation. It's a lot easier to get forgiven for a crime of passion, so fewer use condoms. This attitude makes it a whole lot easier for the bacteria as well as the spermatozoa—and both STDs and teenage pregnancy are more prevalent in this population, with the states in the 'Bible Belt' continuing to win this dubious distinction over the more secular northeast.

It takes time for bacteria to come up with manipulative adaptations that help them infect more people, but when human behavior eliminates the need for it by actively carrying bacteria and viruses to another through sexual contact, epidemics are much more likely, and harder to control. It's the same kind of situation we see in our day care centers where children spread their germs to everyone else in the nursery on the toys they share.

As pointed out earlier the hardest infections to control are those with a vector, carried from person to person by an insect, a toy, a "Typhoid Mary," or any other transmitting agent. With sexually transmitted diseases we act as our own vector. The infecting agents that cause sexually transmitted diseases don't need to be creative and find a better way to infect more people *because we do it for them*. Nor is there any need for bacteria to adapt in the friendly ways that are promoted by blocking their transmission or adherence. We have experienced epidemics of sexually transmitted diseases with syphilis, gonorrhea, and now with HIV/AIDS. And biologists and infectious disease experts know that there will be many more. The most effective way of preventing and dealing with all of them has been through education and by blocking their transmission with condoms.

STDs and sex education

These are social problems; they're called social diseases—and they need social solutions. Antibiotics and antiviral drugs can help deal with the medical aspects of the problem, but control is possible only by society coming together with a comprehensive program addressing both prevention and treatment. Uganda has done this with HIV/AIDS while South Africa, with its estimated 20% infection rate, 5.5 million including 240,000 under age 14, shows the results of social and governmental blindness to the real nature of the infection. As Uganda shows, education is fundamental to controlling HIV/AIDS, and promoting this education should be a function of the CASY that benefits the most—in this case it's the community or state.

The use of condoms as blocking agents is common sense, effective, and necessary. While abstinence also needs promotion, doing so exclusively is regressive, returning us to a pre-World War II mentality where our soldiers and sailors were taught abstinence only. It was only when confronted with widespread outbreaks of syphilis that military leaders began promoting condoms. They worked then and they do as well today.

Currently sex education in our schools is largely limited to the abstinence programs that didn't work with our servicemen in WW II and don't work now. A study and position paper of The Society for Adolescent Medicine shows that "abstinence only" programs do not delay sexual activity and have an efficacy approaching zero. "Abstinence from sexual intercourse," they state, "while theoretically fully protective, often fails to protect against pregnancy and disease in actual practice because abstinence is not maintained." On the other hand broad based early programs that incorporate the many aspects of sex education, with an accurate portrayal of infection risks, the overarching value of abstinence, as well as an understanding of contraceptive devices and their efficacy, does a better job of actually reducing sexual activity, unwanted pregnancy and abortions, as well as STDs.

The biggest force for delaying sexual activity is not making it a sin, but the desire to do something with one's life—where self-actualization goes beyond reproduction. Regulating or coercing human behavior by making sexual activity a sin is the mechanical approach—it treats the agent as an object whose behavior is regulated—and it's abusive. Promoting educational and life goal options is the more creative solution; it is especially applicable in our minority populations where the perception of a respectable and productive future seems more distant and is readily compensated for by the easy ability to reproduce.

Beyond the individual level there is a direct international correlation in the world's countries between birth rate and the lack of opportunity in that country for women to express themselves in areas other than reproduction. Conversely, as women's rights increase in a society the growth rate of the population decreases. The higher the educational level of women in the countries of the world the lower the country's population growth.

This is part of the context of the problem with overpopulation. Self expression is a characteristic of life and it can be creatively done by either reproducing or choosing another means of self-expression. If we wish to do something about overpopulation then we need to increase programs that provide opportunities for self expression in other ways. Careers needs to be a topic of discussion at all levels of education from elementary school on.

Building respect for oneself, one's partner, and for the potential child, is also a major deterrent. It is best taught by recognizing and treating the individual as an agent able to choose wisely when given appropriate information; and by parents, teachers, and societal leaders modeling behaviors based on the principle of not harming, using, or dehumanizing oneself or others. It is not taught by the mechanical approach of regulating behavior. Specific ways of showing disrespect or of hurting another—like giving them an STD, making them sterile with Chlamydia, burdening their life with HIV/AIDS, or saddling them with an unwanted child or child support payments—can and should be taught. And the more these messages are repeated the more effective they are.

While the spiritual nature of procreation and the potent interpersonal bonding of the sexual act are powerful arguments for not abusing sex these are abstract concepts that children can't understand. We can't build models in our brains of concepts like these without some kind of experience. In Riceville, Iowa, Jane Elliott taught her 3rd graders the power of discrimination by having blue eyed children be inferior, and at Stanford Philip G. Zimbardo demonstrated the ease with which young people can become abusive when they are put in the role of jailers. Both of these teachers were heavily criticized for their use of experiential teaching, but it's likely the best way for a student to gain an appreciation for the power that underlies these interpersonal issues. Their students did learn and most were grateful for the experience.

Discrimination and the ease with which we abuse power are abstract concepts that a person is able to deal with cognitively only after the experience; it is futile to try to teach children these lessons where there is no corresponding neural connection. Unfortunately no one has come up with an alternative experiential way of teaching the value of sex as an instrument for bonding—though conjoint hypnosis probably comes close. Conjoint hypnosis is when two people are hypnotized together, sharing and communicating with each other in the same trance. It was done at Stanford University in classes taught by Ernest Hilgard. A common reason his students gave for withdrawing from participation in the sessions was the feeling of the married students that the intimacy they experienced in hypnotic trance with another student was violating their marriage vows. Until we come up with more experiential ways to become intimate experimentation with sex is not likely going to stop. Making it a sin will not stop it. Teaching abstinence will not stop it.

These and other methods represent the mechanical approach of regulating behavior where particular actions are proscribed by fiat without explanation. But children are not machines and they rebel at such treatment. They can and should be taught to respect both themselves and others, the health risks associated with sexual experimentation, and the social problems of early parenthood that include higher divorce rates, child support, increased poverty, the potential harm to an unwanted infant, and how to best protect themselves and those they care about from these risks.

When one is able to prevent the spread of disease so simply it's just common sense to do so. You can get condoms at your local Public Health Department, but they can't talk about them or promote them. Blocking transmission of germs with barriers such as condoms, mosquito nets, window screens, clean water, and other mechanical means, and staying home when one is sick, are the simplest and most cost effective way to prevent the spread of infection and should be actively promoted at every opportunity. And we need to remember Ewald's point that blocking an infecting agent's transmission also helps tame them because if they can't easily get to a new host they must adapt to their current host without killing it.

Respiratory defenses

The respiratory tract goes from the nose to the lungs and is the most commonly infected area of the body. Respiratory tract infections include those in the ears and sinuses, which connect to the back of the nose, as well as those in the lungs: bronchitis and pneumonia. Bacteria in the nose are the common source for all of these infections. In children bacteria from the nose move down the Eustachian canal to cause middle ear infections, whereas in adults they are more likely to climb up into the sinuses. When the nasal mucus is dry and less sticky bacteria can easily get airborne and aspirated to cause bronchitis and pneumonia.

Many bacteria, both good and bad, live in the nose without causing problems—it's called their reservoir. But when the bad ones move into the sinuses, or ears, or lungs, they are by far the greatest source of infection and the greatest reason for using antibiotics.

Besides the infections, irritants in the back of the nose trigger allergies and the bronchoconstriction of asthma. Most allergens have segments that look to our immune systems very much like serious toxins. With the ever increasing number of new chemicals in our environment it is little wonder that our immune systems are sometimes confused, and allergies are increasing around the world. The point here is that many problems, both infectious and allergic, begin in the back of the nose. Like our other openings there are defenses in our respiratory tract that try to deal with these problems.

The primary defense of mucociliary cleaning

The back of the nose has its own built in cleaning mechanism, and a backup. The first-line defense is the mucociliary clearance. If we were able to look at the back of an ideal nose under a microscope we would see that virtually all of the irritants, bacteria, and foreign debris would be stuck to the mucus; mucus that is constantly being secreted from special cells spread among those lining our respiratory tract. We would also see that the mucus was moving to the back the nose—a process that normally takes about 15 minutes. The movement is caused by the sweeping motion of thousands of microscopic hairs called cilia. A similar process is sweeping the bronchi and trachea, but here it sweeps upward. When this mucus from either the trachea or the back of the nose gets to the throat we swallow, and all of the mucus and associated debris (bacteria, viruses, allergens, etc.) is broken down and recycled by the acid in our stomach and friendly bacteria in our GI tracts. The cilia beat about 10 times every second and the whole process works 24 hours a day, 7 days a week—it's a very effective cleaning. Because it is there all of the time we become accustomed to the periodic swallowing of this mucus, but sometimes even this normal post nasal drainage is made into an illness and decongestants used to dry it up. If post nasal drainage is noticeable it is most likely that the mucus is too dry and the person needs to drink more.

Things that make this cleaning less effective tend to increase respiratory illnesses. Smoking, even one cigarette a day, paralyzes the cilia so they don't sweep effectively. Exposure to cigarette smoke is particularly harmful in infants and children where passive smoke is known to greatly increase respiratory infections. Some pediatricians even consider it under the rubric of child abuse.

Dehydration and low humidity dry the mucus so it is harder to move and less able to hold onto the debris. Nasal mucus rapidly absorbs almost 200 times its volume in water and is most effective at both its tasks—holding onto foreign debris and being swept—when it is optimally wet. People with dry mucus commonly exhale large amounts of bacteria because dry mucus is not as sticky. Nor is it moved as easily by the cilia so the bacteria stay around longer and find ways to hold on. The simple inhalation of saline steam for a few minutes eliminates much of this viral and bacterial shedding—even drinking helps. But it only seems to help for a short time. Moisture in the air also plays a role.

We have moved indoors relatively recently in terms of our evolutionary history, and added central heating and cooling even more recently. These factors dry the air in our controlled and comfortable environments and certainly not enough time has passed for us to genetically adapt the cleaning of our noses to our dryer environments.

Relative dehydration is the most likely reason for the association of colds with early winter. Upper respiratory infections cluster around cold spells when we have fewer stimuli to drink, and when we further dry the air by turning on the central heating. Dehydration handicaps this primary defense so infecting agents in the nose are more able to hold on and grow to the point of causing an upper respiratory infection, or break loose to get aspirated into the lungs, or outward into someone else's nose.

The indigenous people of Alaska, to illustrate this problem, have the highest incidence of ear infections in the country, and probably the world, but tribal elders tell us that before they were "civilized" they didn't have ear problems. Indigenous Australians tell the same story. Doctors writing about this problem in the native Alaskans conclude that these people have a genetic predisposition to ear infections and that they just weren't diagnosed prior to the introduction of western medicine. But the identification of a child in pain followed by a draining ear does not need a medical expert; and in 2002 the children in Kotzebue's sister city of Provideniya, across the Bering Straits in Siberia, while sharing the same genes, had neither the conveniences of civilization nor ear problems in their children.

The Alaskan natives were "civilized" in the 1940s and '50s by moving them into communities with heated prefab homes. While these new homes were far more comfortable they also reduced the humidity from nearly 100%, on the ice, to 20-30% when the heat was on. Being out in the cold, as anyone having had the experience knows, makes your nose run; the moist air a person breaths out condenses in the cold, but it also helps to moisten the mucus and helps the nose to stay clean; and the cold air also stimulates more blood flow into the nose that increases the fluid there as well. Noses that are adapted to the cold and humid outdoors have a harder time clearing the mucus when the environment is dry, indoors, and heated. Civilization also gave them access to healthcare and antihistamines, the miracle drugs of the '40's, which sanitized and stopped the baby's snotty nose, blocking what we realize now with his back-up defense. A shift also began then away from breast feeding which by itself is protective for ear infections.

Secondary washing

Just as sweeping the kitchen floor is not sufficient for all spills there is a back-up washing mechanism for the nose. This secondary defense, like diarrhea, also tells us that something is wrong. Sensitive cells in the back of the nose recognize the pollutants and trigger the cleaning process. The main trigger is histamine which opens the taps in the small blood vessels lining the nasal membranes so that they leak more to provide the fluid for the washing. It also increases the mucus to trap more pollutants, and irritates us to makes us sneeze more to get rid of it—and it closes the airway to protect the more vulnerable lungs from the dangers it senses in the upper airway. This secondary defense is the best available and we should honor and support it. But, as pointed out in the last chapter, this is one of our defenses that is routinely blocked in our current humoral based medical practice. Decongestants shut the taps, antihistamines turn off the whole process, and steroids put the immune system to sleep so it doesn't care if the nose is polluted. Honoring this defense would be a much healthier choice than what we currently do with the wonders of modern medicine.

The side effect profiles of these drugs, demanded by the FDA before they can be released, generally are done over a two week period. That is plenty of time to see any side-effects of the drug such as sleepiness or dry nose, but not nearly long enough to see the effects of taking the drug for its designated purpose. One such study reported a doubling in the rate of wheezing and upper respiratory infections, but the total number of the cases did not reach significance. These studies—and this one in particular—are usually done in the summer because upper respiratory problems are less common then. This is reflected by the few numbers of children in either the test or control group having respiratory infections, which was the reason it was not significant. If this particular study had been done in the winter, when school absences for colds are often as high as 20%, and the same doubling relationship prevailed, it would have been significant and we would not likely have these drugs.

One of the ways to address nasal problems that we have begun to use increasingly over the last few years is washing with a neti pot. With a neti pot, or any of the other ways that do this washing, water or a saline solution is poured into one side of the nose while bending over and allowing it to drain out of the other side. The problem with this approach is that it, like douching, is too much of a good thing. Just as douching removes the biofilm in the vagina along with its inherent defenses, copious nasal irrigation removes the protective mucus and opens the nasal tissues to all of the inhaled irritants until the mucus can be restored. Better is to promote the optimal working of the defense itself.

Asthma as a defense

The fourth effect of histamine, shutting down the airway, needs elaboration. If the immune system senses something in the back of the nose that would likely be more harmful should it get into the lungs, where the defenses are not nearly as robust, it is perfectly capable of shutting down the airway to protect the lungs. Allergens, that look like toxins, and chronic sinus conditions are nasal problems that are the major triggers for the defensive closing of the airway that we call asthma—except that no one speaks of asthma as a defense.

An example that may clarify the defensive nature of asthma is a study done in Miami of drowning victims. A frequent observation in bodies found in the water is the absence of water in the lungs. It was commonly thought that these people were killed elsewhere and then dumped in the water, but the Dade County Coroner's study of drowning victims included only people who were known to have drowned. Of the bodies they looked at close to 20% had dry lungs. How did these people die if they did not have water in their lungs and drown? The conclusion of the coroner's office was that the presence of water in their upper airway caused a reactive spasm that closed their airway, preventing the water from entering their lungs—they had an asthma attack.

As pointed out earlier many of our more common allergens, the most common triggers for asthma, have molecular parts that look like serious toxins, so our immune system is really acting in what it thinks is our best interest when it shuts down our airway. Like the diarrhea of cholera, asthma is a defense that can kill us. But it does so to protect our lungs from perceived dangers in our upper airway.

This book is about how to stimulate healthier adaptations; and asthma is very likely an example of the opposite. In many cases it may be a maladaptation to our analytical treatment and use of drugs to block our back up cleaning. Epidemiologic studies looking at the prevalence of asthma in the United States show a steady increase since the 1970s, which is when they began looking. One such study done in Charleston looked back further. What they found was a relatively stable baseline until the early 1970s confirming that the increases began around this time. The authors of the study looked for reasons for this sudden increase. They could find no change in allergen type or intensity, nor industrial change that introduced new toxins, nor any other reason for the increased incidence. What they did not see was that the early 1970s saw two things happen that had a profound effect on our airways. The first is that cold pills and decongestants, which we now understand to block our normal nasal cleaning, were considered safe enough to sell without a prescription. These drugs were formulated in the 1940s, but in the 1970s they were released for over the counter sales. They are what we buy when we need a 'cold pill'; they are also the pills that the FDA recently found to increase the risk of death in children. The second had to do with how they were sold: they began to be marketed on television and they were handed out by the boxful to physicians to use as samples for the many poor patients who now qualified for healthcare under our recently enacted entitlement programs.

While 'after this, therefore because of this' does not satisfy the logic of causality it should at least raise a question. The function of these drugs is to block the histamine that triggers the defensive cleaning of the airway. Stopping the cleaning means the pollutants remain in the upper airway. If the body is prevented from removing them it is under even more pressure to protect the more vulnerable lungs. It is no wonder that we have more asthma. Asthma seen this way is an example of another unintended consequence triggered by treating the body in an analytical manner. The question is: are there more?

Fortunately our immune system is commonly mistaken about the deadly threat of our allergens and toxins because many of them, even the one causing the deadly diarrhea of cholera, are not that serious. If they were, then blocking the bronchoconstriction of asthma, our normal treatment, would allow the toxins to wreak havoc in our lungs, which doesn't seem to happen. It takes an educated immune system to tell the difference between toxins that are really bad and those that just look bad, and people with experienced immune systems do indeed have fewer allergies and less asthma.

An immune system that has been educated by exposure to dangerous viruses and bacteria is less likely to mistake strange allergens for a real threat. Children reared on European farms, where the barn and all of its decaying organic material and accompanying bacteria is adjacent to the house, have better educated immune systems; they have both more antibodies to serious pathogens—indicating prior exposure—and less allergy and asthma. Their educated immune systems can better tell when something is a serious problem. Similar benefits are found in children from day care centers where close contact with other children exposes them to a greater variety of microbes and similarly educates their immune systems. This is called the "hygiene hypothesis" and it echoes the message of CASYs in general: an experienced, or educated, immune system is healthier and more able to tell when a threat is real or when it's really just a similar looking allergen. Perhaps someday we will be able to get better adaptations from our immune systems by giving our children controlled exposure of these pathogens in order to guide their immune systems in a more healthy way.

For now the best way to honor these at times perverse defenses is, first of all, to see that they are trying to protect the body from perceived dangers. The diarrhea of cholera is protecting the body from the toxin of the cholera bacteria, while the bronchospasm of asthma is trying to protect the lungs from a perceived equal danger in the back of the nose. In both cases the best solution includes honoring and supporting the defense in its attempts to remove the irritant or toxin.

Helping nasal defenses

One of the easiest ways to help is to spend more time outside where the humidity is generally higher. Children in the summertime play outdoors more often, breathe more moist air, and have fewer colds and fewer problems with asthma. A humidifier for your home helps the mucociliary part of the cleaning to be more effective if it is kept clean of the molds that can easily grow in such appliances.

Another common and simple way to help is with saline sprays that are available just about anywhere in the U.S. These sprays became common soon after antihistamine use became widespread and are helpful at moistening the dry nose these drugs cause. They also help restore some of the fluid, which helps loosen the mucus. But they don't seem very effective at helping this cleaning because their regular use doesn't significantly reduce ear or sinus infections, or asthma.

Harvard researchers have found some people they call heavy producers who commonly exhale extremely large amounts of bacteria. They also showed that inhaling vaporized saline for a few minutes rapidly reduces the amount of exhaled bacteria. Likely such treatment done regularly will also reduce infections. Irrigation does a better job at reducing infections than the sprays, but is bothersome and time consuming; and it risks washing out the mucus and removing that defense. If the spray loosens the mucus and helps to clean the nose it should help reduce ear infections, but saline sprays don't help much. Even using them aggressively doesn't help prevent recurring ear problems. The problems begin in the back of the nose where these bacteria live, and from where they spread to other areas to cause infections, but putting saline there doesn't help. Something else is needed.

Heather

The need for this something else became critical during the winter of 1997. Our granddaughter, Heather, had been born in the spring and in August her parents put her in a local day care so that her mother could return to teaching. She promptly began getting ear infections, just like her father had. Jerry has had extensive experience teaching in special education and noticed long ago that many, if not most, of the children in special education had had ventilation tubes placed in their ears to deal with these recurrent infections. When Heather's doctor brought up the subject of tubes Jerry was concerned to say the least.

Whenever a child has an ear infection the inflammation in the middle ear causes fluid to be secreted there in the attempt to wash out the infection. Untreated ear infections are commonly painful because of the pressure of this fluid on the ear drum. Sometimes the pressure causes the ear drum to rupture. Then the child recovers as the infection drains. Early treatment for ear infections used to recognize this process and help it along by lancing the ear drum to allow for the draining, but antibiotics were just as effective early on and far simpler, for both the doctor and the patient. Antibiotics also prevented a major complication of ear infections; when the pressure in the middle ear was not relieved by draining through the ear drum it occasionally would extend into the porous bones around the ear and from there into the brain causing infections that killed many children. But that was then. Antibiotics seemed to be a better choice, but because of our overuse of them, and the resistant strains of bacteria that have come from this overuse, we now need nearly twenty times more of the antibiotic to do the job; and as we saw earlier the problem is not likely to get any better.

Often, especially when ear infections get chronic, the fluid has no where to go and takes time to go away; when it stays around it gets thicker and stickier—the English even call it 'glue ear'. The middle ear, where this fluid collects, is also home to the small bones that conduct sound from the ear drum to the brain. When the fluid persists the sounds are dampened and children don't hear properly. If they can't hear properly they can't learn the sounds that make up our words, and this is why ear infections are associated with special education. Most ear infections, like Heather's, begin when children are about six months old which is right in the middle of the developmental window for our brains when we can best and easiest learn to discriminate the sounds that make up our languages. Again poor sound discrimination leads to poor language development, which in turn leads to special education.

It is also now being associated with other developmental problems. The conditions of Post Otitis Auditory Disorder (POAD) and Central Auditory Processing Dysfunction (CAPD) are relatively new concepts that are being traced back to this same problem. As with all CASYs, input from the environment is critical in early adaptation and sound input plays a significant role, and not just with language. This and all other inputs to the developing brain need to be optimal.

The critical nature of these problems has not been fully realized. Ear infections are so common we can easily overlook their potential for damage. Children are CASYs and extremely sensitive to initial conditions—the 'butterfly effect' is working. Handicapping one's recognition of the verbal symbols used in the development of a child's brain can have profound effects later. Studies looking at the social costs of ear infections look only at the medical and familial expenses, but these are eclipsed by the educational expenses. Ear infections were estimated to cost Americans over $5 billion in 2000, but this is peanuts compared to that of our special education programs. Close to forty years ago Jerry recognized the association of learning problems with tubes. These tubes are placed in the ear drum to drain the fluid that accumulates in the middle ear so that children can hear better, but long term studies done in Europe show that they don't correct the learning handicaps. That experience was long ago, but well remembered. Jerry, in the mean time, moved from special education to counseling; and she loves what is called "Reality Therapy" which asks often embarrassing questions about why we persist in doing things that don't work. When Heather had her fourth ear infection in as many months and her doctor opened the subject of tubes Jerry used it on me: "WHAT YOU ARE DOING IS NOT WORKING!!" she said. "DO SOMETHING ELSE!!" Indeed something else was needed.

Heather's parents had tried saline, but to no effect. Looking for the missing something I found a study showing that chewing gum sweetened with xylitol reduced recurrent ear infections by more than 40%.

Xylitol

We have already discussed xylitol's ability to block the adherence of many different bacteria and to exert pressure on bacteria to 'shape up or ship out.' Xylitol's ability to do this is another example of success preceding science. Xylitol, the sugar alcohol of xylose—wood sugar—is a natural substance that is found in many foods, and the body itself makes some. It looks and tastes like sugar and has been a common sweetener in Finland since their isolation during the Second World War when other sugars were not available. It is also safer for diabetics because it is metabolized in a totally different pathway than glucose. It took the Finns close to thirty years to see that the people using xylitol had less tooth decay and close to thirty more to see its benefit in preventing ear infections.

The "Turku Sugar Studies" began in 1972 and with follow up studies on the initial population now number 23. They have been carried out largely by Kauko Makinen and his colleagues and published primarily in *Acta Odontology Scandinavia* beginning in 1974. In these studies and many others done by other researchers and published in other journals they found that high oral concentrations of xylitol at frequent intervals, was the best way to prevent the tooth decay; and that the most effective time for such use is in childhood during the time that primary teeth are lost. It is in this period where the child can realize the long-term benefits described earlier with cranberry-lingonberry extract and urinary infections.

Most of these studies used gum sweetened with xylitol. High concentrations are released into the mouth by chewing this gum and it's easy to chew gum several times a day—it's an ideal delivery system for getting xylitol to the bacteria that live on the teeth. It also makes clinical studies that look at dosing a whole lot easier. As stated earlier the bottom line for all these studies is that once a day doesn't provide much benefit, but five times a day reduces tooth decay by about 80%. When you go to a dentist in any of the Scandinavian countries, Japan, or Korea, they don't give you a toothbrush, they give you chewing gum. And when you go to school in Finland you are given two pieces of this gum three times a day, paid for by the state because they realize they are saving money in the long run. The U. S. military has recently acknowledged these benefits and now supplies xylitol sweetened gum in every packaged meal provided our troops in the field.

It took this kind of promotion and more time to find out that chewing this gum also reduced ear infections. The study I read in the *British Medical Journal* showed that two pieces of gum five times a day reduced recurrent ear infections by 42%. The authors pointed out some of xylitol's antibacterial properties and credited them as the reason it worked.

Since Heather was too young to chew gum, and since the bacteria causing the ear infections, which the xylitol works on, are in the nose we thought it prudent to put it there. Heather's ear infections disappeared when her nose was sprayed before every diaper change. I began using it in my practice with children having recurrent ear infections. Ten similar children with recurrent ear infections decreased their earaches and visits to the doctor by 92% when they used it with the same frequency. The percentage is actually higher because four of the seven ear infections that occurred during the year that I was watching these children happened when the parents stopped spraying the child's nose. A recently completed study of this spray in older children done in the Czech Republic looked at its use three times daily and reported a 60% reduction in ear aches and doctor visits. Jerry and I had found the something else, another example of success preceding science because, except for giving bacteria indigestion, we had no idea how it worked. This was ten years ago and the adherence studies had not been published yet. Much has happened since then.

In order to find out why the gum worked to prevent ear infections the same group that did the clinical study on chewing gum and ear infections did a laboratory study showing that xylitol decreased the ability of the major problem causing bacteria, living in the back of the nose, to hold on there. We have already discussed the ability of xylitol to decrease bacterial adherence and this study was one of the earliest to show this effect. Many researchers see the effect of xylitol as due to a metabolic inability of the bacteria to deal with xylitol. Bacteria eat the xylitol but can't use it properly for food. Studies have looked at some of these bacteria and the structure of their cells is radically disturbed after they eat xylitol. It's an appealing argument, but it doesn't explain a particular aspect of the adherence study. In the adherence study the researchers combined pathogenic bacteria and cultured cells from the nose and counted the number of bacteria that were holding on to each cell. This was their baseline. Then they added xylitol to a group of the cells and to a group of the bacteria before putting them together. They showed that the adhesion was much less in all the groups, *but it was decreased by much the same amount whether the xylitol was added to the cells or to the bacteria.* If bacterial indigestion was the only reason for the decreased adherence there should be no effect when treating only the cell, but there was. The most reasonable explanation for this is that xylitol interferes with the lectin binding as we argued earlier, but this view has not caught on.

Again, the ability to adhere represents a bacterial adaptation that needs to be blocked. If bacteria and viruses can't hold on they are easily washed out and can't cause infections. This understanding of the problem had to wait for our paradigm to change to one that allows for the importance of adaptation and evolution, but even before this understanding putting xylitol in the nose seemed a reasonable thing to do if its effect was due to its interaction with the bacteria.

Xylitol in the nose

Seeing the decreased bacterial adherence shown by the Finns, researchers at the University of Iowa looked at more of what xylitol does in the nose. They found that xylitol is not absorbed but acts locally to pull water into the nasal airway. This movement of fluid is the same thing that happens when histamine opens the blood vessels so that they leak; both turn on the taps that wash the nose. This fluid also decreases the salt concentration in the back of the nose and this is what these researchers focused on. Natural antibiotic substances, called *defensins*, in the fluid lining the cells in our nose are salt sensitive. When there is lots of salt they don't work well so the people get more respiratory infections. This is particularly the case in children with cystic fibrosis, who were the focus of the Iowa study. In these children the first-line defense of the mucociliary clearance is handicapped because their mucus is so much thicker. This handicapped defense means these children get lots of complicated respiratory infections with hard to treat bacteria, and they usually die much sooner than normal as a result of these infections. Reducing this salt concentration with xylitol enables these defensins to work more effectively. The Iowa researchers proved this by using a nasal spray with xylitol on normal subjects four times daily for four days. All of these subjects had fewer bacteria in the back of the nose after the four days of treatment. It worked six times better than their control group using a saline spray, and a more concentrated spray with more xylitol, like the one we used, should work even better.

The reason a higher concentration works better is another aspect of its mechanism of action that was demonstrated by researchers at Johns Hopkins in 1988. They used a concentrated solution of mannitol, the sugar alcohol of mannose, in the noses of normal subjects, and they used, not a spray, but enough to fill up the nose. Like the later Iowa study also showed they found that it pulled fluid from the cells in the nose, and there was enough that it stimulated histamine release—it thus mimics and stimulates our own defensive washing. At that time, in 1988, and even mostly today, histamine's defensive role was not even considered; it was only seen as associated with inflammation, so they didn't even pursue the research further. Understanding that histamine is the trigger for the defensive washing puts it in an entirely different light. A concentrated solution of xylitol turns on the washing, just like the mannitol, as well as decreasing the ability of several infection causing bacteria to hold on. Jerry and I had developed soap for the nose. Regular use of this spray has also helped to eliminate sinus problems and asthma in most of my patients.

This spray is not well known because xylitol is a food, not a drug. Making xylitol into a drug has the same problems as oral rehydration: without it being a drug one cannot make the medical claims that are appropriate, but a pharmaceutical company cannot be assured of a profit when the ingredients of the drug are available at your local grocery store. I searched for pharmaceutical interest when I saw what it did in my practice and got some initial interest, but it evaporated when they found out that xylitol was available without restriction. Several xylitol containing nasal sprays are available through health food stores, but only one has sufficient xylitol to reap these benefits. This marketplace voted it the country's "Best New Natural Medicine" for 2004, but the company manufacturing it doesn't make any medical claims—it's just a very effective way to clean the nose.

The information on both the oral and the nasal benefits of xylitol has been out long enough that businesses have become aware of its potential. Many manufacturers of both gum and nasal sprays put xylitol in their products and display that on the label, but the amounts are not able to produce the benefits that are there with more concentrated amounts. The gum used by the military is even in this class. When looking for xylitol in either gum or spray read the 'ingredients list' on the packages; and choose the product where xylitol is listed as the first ingredient in the gum, or after water in the nasal spray. It may cost a little more, but it will be more effective as well.

Both oral rehydration and the nasal use of xylitol show that there are safe and beneficial ways to honor our defenses, and that doing so helps to eliminate many of the problems we deal with in America and world wide.

Conclusion

These are the defenses that have developed in our evolutionary history to protect these necessary openings in our bodies. Their expression in us means that they are the best defenses that are available. The fact that our immune systems overreact occasionally should not dissuade us from honoring and promoting these defenses and trying to help and guide them to be even better. The fever, diarrhea, and rhinorrhea, which we routinely block because of our persisting mechanical paradigm of balancing symptoms, are defenses that need to be honored.

While we have not gotten to the point of asking the question, we should expect that blocking these and other defenses is just as damaging to our health and lives as was the practice of blocking the inflammatory reaction with blood-letting. This is very likely the reason behind the deaths associated with the use of antihistamines and decongestants released by the FDA in the fall of 2007. Blocking defenses robs us of their survival advantage. Instead we should try to honor and assist these defenses, best done with oral rehydration supporting our GI defenses, abstinence, monogamy, and condoms for our genitourinary defenses, and a nasal spray containing xylitol for those in the respiratory tract.

Few know about the benefits of either oral rehydration or nasal xylitol because they are not drugs, so their manufacturers cannot tell the public of their real value in preventing illness. Besides their overwhelming effectiveness at preventing problems in both the GI and respiratory tracts another real value of these treatments is that they clearly show the benefits of seeing the washing symptoms as defensive adaptations. Trying to explain the success of the nasal spray containing xylitol in the mechanical model, where the focus is balancing symptoms, was the anomaly that we could not get past; it forced us to see that the body is a CASY with defensive adaptations that need to be honored and not blocked. We could see that this concept is invisible in the mechanical paradigm. The importance of honoring defenses opens us to accept the paradigm biologists call Darwinian Medicine—the paradigm that recognizes that we are CASYs with the ability to adapt. We need to find out why a symptom is there before we treat it; and if the name is not palatable to some American's let's just call it *Common Sense Medicine*—because it is.

Part II
Social Systems as CASYs

In Part I we saw how living agents adapt to their environments and that with natural selection the beneficial adaptations are spread to the larger population. In Part II we look a a few of our social CASYs to see that they also adapt.

But while adaptation in living agents to their physical environment is at the level of their DNA, adaptation in our systems is at the level of our neurons and our mental models; and it is much faster. In our social systems we also play the part of nature in natural selection by choosing what we want to succeed. Those choices need to be informed.

CHAPTER 7
Shopping for Healthcare: Shop 'til you Drop

That any sane nation, having observed that you could provide for the supply of bread by giving bakers a pecuniary interest in baking for you, should go on to give a surgeon a pecuniary interest in cutting off your leg, is enough to make one despair of political humanity. But that is precisely what we have done.

G. B. Shaw. The Doctor's Dilemma. Preface

They got AIDS out there. You think they gonna cure AIDS? No, they ain't gonna cure AIDS. They ain't never gonna cure AIDS. Ain't no money in curing it. The money's in the medicine. That's how you get paid. Sick people comin' back and back.

Chris Rock

We move now up the CASY scale a couple of notches to look at a social CASY that is in trouble. Health care has gotten increasingly expensive over the past years and we are not getting what we pay for. That's the conclusion of the experts from the National Academy of Sciences that were organized into The Institute of Medicine and given the task of fixing the system. There are many reasons for the failure of our system to deliver, but chief among them is our mechanical model. A regulatory approach that tries to treat an ailing complex system by balancing the parts doesn't work on ecosystems, or on any CASY—and it doesn't work on our healthcare system.

The problems in our healthcare industry have been brewing for some time and, because we continue to use the model that created them in the first place, current attempts to fix it are likely compounding them. We are at the point where many consider it our major social problem. It costs too much and many aren't served. We pay more for our health care than any other nation in the world. Employers, like our auto manufacturers, that pay a large part of those costs through employer based insurance, are handicapped in competing with manufacturers in other countries, so manufacturing is sent overseas and people lose their jobs and their insurance. Those with medical bills who are unable to afford insurance, or who are faced with health care costs not covered by their insurance, are being forced into bankruptcy at unprecedented rates. Many small employers don't provide insurance. In Texas, the worst state, more than one out of five people are uninsured.

Other reports show that our small increases in life expectancy don't keep pace with those in the rest of the developed world. In 1977 we ranked 11th in life expectancy among the developed nations and in 2005 we were 37th, and at latest count we were 43rd. As with the productivity index mentioned earlier, many within the system have a problem with this trend and argue that longevity is more often cut short by homicide in America, or that it is mostly hereditary and not due to health care. However, the most significant gains everywhere in life expectancy occur when infant mortality is decreased—a problem with health care, not heredity. In 1980 we ranked 19th among developed nations in infant mortality and CIA estimates for 2005 have us dropping to 43rd. The other major causes of early mortality—smoking, diabetes, obesity, and even homicide—are social problems that should be addressed by our healthcare system at that level, but aren't. Since 1960 our relative performance on most health indicators declined when compared to 28 other developed nations and, as pointed out earlier, the productivity of America's health care has dropped by almost 70% since 1930. The Institute of Medicine is right to conclude that we are paying more and getting less.

These are the most visible problems, the ones that get the most attention. But our actual health is falling behind. A recent comparison of health in America and England points out that Americans have higher incidences of diabetes, hypertension, heart disease, stroke, heart attacks, lung disease and cancer, despite the fact that more people smoke in England. Not just with HIV/AIDS, as Chris Rock says, but the orientation of the whole system seems to be on using drugs to live with illness because that is where the money is.

There are many factors behind these problems, but underlying them all are the facts that: the major players in our system are aligned defensively where the focus is on size and profits; they have a regulated system they can game to these ends and; they work in a marketplace where they have more information than those they serve and they don't hesitate to use it to their advantage. Historians looking at past attempts to fix our ailing system point to its variety of players with their vested interests as the road blocks to progress. Chris Rock is right!

Chronic conditions, like anti-retroviral treated HIV/AIDS, are those that affect ones life style, but are not usually life threatening. Forty five percent of Americans have a chronic condition, but 75% of the money paid into the system is for chronic care. For the system to cure a chronic illness is like shooting yourself in the foot, so there is not much interest in finding cures. Instead research concentrates more on how to deal with the symptoms; on drugs which help us live with the problems, but also insure that we keep coming back. What is sold in our current system is health care that feeds the system.

Earlier we told about Dr. Sara 'Jo' Baker and her experience dealing with typhoid and cholera in New York a century ago. Her program educating about the value of hand washing helped to resolve this epidemic; in public health that's considered a success. Left out of that story earlier was the fact that in the midst of her success thirty Brooklyn pediatricians petitioned the mayor to stop her program because the lack of sick children was hurting their practices. In the healthcare marketplace success is measured by an agent's bank account; yet, reflecting a bit of Shaw's despair, the marketplace is what we chose.

Over the intervening century we have built a system of marketplace medicine that feeds the pediatricians and starves the Dr. Baker's. It gains and is satisfied when we are sick or injured and loses and is frustrated when we are healthy and whole. For the first seven or eight decades of the last century we trusted the pediatricians, doctors in general, and their voice, the American Medical Association, with making the right choices in regard to our health care. What was built is not a healthcare system, but an illness care system that has little interest in health.

Since the rise of third party payment and the passing of Medicare in 1965 organized medicine has lost much of its control in health care policy and planning. Government agencies are busy trying to fill this void, but their actions have been only to regulate. As with all CASYs, regulation is not the best way to handle this system; better is to address the context, make it safe, empower the agents, and allow some time for it to adapt.

As it exists today the system is heavily regulated and defensively aligned so the focus is mostly on increasing both size and profits, and agents game it to these ends. How successful they are is shown by the inflation in health care costs that is at least two to three times that of the rest of the economy, and its growth to eat more than 15% of our gross domestic product. It is an excellent example of the problems associated with a defensive alignment.

We also have justifiable concerns about the sustainability of this system, especially as it expands even further to care for the epidemic of diabetes, the complications of which are just beginning to surface. No entity, government included, is going to be able to satisfy the demands of an illness care system that is fed from and grows from these complications. Realizing the complex and adaptive nature of our healthcare system is the first step in realigning it to one that places more emphasis on prevention and on maintaining health. Reviewing the steps we took that got us here will also show us how many of those steps were mechanically designed with results that were not those intended; adverse 'unintended consequences' are almost the rule in such situations. This review also requires a look at the "marketplace" because that is where we have chosen to provide these services.

"Boid" rules in the marketplace

As pointed out earlier a CASY's alignment shifts between creative novelty and defensive protection, and the most common factor affecting this alignment is the level of perceived threat. The marketplace is a CASY and activity in the marketplace reflects these same dynamics. All markets have, or have had, elements of creative novelty that increase their diversity and complexity. But once the novelty is established the threat of competition or outside regulatory control pushes the alignment toward the defensive, which generally leads to the search for efficiencies and eventually a reliance on size and profits. If one focuses on the end stage of this defensive position, looking at what is commonly done to maintain market position and profits, readily demonstrated by Enron, Tyco, and now most of our investment banking system, then one sees clearly the shadow side of capitalism and has to agree with the play on Acton's famous aphorism that says: "All capitalism corrupts, and consumer capitalism corrupts consummately." This shadow side of capitalism is revealed when we look at sweatshops and other unfair labor practices, or blind contracts with the cheapest subcontractor, or the use of one-sided or privileged information to increase one's financial advantage. The moral hazard of profiting from someone else's disadvantage is a common problem in a defensive alignment, but it is a substantial part of capitalism as commonly conceived. It's why Shaw, as pointed out in the opening above, had misgivings about making an amputation profitable for the person recommending it.

The wise administrator tries to avoid placing moral hazards like these in the pathway of agents, but such hazards are often seen as the mainstay of the free market system, especially by its defensively aligned agents like the Brooklyn pediatricians where profits are more important than people.

Seeing and not wanting these hazards in the area of healthcare, most of the world's nations have chosen to bypass them by choosing varying forms of government sponsorship. This distrust in the profit incentive and the resultant shift toward socialization, however, ignores the rewards that are present only in a free market system for the initial novelty and its stimulus of diversity. No other economic system compares with capitalism when it comes to creating and rewarding novelty and diversity. This is the reason America's healthcare system, and capitalism in general, is as successful as it is. If we wish to find novel ways to prevent, treat, or cure our illnesses, as well as deliver that information efficiently, marketplace medicine is a necessity. The problem is not in the marketplace, but in its defensive alignment. If we want it to work better we need to play with its context and make it less threatening to the agents so that their play can be more creatively aligned.

Regina Herzlinger, in her *Market Driven Health Care*, shows elements leading in this direction, such as the rise of consumer friendly specialty groups. But more often these groups are just more efficient and profitable; the adaptations behind them are more defensive than creative. She does not have the advantageous 'boids-eye-view' of seeing the system as a CASY; nor does she see how powerful and profitable defensively aligned agents can control much of this marketplace, to the detriment of diversity.

Just as with all CASYs the problem in dealing with the medical marketplace is how to stimulate an alignment toward creative novelty, with its systemic benefits, while at the same time fostering the efficiencies seen with the defensive alignment, but without the shadow that comes from excessive focus on profits. How can we alter the context of this system so that its alignment moves to the creative and the marketplace becomes as interested in discovery, novelty, and diversity as it now is in profits and power? In health care we need a system that is as interested in the cure, as it is in the come back—in our health, as it is in our money. Herzlinger correctly sees informed patients as a major driver in moving the system in this direction, but their voice in her system is still muted by the fact that they are a weak part of the contract. The contract is increasingly between the provider's billing agency and the third party payer and the question now becomes how to get the patient's voice back.

For years we trusted the doctors to lead the way in forming our system and representing our interests. We now see that feeding Brooklyn's pediatricians is one reason why our system is as expensive as it is. We turned to government to control the costs, but more often government panders to the powers—after all they put them in office—and its sole approach has been the regulation that has led to more defensive gaming. We have seen that insurance and corporate interests have little expertise or interest in leading, but they are the ones with the power. With the patient out of the equation the shots are called by those profiting.

Adam Smith, the 18th century patron saint and founding prophet of capitalism with its marketplace, argued that an "invisible hand" will guide the market to increasing social values. If we are committed to a capitalist oriented health care then we need to understand more about this invisible hand, how it works, and how to empower it.

The "invisible hand" of the marketplace

The marketplace is a CASY that has been the basis of western economy for more than two hundred years, ever since cottage industries gave way to the industrial revolution. Thanks in large part to the fossil fuels that provide the energy needed to support our economy, and its marketplace, the system has passed the test of time and worked better than any alternative. If there is any way to make the market more friendly, more interested in the cure than in the come back, we need to find it.

Some believe that in today's marketplace there is no invisible hand; that the lack of transparency has eliminated it, or that people do not make the rational decisions needed for it to work. They believe that capitalism needs to be managed. But managing healthcare did not work, nor does managing ecosystems, and there is little chance that managing capitalism will do any better. On the other hand many believe the answer to all of our current health care problems lies in expanding the marketplace—that "market forces" will correct the problems if regulators withdraw—and that the invisible hand still works.

Basically Smith's description of this process was that those involved were under social and ethical pressure to be honorable in their actions. More recently the school of economists following Milton Friedman expanded the idea to cover more marketplace actions; if someone makes a really good product then people will be willing to pay for it; the more they are willing to pay—the more profit is made—the more others will be drawn to make more of the product at a lower price. More good products at lower costs mean value is added to society.

This concept of value identified as inexpensive commodities is now a part of our conventional wisdom. It is the foundation of the 'Wal Mart' mentality where commodities are central, where our purchasing of commodities is a major bulwark of the world's economy, and where in a crisis we are told to go shopping. But it twists reality. It ignores the fact that real human and social values are found in relationships, friends, family, and community—and largely in altruistic behaviors towards others both in and outside of one's local community. Once basic needs are met happiness is associated with neither wealth nor commodities. But the mechanical way in which our marketplace is set up with its defensive alignment tends to ignore human values. The invisible hand of the marketplace in this setting works only with commodities so unfortunately that is our conventional wisdom.

This is an inborn weakness of capitalism where commodities are the focus of the system. It reflects the fact that capitalism, as commonly understood, is based on individual agents working to maximize their survival and with their defensive alignment they associate primarily with those in the same family who are best able to help them—their relationships are incestuous.

But the power of the invisible hand goes far beyond capitalism and commodities—it's that of natural selection; it promotes what works. The invisible hand in capitalism promotes commodities that are helpful to the consumer and the overall economy just as natural selection in nature promotes those characteristics that help both the agent and the system to better survive. The underlying difference between the two is that the consumer is playing the part of nature.

The working of the invisible hand in leading to continued progress is a nice argument for those believing in marketplace freedom; and it's clearly the case with something like the sewing machine that brings a great deal of economic value to society. But just as clearly it is not the case with the machine rolled cigarette that has brought a great deal of harm to society. The difference between the two, *and what makes the invisible hand work in the marketplace*, is the consumer's understanding and knowledge about the product being sold—and their ability to act on that information. Natural selection works to expresses adaptations that have a survival benefit. The invisible hand as seen by Smith works to promote adaptations in the marketplace that are beneficial to the consumer in that market. Natural selection works because of the survival benefit; the invisible hand relies on the wisdom of the consumer. Both represent the forces we have seen in evolution as agents adapt to changes in their environments; and the same pressures forming the agent's alignment—defensive or creative—are present as well. Despite those saying that the invisible hand does not exist today, adaptation to one's environment will continue; it's just that it risks being maladaptive, leading to confusion and chaos, without adequate information. In order to be effective in their adaptation, in order for the invisible hand to work in our systems, the consuming agents need to be both informed and empowered.

Lack of information on the side of the consumer is the basis for Joe Stiglitz's argument that the invisible hand doesn't exist. Most of the time, he points out, we make decisions based on advertising that focuses on emotions such as fear or sexuality, with little to no information about the product in question. Such decisions are swayed more by conventional wisdom or group pressure than by reason. Information relating to a transaction is more likely to come from the selling party, and is also more likely to be incomplete in order to preserve the seller's advantage. The name for this in economic language is "asymmetric information": the seller has more information on the product than the buyer, and is not inclined to share it. But while Smith's invisible hand may be hamstrung by asymmetric information, the adaptation of the consumer that we see as buying and selling is not going to stop; it is just going to be increasingly manipulated by those in control as they search for profits, and agents in the system relying on asymmetric information will game those profits into existence in any number of bubbles.

To counter this disaster in the making it is in our interest to try to get impartial and correct information to those who are adapting. The invisible hand represents the power of informed adaptation in any system, not just capitalism, and it should be empowered wherever it is found. It was invisible to Adam Smith because his mechanical paradigm did not allow him to see a role for adaptation. It was even invisible to Marx, Smith's archetypal critic, whose critique was nonetheless rooted in rigid cause and effect.

Two hundred years ago when people bought products like machine woven textiles and later the sewing machine, they could see and understand their economic benefits. The benefits of many products today are just as clear, but more often today what is sold with the cigarette, and many other products, is not the product, but sex appeal, or fear of not belonging, of not fitting in. Demand is created by clever advertising and marketing that appeal mostly to primitive and largely unconscious fears rather than the particular benefits of the product. Investment opportunities and home mortgage refinancing, similarly, are often based on the appeal of rapid labor free wealth. These appeals have, not a beneficial, but a corrupting influence on society; they guide the invisible hand into making irrational and maladaptive decisions that lead analysts like Stiglitz to conclude that its beneficent pressure doesn't exist.

The difference between the sewing machine and the cigarette, and why the invisible hand is handicapped today, is the lack of consumer information about the product in question; the efficacy of the "invisible hand," as many economists point out, is directly related to information. Without proper information the consumer cannot make wise decisions and the invisible hand is handicapped—but the marketer is more able to make a profit. Moral hazard, the opportunity to profit from someone else's loss, made possible by asymmetric infirmation, is thus on the ground floor of the system.

A major role of government can be seen as coping with asymmetric information. The role of Public Health, as Dr. Baker shows, is to share information on how to deal with, and hopefully prevent, health problems. Similarly our Public Schools are there to teach our young people how to gain, find, and use information in order to make wise choices. Though their responses are only regulatory many governmental agencies, such as the Federal Trade Commission and the Securities and Exchange Commission, exist to prevent the misuse of asymmetric information. Activity that informs and empowers the invisible hand enables wise and capable agents to make decisions that bring value to any CASY, and information that enhances the breadth and variety of an agent's available elements brings more diversity into the system. Stiglitz argues that the invisible hand doesn't exist because our information is seldom if ever shared equally so those choosing make less rational choices. But we will continue making choices and adapting, and one of the best ways to help the public make better decisions is to increase the information available to them.

Empowering the "invisible hand"

In order to use the governmental agencies designed to level the playing field in a proper way we must see the system as a CASY. Adam Smith saw the system as a machine. Individual agents became tools as the manufacturing of a pin was broken down, analyzed, and made more efficient by the separation of labor. People were not agents, but cogs in the machine—and the 'invisible hand' for Smith was *invisible*. Kuhn stated that, "You can't see something until you have the right metaphor that lets you perceive it." While Toyota has seen the value of reversing the trend toward separation of labor we haven't learned yet the principle behind it which was seen clearly by 18th and 19th Century reformers, but lost in our acceptance of the mechanical paradigm—separation of labor objectifies the agent. As long as we see ourselves and our systems in mechanical terms we remain blind to the role agents play in adapting to the products in their environment. We remain blind to the value of their informed choice, and the diversity and novelty that come from the agent's adaptation is ascribed instead to an invisible hand. The invisible hand is empowered by informing the agent who is making the choice.

Our federal agencies continue the mechanical error by doing a lot of regulating, but very little sharing of information. Nor does there appear to be much interest in breaking down the asymmetric information that is contributing to the polarization and weakening of our society; information is power and both government and business seem intent on consolidating and using it to increase their influence, power, and profits. The 10-fold increases in the use of secrecy in the Bush administration, together with the scandals in both the tobacco and pharmaceutical industries when hidden information is brought to light, are example enough of this process. Governments correctly argue that less regulation aids industrial growth, but they forget the need for consumer safety in their need for more growth. Nor do they appear to realize that it is information that empowers the agent to make the decisions that bring value to society in the same manner that creative adaptations bring value to their larger systems.

In a defensively aligned adaptive society such as ours information has value and is sold or otherwise used to increase ones power, profit, or prestige. The survival edge goes to the individual who can accumulate the most power so agents in such systems will become wealthier or poorer depending on the information they have and how they use it. According to surveys from the World Bank the United States is one of many nations to have moved backward over the last decade in the areas of "controlling corruption" and "voice and accountability," falling below the 90th percentile in both areas. This is not the direction to help a creative alignment. The only governments showing progress in controlling corruption were Serbia and Tanzania, countries with new governments. When information is used to accumulate power individuals survive better; when it is seen as a social good and shared, agents are able to make better decisions—value is brought to the system.

Members of the healthcare family share a defensive alignment where there is little effort to share information. Pharmaceutical advertisements generally provide little information about the product, but focus on sex appeal—the focus with Vioxx (until its withdrawal) almost as much as with Viagra. And health care practitioners are much more likely to give a patient a prescription that helps them deal with their current problem, than information on how to better cope with or avoid it.

A lot of medical information is now being provided on the Internet. It is challenging because of the technical language, emotionally charged and often sensitive nature, and the fact that there is little financial support for the process. Most sites so far are associated with private health care interests, those in a position to profit from the information they present.

Historically this educational role has been, and should be, that of Public Health, where the purpose of the organization is to educate people to promote and maintain health rather than on treating disease or selling something. Ex-Surgeon General Koop's web site is a good example of how to start, as is that of the World Health Organization, but this education also needs to be carried into our communities for those not familiar with Internet use. And those providing it locally need to be able to translate the technical language to the level of the individual. Transparency is the term for the openness in transactions that is the opposite of asymmetric information. Maximizing transparency is a critical step in empowering the invisible hand since the adaptation of any CASY that is based on clear, correct, and non-threatening information is more likely to be creative and bring value to the system.

Local support and the plasmid model

This local access to high-quality health information through an empowered and enhanced Public Health Service also opens a door to one of the best and most proven ways of both reducing the cost of chronic illness and improving the condition of the sufferers. Groups of people sharing a common problem enable all participants to deal more effectively with their problem—whatever its nature. They work because they address the social, emotional and spiritual aspects of our CASY natures, as well as providing medical information about the particular illness that does best to level the asymmetry.

While programs such as Dean Ornish's have demonstrated the efficacy of such programs in preventing heart disease there is interest in our current system neither for establishing and supporting such groups, nor of insuring the correctness of the information shared in them. Educating patients often amounts to curing them, and again is like shooting yourself in the foot if your own living is based on treating their illnesses.

Insurers should have an interest in this preventive education except for the way our health insurance is set up. When insurance is tied to employment and people change jobs, and insurers, about every five years it makes no financial sense for Insurance Company A to support preventive services that will help, not them, but Insurance Company B five years down the road. Insurance portability has helped improve this situation, but it needs more. People need to own their policies and carry them with them before insurance companies will become interested in long-term benefits or prevention. The issue of insurance will be discussed in a following section.

Profitability is a key issue when the markets are established in a defensive alignment. Preventive treatments that make money, like immunizations, are supported; but others, like dietary and exercise treatments, or natural treatments that promote and honor our defenses, like oral rehydration and the oral and nasal use of xylitol, don't make much money and have no way to fund the large clinical studies that the system requires to show efficacy. While the science is there, non-profitable products cannot fund clinical trials, and without such studies insurance companies are not willing to support the novelty. Preventive treatments are much more likely to be promoted with a change to the system that honors health rather than profits from disease.

Yaneer Bar Yam is the president of the New England Complex Systems Institute and a leader in applying the ideas and models of complex systems to our real social problems. When looking at healthcare he argues, as we have here, for two parallel systems: one, a Public Health System, for high efficiency problems and a focus on health, and another, similar to our current illness centered one, for critical problems. His model is based on his experiences in physics studying turbulent flows. While reaching the same conclusions we come from a different path.

The plasmid model and Public Health

Groups sharing similar problems promote a cooperative state that makes the plasmid model work. The model requires a community to support it; without the support from the rest of the colony bacterial mutation would not be triggered, and without the support from somewhere else those participating in Linux or the Wikipedia would not have had the time to do so. Adapting agents need support from the system that their adaptations are going to benefit. In the case of healthcare the most likely source for this is found in Public Health. BRAC's carrying the information about oral rehydration to the people of Bangladesh is an actual example of how beneficial this can be. Consider its potential use in the nasal spray we developed.

Progress with the nasal spray that helps wash the nose is now nine years and ongoing. Alternatively, had we been able to use the plasmid model: go to our local health department, tell them of our experience and success with this spray, assure them, as we did the FDA, of its safety—and had they been organized in the community so as to be able to bring it before a group suffering from nasal related problems—knowledge of this product would have spread much more rapidly, saving billions of dollars, and thousands of lives. This same scenario could reduce coronary mortality by spreading programs like Dean Ornish's. Again, the plasmid model, where informed and empowered agents adapt, share and refine those adaptations, is likely the most efficient way of improving novelty in existence. Another potential is with autism.

Autism is rapidly growing in our country and there are many potential reasons. Exposure to heavy metals such as lead and mercury causes central nervous system problems similar to those seen in autism, so a major focus of parent groups trying to cope with this problem is looking at such exposure. The pharmaceutical industry studied the mercury used as the preservative in immunizations given to our infants and children and demonstrated no clear connection, but because this industry is often more interested in protecting itself than in finding the truth their studies do not convince the parents. More in their favor is the fact that the incidence of autism has not diminished since the mercury was removed from the immunizations. But there also are other sources of mercury: the amount in fish is increasing and may be contributing; it's emitted in ever increasing amounts in the unclean burning of coal in our many power plants that have escaped the Clean Air Act because of government laxity and malfeasance; and it's in the amalgam used in dental fillings. Community wide studies looking at these factors may help in understanding the causes behind this illness. They could play with these different factors, as is done in the plasmid model, and find out what happens.

Many see autism as a developmental disorder resulting from some type of early childhood deficiency. The earliest idea of the "refrigerator mom" has been ruled out, and researchers swung to the opposite pole of chemicals and genes; but there are many other social and environmental factors that need to be questioned. Many autistic children have a history of ear infections which lead, as we have seen already, to decreases in auditory development and handicaps in that part of the brain.

Another factor may deal with faulty imprinting. Since the earliest physical lesion in autism is in the part of the brain dealing with facial recognition a problem with early imprinting may be a factor. Just as birds imprint 'mother' with the first moving thing seen after hatching, human infants similarly imprint mother's face. This early, if not first, developmental construct becomes the critically important foundation of other mental constructs in the development of a complex adaptive and self organizing child—an understanding of CASY development demands that this experience be optimal. Most often this imprinting is done during nursing. With the decrease in nursing mothers is there a defect in the imprinting? Would teaching its importance make a difference in the incidence of autism? Interference with this imprinting may also occur from early exposure to television where the 'face' changes every ten to fifteen seconds leading to over-stimulation that can exhaust this region of the brain. Early television watching has recently been implicated by association because the rate of autism in a community correlates well with the amount of inclement weather, which is tied to more exposure to television. The rate of autism in Amish communities, where there is no television and breast feeding is the norm, is at least 30 to 40 times less than in the general population, and since at least some of the autistic children in these communities were adopted in after the diagnosis it may be even less. Would the elimination of television exposure for the first six months to a year of an infant's life, as is recommended by the American Academy of Pediatricians, make a difference? Would increased nursing make a difference? These and other questions could be readily answered by a strong and well funded Public Health Service using the plasmid model. Within a year or two we could have a good idea how to prevent autism in the whole population.

Both autism and the learning problems associated with recurrent ear infections are early problems that can have a profound effect on the development of the child. The stimulus for our nasal spray came from Jerry's forty year old experience with the prevalence of ear tubes in her special education students—a connection that is by far the greatest cost of ear infections, and which health care doesn't even consider since it is an educational problem and not medical. Just as the facial recognition and imprinting of 'mother' is a crucial foundation for the later discriminating and understanding of self and other, the use of symbols, or words, by the brain is fundamental for reasoning. The structure of language, the grammar, provides the logical rules for reasoning in our brains and likely contributes to our logical, causal, mechanical way of thinking. Conditions that impair the ability of the child to sense and play with these auditory elements in their environment can lead to major problems later.

In self organizing systems, CASYs, the butterfly effect is operative and the early context is critical. Both the defect that leads to autism and that leading to middle ear infections are in this early context. Nowhere is the importance of this early context as clear as in the extreme case of Helen Keller. With the twin defects of sight and hearing the input to her developing brain was limited to touch, taste and smell, and the learning of language was nearly impossible. Language is the basis of thinking. Without language there is no productive thought. Without language we are little more than animals; and this is how both Helen and those caring for her describe her childhood behavior. Helen had no language prior to her realization that the symbol repeatedly inscribed on her hand between shoving it under the pump meant "water". This 'A-ha' experience laid the groundwork for the change in her from the animal she identified with to the humanitarian we remember and honor. The context of our early formative months is the basis of our adaptation, the foundation for what we later become. It needs to be optimal.

Unfortunately our "illness" care system has not learned any of these lessons because it is defensively aligned, and illness pays much better than does good health. Countering this defensive alignment by supporting Public Health, where the alignment is on health, prevention, and the education that levels asymmetric information, would be the best place to start—especially in an environment supporting creativity.

Public Health has been limited in this country because of our fear and flight from socialism. But Public Health is no more socialistic than public education; both are about decreasing the asymmetric information that handicaps the invisible hand and reduces its ability to bring value to society. If there is any 'proper function of government' it is to secure its own future by assuring its citizens every opportunity to maximize their self expression.

Capitalism's shadow side is rooted in using asymmetric information to increase one's own profit, and the best countermeasure for that shadow, the best way to insure a working "invisible hand," is for government to increase its role in education and decrease the asymmetric information that now empowers that shadow. Those profiting in the marketplace from commodities, health care, or any other marketable good, get no benefit from a decrease in asymmetric information, but this transparency is critical for the progress of the society. Again, the highest function of government is to educate the public in all areas—to insure as much as possible that the invisible hand, the adapting agent, is optimally informed. The informed agent's choices are the best way to lead us into a better future.

Providing high-quality health information that enables healthier decision making resolves part of the problem in our health care system. In Shaw's metaphor at the chapter's beginning, this type of information levels the playing field by enabling the patient to discuss options to amputation with a knowledgeable person who has no financial stake in the matter. Empowering Public Health to do this task satisfies Plsek's fourth criterion of the solution coming from within the system.

An example for how effective this kind of system would be is suggested by the experience of the Alternative Medicine Integration group in Chicago, a group that has discovered a novel way to practice medicine that should be put into a plasmid system and tested and refined. This group of physicians provides primary care for an HMO in the Chicago area and has kept comparative records with other conventional providers in the HMO for the past seven years, representing 70,274 member months. Primary care provided by the alternative group focuses on prevention and information. When compared to conventional medicine the care they provided resulted in decreases of 60.2% in hospital admissions, 59% hospital days, 62% outpatient surgeries and procedures, and 85% pharmaceutical costs—and more satisfied patients. These satisfied patients are a critical part of this study because HMOs profit when healthcare money is not spent on illness so a common finding is patients who feel that they are given less than appropriate care. In this case they were satisfied. Satisfied patients could become a powerful part of the invisible hand, but their voice is still muted because their health care is still paid for by someone else. If we want to empower them we need to look at how the system is paid and at the marketplace where it works.

Paying Aesclepius

Hippocrates, the father of western medicine, said that the patient should pay the doctor for his services, and it worked that way for close to three thousand years. Four hundred years before the birth of Christ, Socrates, when he realized that the poison he drank was the final healing of his physical ailments, honored this method of payment with his last words when he asked his friend Crito to pay a cock to Aesclepius for him. In the intervening centuries there was a simple two party contract between the physician and the patient wherein the patient paid the physician to restore his health.

Over the last century, however, this contract has become much more complex as other agents have been included. Life saving surgery required hospitals to provide nursing care; laboratory and radiology services help us find out what is wrong; therapeutic technologies help us fix it; and pharmaceutical companies manufacture the drugs that are supposed to help; and all expect to be paid—to say nothing of the insurance industry that pays them. Hippocrates's two party contracts were much simpler and more transparent in that you had a better idea of what you were getting. It was also controlled by the patient. The added services have complicated the contract. They have led to our acceptance of the marketplace because of its ability to appropriately value a variety of services, and of insurance because of the increased expense as technologies were added. But the patient's role has been hobbled in our marketplace, the invisible hand is paralyzed, and as the alignment became more defensive all the other agents have gamed it for their own benefit. We need to look more at the role of the market in healthcare.

Elements of a marketplace

Besides the foundation of informed consumers a well functioning marketplace requires a legal system protecting the agents—the ideas of the innovators, the safety of the consumers, and ideally the rights of the workers—though the Chinese brand seems to do well, initially anyway, with none of these. In addition it works best and most equitably when: the buyers and sellers are representing themselves; there are a variety of commodities from which to choose; it is unregulated and transparent (i.e., asymmetric information is minimal); and ideally the commodity is not something critical that you could not go without. These elements form the physical, relational, and ideological context of the CASY that is the marketplace; they provide a means of looking at our healthcare system as a CASY and of seeing where small changes can be made that may elicit healthier adaptations. The often critical nature of health care shows how this factor complicates the marketplace.

Elements in the marketplace—Critical commodities

In an open market people are free to not purchase the commodity, and the need for most commodities is not critical. The world's need for oil today shows how a critical need can skew its cost. In much the same way the *need* for pain relief, longer life, and repair of injuries is on an entirely different scale from that of most other commodities—we are not in a position to say "No."

Life-saving services are mostly surgical procedures developed over the last 150 years, since the advent of anesthesia and antisepsis made them possible. They complicate the market because their perceived value is immeasurable—a life is saved. That's why surgeons are paid more. The understanding and utilization of painless, infection free, surgery meant that critical internal problems could be fixed and patients restored to full functioning—a far better deal than the trade off of saving your life by cutting off your gangrenous leg that had been surgery's beginnings.

At some time or another most people have a need for health care that they see as being necessary, and there is no real consideration for going without it. Putting a necessary service in the marketplace runs into the same problem that privatizing the water supply did in Bolivia, Ghana, Peru, Trinidad and Tobago, and other developing countries where such action led to protests, revolts and riots. It's not right to charge for, and thereby make unavailable to the poor, something that is essential to life. Bread riots, a relatively common occurrence in times of shortage and famine, have the same message—when the charge for something seen as essential to life makes it unavailable to some it breeds hostility and revolt. And whether that something is given by nature, as is the case with water, or is in the form of asymmetric information or expertise held by a professional cabal, as in the case of illness care, doesn't seem to make much difference to those in need. Critical services distort the marketplace and relying on marketplace pressures to provide them skews the cost upward, especially when the marketplace is aligned defensively as we can readily see in the case with both oil and healthcare.

A defensively aligned marketplace is also a questionable place to seek quality. When a defensively aligned CASY has to balance profit and quality it's usually the latter that gets shorted. Hospitals are a current example as the need for profit leads to fewer nurses and more work—and consequently more mistakes—for the ones they have. The Canadians looked at this problem when they were seeking direction for their health care programs. They found that for-profit hospitals in the United States came with an increased mortality rate. And it's not a new problem.

The condition of our canned foods in the 19th Century shows the same shorting of safety in the face of increased costs. Books like Upton Sinclair's *The Jungle,* that portrayed the careless and filthy nature of many food industry practices, eventually led to the creation of the Food and Drug Administration, the government agency with the responsibility to assure us that our food is safe. This regulatory agency was seen as necessary because our political leaders could not see any other way to get private interests to improve the food supply when it cost them more.

While we have more often chosen private enterprise to provide these necessary services, and the regulation it requires to cope with the market's shadow, most of the world has chosen to deal with the problems of quality by some measure of state sponsorship. In the matter of health care they realize that the health of the populace is a systemic benefit, and accept to that measure that public agencies have some responsibility to provide it. This is the case with the safety of the food we eat, the water we drink, and the air we breathe, as well as some measure of health care itself. It's the reason behind the Finnish government and our military providing xylitol sweetened gum to the students and the troops.

This is not the place to argue the merits or faults of their position, or of those favoring privatization, but only to show that privatization, with its implied profiteering, is problematic when dealing with something viewed as essential to life—whether it's water, food, or health care—and that the most reasonable way to deal with it has already been discovered by the rest of the world—assuring that everyone has access.

Elements in the marketplace—Diversity

The health and wealth of an ecosystem, and any other CASY, is proportional to the diversity of elements within the system. The more elements there are to play with, the richer the potential for novelty and creative adaptation.

On the simplest scale bacteria play with DNA and have anywhere from a few hundred to 7000 plus genes. Compared to the 35,000 that we find in a much more complex human, bacteria are much richer in these elements than they need to be. Bacteria with the lower numbers live in safe and stable environments, where there are few challenges or need for novelty. Bacteria with higher numbers are those that are challenged more often; they are the ones that can speed up their rate of mutation. Many of them live in our gastrointestinal systems. One reason for their success in surviving may be that they have more diverse elements with which to play.

On the scale of our immune systems the elements are the proteins that our immune system uses to recognize invaders, those it uses to combine with viral, bacterial or tumor cell proteins that it wants to eliminate, and the antibodies it builds to deal with them. The healthiest immune system is one with a sufficient supply of these proteins that has been exposed to, and has tabs on, the greatest number and diversity of foreign agents. These are those, discussed earlier, who are less likely to be bothered with allergies or asthma.

In a similar way children adapt to their varied cultures by playing with their neural connections and there are several periods in child development when unused connections are pruned and deleted. The connections used the most are preserved so a child who has played the most with a variety of elements should have greater potential. We can readily see this demonstrated in the success of early child education programs.

From the viewpoint of a market, *Wal Mart*, the world's healthiest retailer, has the greatest diversity in products. A healthcare system, like other CASYs, is better and healthier when it encompasses the greatest diversity. But that is not what we chose.

Diversity in health care. Health care in the United States a century ago was diverse. It was a hodgepodge of disorganized physicians practicing with a variety of treatments, still largely based on balancing aberrant humors, but with pockets of resistance and novelty. This was the time spoken of by Oliver Wendell Holmes when he said that if all our medications were dumped in the bottom of the sea it would be better for mankind and worse for the fish. He was far from alone in his criticism, but health care was gradually improving. We understood the germ theory and the paradigm of medicine was shifting to encompass it—just not fast enough for Dr. Holmes.

With anesthesia it became possible to surgically correct internal problems, like appendicitis, that had previously been almost universally fatal; and with antisepsis people no longer died from infections introduced from the dirty hands of the physician. And we were asking the right questions about our accepted treatments.

One of the earliest examples of a longitudinal study, for example, was on the practice of blood-letting. As discussed earlier it showed that more people died after the procedure—so we didn't kill people as often by mistakenly treating their inflammatory response with blood-letting. Health care was getting better.

By far the greatest benefits to our overall well being and life expectancy, as Dr. Baker's experience during this time suggests, came from the public rather than the private sector of healthcare. With the understanding of the germ theory, clean water, sanitation, Pasteurization, and vaccination (for small pox) and immunization made sense, and the pursuit and application of this new understanding did more to extend life expectancy than all of the other medical advances put together. Life expectancy shot upward in the first decades of the 20th century as this paradigm shift led to effective changes that prevented many of the infectious diseases that until then had been major causes of infant and childhood mortality.

Most diversity and true novelty in large systems comes from the margins and these advances were no exception. While they are commonplace and accepted today, immunization, clean water, and sanitation were long fought battles against vested interests in the 18th and 19th centuries. Jenner's idea of infecting people with the relatively benign cow pox to prevent the much more lethal smallpox went against the first principle of medicine, "first of all do no harm," by actually giving people a disease. It was bitterly fought and tantamount to malpractice. Fortunately much of that battle had already been fought and won by the success of variolation where puss from a person with a mild case of small pox was used to infect and thereby develop immunity in others. But this victory did not translate to acceptance in other areas. Semmelweis was kicked out of his hospital for suggesting that physicians were carrying bacteria on their hands that killed new mothers, and Pasteur was booed and shouted down when he supported the idea.

The margins increase diversity and produce novelty because that is where cross-pollination with other ideas and other systems is more likely to happen. Jean Piaget, the great pioneer of human development, recognized this when he counseled researchers to read in fields other than their specialty. As with the bacteria and its DNA the more elements there are for the agent to play with the greater the potential for novelty. The varieties of elements on the margins of a field are greater than those in its center. As Wendell Berry puts it, "it was the desert, not the temple, that gave us the prophets." Jenner was an observant country doctor working with milkmaids that had cowpox; Semmelweis was an equally observant low ranking physician working in a birthing hospital where he watched mothers die of infection after being examined by their doctors fresh from the dissecting lab—and not get infected and die with the midwives, or if the doctors washed their hands prior to the examination. And Pasteur did not begin his work in the prestigious Pasteur Institute, but in the equivalent of his garage; and their new ideas were usually resisted by the establishment.

Osteopathic and Homeopathic medicine added to the diversity as they arose from the margins during the 19th century as reactions to the problems seen in traditional medicine. Osteopathic medicine took from biology the interrelationship of structure and function, and from Newton the idea of forces, and applied them to the body. Its founder, Dr. Andrew Taylor Still, proposed that optimizing the body's structure would improve its function and help the patient's own defenses against illness to work more effectively. The decreased mortality of Osteopathically treated victims of the 1918-19 flu epidemic is strong indication that he was right.

Homeopathy is based on the observation that very small amounts of toxic substances act as stimulants in the area of their toxicity. Examples of this principle from standard medicine include salicylic acid, or *Aspirin*, which in small amounts is used to lower temperature, but in large amounts is toxic and raises the body temperature; and digitalis, which in large amounts creates all kinds of abnormal heart rhythms that can easily kill us, while small amounts are used to regulate some abnormal rhythms. These examples show the principle, but therapeutic amounts of these drugs used by western medicine are many orders of magnitude larger than the doses used by homeopathic practitioners.

These are just two examples of the diversity that existed a hundred years ago in the marketplace of medicine. But instead of letting this diversity evolve and promoting the margins we took a different, a regulatory, mechanically oriented, path, because that was the way we saw the world.

Squelching diversity. Early in the last century the Carnegie Institute sponsored research on medical education in the US and Canada. The study was led by Abraham Flexner, a noted educator and later the first person to lead Princeton's Institute for Advanced Study. He concluded, in his 1910 report, that of the 155 medical schools currently on the records only those with a program based on that of Johns Hopkins were doing an adequate job of training physicians. Over the next few decades, as medical education lined up on the Hopkins model and states increased licensure controls to assure the public that their physicians were adequately trained, organized medicine got its shot in the arm. The American Medical Association, organized in 1847, had been trying for some time to organize America's doctors and Flexner's report gave them the support they needed. Doctors, threatened by the risk of losing their license to practice, came together; they flocked—the cohesion rule at work. From the mechanical perspective of the time this was a positive result. The system, if it could be considered a system at that time, became more cohesive, and as such, more predictable and manageable.

These changes affected both the increasingly standardized practice of medicine as well as the system in which that care was delivered. Both shifted toward the predictable and mechanical side of the systems' spectrum, but the diversity disappeared.

Few have seen the down side of these changes since our medical education and practices are still largely based on the Hopkins model, but treating CASYs in mechanical ways is abusive. Treating the body as if it were a mechanical contrivance is abusive and ignores its ability to adapt. Treating our healthcare system and its schools as if it were mechanical is just as abusive to that CASY.

Shutting down the margins stifles novelty. Homeopathic colleges were closed and almost osteopathic medicine as well. Osteopathic medicine survived in large part because many Osteopathic physicians bought into the standard model. The openness, on which systems and markets thrive, decreased; and so did the diversity—the source of novelty and the measure of a system's health.

Fortunately those changes have been temporary. The continuation and growth of Osteopathic Medicine, the resurgence of Homeopathy, the growth of natural medicine and other alternatives like chiropractic, and the public's utilization of these alternatives, demonstrate that diversity is strong in this marketplace. So also does the inclusion of other paradigms of illness in the National Center for Complementary and Alternative Medicine at the National Institutes of Health. But while more people seek these alternatives they continue mostly to be considered "non-scientific" and marginal—except for Osteopathic medicine, which often is more of a "medical" clone and hardly "osteopathic." Fewer insurance companies pay for alternative medicine, and there are other pressures attempting to keep the healthcare marketplace uniform as well.

One of the latest, for example, is called "evidence based medicine." But as nice as the name sounds the science behind it is more often than not biased toward what makes the greatest profit. Its stated aim, much like Flexner's with medical education, is to assure that treatments have been shown effective in "gold standard" randomized, double-blind, placebo-controlled, crossover, clinical trials. The problem is not so much with the stated goals of these standardization measures; we want effective treatments. The problem is with how the studies were and are carried out, and on what they look at. The analytical clinical trial, just as Flexner's analytical approach to medical education, ignores the importance of adaptation and the networked interconnections in their respective systems. Indeed the placebo part of these trials is specifically designed to eliminate adaptation as a factor and shows how really powerful it is. In most such trials about one-third of the people taking the placebo get a benefit that can only be explained by their ability to adapt as if they were getting the real drug; and in psychotropic trials for drugs like anti-depressants it is often more than double this. Clinical trials are very expensive so they are short and they look only at the symptom(s) the drug was designed to address. Because of this they are often too short to find out long term effects, like the increased cardiac risks of those taking Vioxx. These gold standard trials focus on the efficacy of the drug to balance the symptom rather than the healing of the patient. They focus on the statistical result of using a drug and eliminate as much as possible any human, adaptive, or individual effect there is from any particular patient. While they are the best way to tell the efficacy of a drug for treating a particular symptom they are likely the "worst way to assess who will benefit." The expense of these studies also inhibits low profit natural therapies from having a voice since few have profit margins that could afford the expensive 'gold standard' trials. Even older generic drugs with time tested efficacy for the condition are commonly left out because they no longer make the needed profit. Furthermore the trials are often open to the interpretation and manipulation of the interested funding and profiting parties as the result of the incest that was discussed earlier.

The effect of evidence based medicine is to promote the treatments that make enough money to pay for the expensive tests. At the same time the decrease in the remaining options reduces physician and patient choice in drugs as well as the use of alternatives from the margins. Needless to say evidence based medicine is promoted mostly by the pharmaceutical industry that is the primary profiteer.

Evidence based medicine continues the error of our current medical model of treating the body mechanically; it attempts to analyze and reduce the problem to its one fundamental imbalance that can be treated with a drug. The body, however, is a CASY with many paths to healing. Evidence based medicine ignores this variety in the individual and works to reduce the diversity of therapies that is part of the health and wealth of the CASY that is our healthcare system. It takes us in the wrong direction.

Elements of the marketplace—Buyers, Sellers, and Insurance

With the closing of the margins advances in health care came increasingly from the scientifically approved high tech sources and the life-saving surgical procedures that accompanied them. The upward spiral of health care costs began. Seeing the increasing costs doctors began promoting the idea of health insurance as a reasonable way to guard against these often unforeseen expenses. Most of what are commonly called the "blues" began as insurance sponsored by local groups of physicians.

Even better, we thought, was the idea of the automobile manufacturers who gained their needed workers during the post WW II wage freezes by offering a health insurance package. Why should we pay for our health care when our employers can deduct it from their taxes? Employer based health insurance has become the norm in this country and has expanded far beyond the definition of insurance; and as insurance got bigger the 'blues,' with their physician control, were edged out.

Insurance is properly designed to cover unforeseen events like accidents, illnesses, or injuries. But employer based health insurance, because it was paid by the employer before taxes, has expanded to pay for everything. Employees could gain more, because of the taxing difference, by a larger benefits package that included broad health care coverage, than by a wage increase. Health insurance expanded to cover all health care, even the drugs. Medicare, initially providing hospital care for the elderly under Social Security, has eventually done much the same thing. But as nice as these measures were for the patients and their pocketbooks they essentially destroyed the contract that had existed between the patient and the doctor; and with its demise costs began increasing even more.

The system was now being fed by third parties that included the government—the deepest pocket of all. But this shift disconnected the patient from any financial responsibility in their treatment—they could choose without having to pay. If we could buy automobiles that way we would all drive luxury cars. The buyer and the seller became the *user* and the seller and like users of narcotics there was some addiction, in this case to more expensive treatments. Inflation in health care cost followed, then regulation to try to control the inflation, and then the inevitable response of a CASY to regulation that is seen as outside interference—defensive realignment and gaming. The presence of third party payers made this gaming easier as well as more profitable.

The relationship between the buyer and seller is altered when a third party pays for the service. Normally market pressures from increased demand lead to higher costs which in turn lead to increasing the supply, but in a regulated and insured environment this doesn't work. Third party payers mostly pay the same to everyone so there is no pressure to increase supply; and when there are more providers the doctors don't compete and prices don't go down, they just do more procedures. Demand and costs rise together in this situation. So we began looking to the government for cost controlling solutions; solutions that were in retrospect mechanical, regulatory fixes that didn't control anything because they just promoted more gaming. As Plsek pointed out in his appendix to *Crossing the Quality Chasm*, all the regulatory fixes failed to control health care costs; regulation, in a friendly environment, promotes the playful, but mostly defensive, adaptation we see as gaming.

Unmanageable regulatory fixes. One of the problems regulators confronted was that healthcare costs differed from one part of the country to another. In CASYs such variation reflects the diversity of the system, but in mechanical systems it's unmanageable, and of course we chose the mechanical option. In order to address this issue the AMA divided healthcare up into hundreds of specific service codes for every type of interaction a person could have with the healthcare system and, together with Medicare and the major players in the insurance industry, agreed on the value to be paid for each service.

In this coding fix the service, or code, was given a particular value that was based on the time needed, complexity of the problem, and the training needed for dealing with the problem; and the same thing was done with procedures, which are generally pricier because of the increased training needed for proficiency. The value was determined, not by the marketplace, but in committee. A similar process assigned codes for medical diagnoses that replaced networked conditions with isolated codes and disregarded completely the complexity of the human body. These codes then became the commodities of healthcare; and at almost the same time they became the focus both of the gaming of the system by the agents and the attempts at control by the regulators.

This is a mechanical fix on a complex system. It tries to control output or behavior. It's like the father who tries to control his child's outward behavior by his control of the pocketbook. It might work when the authority is watching, but that is about the limit. It's treating the CASY as an object to be used and manipulated, and despite the role of the AMA in this process it was seen as outside interference, as something demanded by government, as coercive, abusive and threatening; so the system responded by shifting closer to chaos and to more of a defensive alignment. And the focus of the system shifted from the patient and their problem to the diagnosis and the service code, and how to game them to increase the profit.

Another mechanical attempt at control was payment by diagnostic related groups, which resulted in much the same kind of gaming. Under this program payments to hospitals were based on the optimum (shortest) time it took to resolve such problems with the best care possible. But one can easily game this by shifting from a diagnostic group that doesn't pay very much to a more complex one paying substantially more just by including a few more laboratory tests or detailing a few more clinical signs in the exam. Again, treating the patient became secondary to the manipulation of their symptoms in order to maximize profit as participants in the system rapidly learned to game it for their own benefit.

Managed care, the latest attempt at regulating the system, has also succumbed to the gaming it promoted. Regulating CASYs is mechanical and abusive; it promotes a defensive alignment and is not the best way to deal with them.

The two factors of the third party payer, that removed the patient from the contract, and the transformation of health care into a commodity, where a procedure code and a diagnosis determine payment, have together pushed the alignment of our healthcare system from enhancing health through creative novelty to defensive gaming for profit. The two factors succeeded, not at making the system more mechanical and predictable, but of eliminating its professionalism. They led to what Dr. Marcia Angell, past editor of the *New England Journal of Medicine* and professor of Medicine at Harvard University, calls the commodification of health care. This, she says, is the major problem with our current system. Making healthcare into a commodity is consistent with the marketplace model and manipulating it consistent with the mechanical regulatory model, but objectifying the healthcare system is the step that shifted it to the defense and began the gaming.

Gaming the system means that the complexity of illness increases because more complex problems pay more. It means that less expensive preventive therapies are ignored in favor of those paying more. It means that more procedures are done than may be necessary, like our rate of Caesarean deliveries. It means that a person outside the umbrella of a regulating body—whose health care is not paid for by Medicare, Medicaid, or a large insurance company—pays substantially more despite often being less well off, because, the system argues, the regulated price is too low; so they charge more to make up for their shortfalls. It means that when the regulators reduce the payment for one code, providers just move up a level of complexity to the code that pays more. It means that the insurers respond by downcoding, where the provider is reimbursed for a less complex and expensive code, and bundling, where the billed charges are lumped together and some of the services are not paid. It means that the active agents in the CASY of healthcare are so busy dealing with the hostility and frustration of working and gaming in the dysfunctional system that they have little time or interest to seek creative novelty in caring for their patients.

Because the patient doesn't pay the bill they are not usually concerned with these family squabbles. Indeed, the greater the charge to the third-party-payer the more there is a sense of greater service and greater bargain on the part of the patient.

All of these fixes, from establishing the codes and the diagnostic groups, to regulating the prices, are mechanical attempts at cost control, but they all stem from the introduction of the third party payer and the commodification of health care that logically followed. These two changes determined how the system was fed and established the "for profit" alignment of our current system. Newt Gingrich is absolutely correct when he sees the primary reason for skyrocketing health care costs in our failed third-party-payer system. Most agents in the healthcare system attribute its decline in quality to the advent of Medicare and government intervention in the healthcare marketplace, but the significant drops in healthcare productivity began in the 1950s as insurance expanded, not in the 1960s when government entered the field. If there is one point that marks this change it is the passage of legislation allowing companies to deduct health insurance premiums from their corporate taxes in 1954. We need, Gingrich says, to get back to the idea and simplicity of buyers and sellers.

Political solutions. Skyrocketing costs are by far the most visible problem in our system and we look to our politicians for solutions. But most politicians seem more attentive to the powers than they are to the problems, so all they have come up with have been mechanically oriented regulatory solutions which don't hurt the powers, have not worked in the past, and do not work with CASYs in general. If the latest Medicare drug bill is any indication government will look to the system itself for its own regulation, which openly allows the gaming that pads the pockets. Current proposals are focused in three areas: mandating employer based insurance, increased governmental underwriting of insurance or edging toward the Canadian system of one party payer, and promoting a voluntary "ownership society" that has health savings accounts—where we get away from our failed third-party-payer system and back to Gingrich's favored binary based system of each paying for our own health care.

All of these options in their current form are primarily mechanical designs to control costs and address availability. They regulate elements of the system with the hope that control is possible, without realizing the adaptable nature of our healthcare system. But their effects on the context of this CASY are far different.

Mandating employer based insurance will continue the trend of making our manufacturers less competitive and driving manufacturing out of the country. It's not our best option. Albert Einstein is quoted as saying that, "Insanity is doing the same thing again and expecting different results." William Glasser, father of "Reality Therapy" says much the same thing: "If what you are doing is not working, do something else." Gingrich is right and continuing with more of the same will get us more of the same—it's insane.

Increasing the government's role in underwriting will eventually lead, because of its efficiency, to their doing it all. But at the extreme of socialized medicine it means the rationing of services: as in Romania where the treatment of cancer by specialists is not funded; or Oregon where they attempted, but failed, to limit government funded services to core problems.

The lesser extreme of the Canadian system makes more sense. Since close to 30% of health insurance premiums goes to the non-medical expense of feeding the growing bureaucracy, going to a single insurer would have some immediate benefits; and despite the well advertised waits and delays, the Canadians are far happier with their system than Americans are with theirs. But Canadians too are finding out that they are not immune to cost escalation. As Gingrich points out, any time a third party pays the bill for a service the demand for the service goes up, whether that third party is an insurance company or, in Canada's case, the government acting as an insurance company. And it is not just the demand for the service that rises, but the demand for expensive services, because as long as someone else is paying for it most people erroneously see high tech and expense as indicating better care.

The largest problem with government as insurer, however, is perpetuating the dysfunctional relationship and the gaming between government and the healthcare system. As long as this relationship remains dysfunctional and the government seeks to overtly control and regulate the behavior of the healthcare system, it leads, as it does in any CASY, directly to a defensive alignment in the objectified agents. Costs will continue to increase as the agents resort to defensive gaming. Most people are uncomfortable in such an environment so while most Canadians are happy with their system, most of their doctors are not.

With Health Savings Accounts (HSAs) we take a step back to what Gingrich calls the binary payer system, where the individual pays for his or her own routine health care. These accounts are a combination of a high deductible catastrophic health insurance policy, with premiums that cost much less than regular health insurance, and a savings account, that can be converted to a retirement account at age 65, to pay for routine care. The catastrophic part of these policies gets us back to the nature of what insurance is for.

The 'savings account' part of HSAs allows the individual to pay for their routine health care as well as the deductible part of the catastrophic coverage. In these policies even employer funded accounts are under the control of the individual and it's the individual, not the insurance company, who writes the check. Supporters of HSAs point out that they will be effective at reducing costs because people will be more conservative in their purchase of health care when they pay for it from their own pockets. And they are. Seen in this way HSAs are little more than a manipulative tool that benefits the healthy agent by allowing them to exit the more expensive system. Their real value lies beyond that in the fact that HSAs return the buyers to the marketplace; if there were enough of them they could effectively realign the system.

With their current voluntary nature HSAs offer a form of "cherry picking" for the healthy person who can withdraw from an average risk insurance pool, pay lower premiums, and save for retirement—and do it with mostly pre-tax dollars. "Cherry-picking" refers to the practice in the insurance industry of selecting those with low risk for the accident or disaster that they are insuring against—like insuring someone living on a hill in Las Vegas against flood damage. Lower risk means less insurance money paid out so the practice makes money for the insurance company. It is common practice in today's marketplace where there are many insurance companies vying for customers and a benefit of a single payer system would be its elimination. In HSAs the one who benefits most from the cherry-picking is the healthy person who gets to save for retirement. But their less healthy partners who stayed with their traditional insurance wind up paying more because the remaining group is less healthy and their premiums must increase to cover costs. There is little interest in HSAs among the chronically ill or the poor, and leaving them voluntary will remove the healthy from the pool and therefore increase this financial burden on those less able to pay. This problem needs to be resolved before HSAs can reach their potential of realigning the system.

Another problem is their uneven tax status. When paid for by a company or even a small corporation they are fully deductible, but when purchased by an individual only a percentage is tax free. Any HSA policy needs to be fully deducible. A final aspect that needs a solution is the down side of HSAs.

There are two sides to everything and HSAs have their critics as well as their supporters. The supporters correctly say they will work because of the hesitation we all have of spending our own money, but the flip side of this is that people will be more likely to delay evaluation of a problem so that a stage 1 cancer has time to grow and spread to stage 3 or 4, shortness of breath with exertion becomes a heart attack, or strep throat develops into rheumatic fever. So from one point of view, looking at the expense of the system, they appear a solution, but from the other side, looking at the health of the people, they appear a problem.

This problem is that of asymmetric information; the patient lacks the information needed to make a wise health care decision. The resolution of the problem comes again from empowering Public Health to do the preventive health education and screening that is needed to insure our improved health; Public Health needs to be able to help people decide whether or not their condition needs further medical care. The role of government is to assure, as much as possible, a good future for the society, and enabling the 'invisible hand' by addressing and eliminating asymmetric information wherever it exists is the best way to accomplish this goal. Access to screening tests designed to help the person know whether their particular problem requires "illness care" or is not of medical significance should be available at one's local Public Health office. This is the kind of health care provided by the alternative group in Chicago's HMO mentioned earlier.

Health care designed to keep our people healthy is a public good and should be widely available and subsidized. Illness care should be prevented if at all possible, but available to all and insured if it turns out to be a major problem, and the person should have access to independent information that helps them to make wise decisions as to where to go as well as access whenever possible to a group of patients sharing their experience with the particular problem. The individual agent not only owns their HSA with an interest in its long term appreciation, but this is now coupled with financial pressure to improve their own health; they are responsible for using it wisely and making appropriate decisions about their health care. The information to do this wisely needs to come from some place other than the illness care section lest we continue the moral hazard portrayed by Shaw's amputee.

Shaw's analogy is not unreal. Several years ago when arthroscopic surgery was first becoming popular I attended a lecture by an orthopedic surgeon entitled, "Is arthroscopic surgery damaging to your knees?" In arthroscopic surgery an orthopedic surgeon uses a small camera to look inside a joint, usually the knee, to try to find the source of the patient's problem. Used in this way it is *only* a diagnostic procedure. But if the surgeon sees a rough edge and snips something it becomes a therapeutic procedure and is paid significantly more than a diagnostic one. This places a moral hazard in front of the surgeon who can increase his income by a simple snip. The fact that they often succumb to this hazard justified the conclusion of the speaker that this type of surgery is damaging because more knees are snipped than is necessary.

Moral hazard is also present for the well insured patient to seek unnecessary care, for the insurance industry to "cherry pick" whom they will insure, and for all players to game the system for their own benefits. Moral hazard on all levels is best constrained by eliminating asymmetric information, by leveling the playing field. While some information needs to be private in order to eliminate cherry picking by insurance companies who look at an applicants past history, their personal habits like smoking, or unhealthy occupations like working with heavy metals or solvents, in order to reduce their exposure. While it seems sensible to pass the expense for these riskier exposures on to the patients there is often, in the case of genetic risks for example, nothing they can do about it; and often the agent is exposed without his or her knowledge. While such health related questions as smoking history can provide stimulus for improving that behavior insurance companies should not be able to ask for information that the patient cannot change such as family history, genetic handicaps, or past medical history, which allows the company to do this kind of 'cherry picking.' The wide spread use of these blinded HSA's empowers the insured agent with the financial ability to guide the system, and enabling Public Health to educate them provides the healthcare consumer with the information needed to guide it in a healthier way.

If they are going to be effective HSA's must be wide spread enough to impact the system, meaning that they must be promoted and supported to the extent of building our entitlement programs on them. In a recent effort to stimulate our domestic saving, politicians proposed, but did not pass, the "KidSave program," where the Federal government would set up, and initially fund, a savings account for every child born in the country that could only be withdrawn at death, disability, or retirement. The intent was to encourage savings and to reduce the burden on Social Security. We should look at this idea again as a way to establish an HSA for America's newborns. For the cost of a few days in Iraq every newborn child for the year could have an HSA contribution of $1000.00. Continuing this program would gradually make the base universal, and any means of increasing our domestic savings would also be beneficial for our own, as well as the worlds', economy. Subsidizing this program for the poor would encourage their cooperation as well because they have shown a willingness to save some of their own money if it is matched by enough to overcome the weight of current needs. A side benefit of HSA's would also create a context in which the agent, the patient in this case, would be encouraged to adapt in ways that would actually make our public healthier.

In our mechanical model illness is mostly defined in terms of bothersome symptoms, or a physical or chemical imbalance. The World Health Organization's definition is more inclusive: health is a state of complete physical, mental, and social well-being and not merely the absence of disease or infirmity. Social well-being is of interest because sociologists looking at illness have found what are called 'hardy' people who tend to have fewer problems and deal with them in ways other than relying on the healthcare system. They find that hardy people have more of a sense of coherence or fitting in with their environment and to them that environment is understandable, manageable, and meaningful. Those in our society that currently benefit from the lower costs and the savings benefits of HSAs are far more likely to be those enjoying this sense of coherence with, and manageability of, their world. A significant result of giving a wider population the responsibility to cope with their own health care, the financial means to do so, and the information needed to do it wisely also gives them the context of the hardy individual and would encourage adaptation in that direction. It's the equivalent of giving a starving person a fishing pole and teaching him how to fish.

With wider utilization of HSAs we will also see the most important change that is not brought out by their supporters—the adapting, empowered, and informed agents can change the alignment of the system. HSAs restore the contract between the patient and the physician. With the patient paying, the physician's alignment is no longer defensive so they can focus more on creative novelty in their treatment. Other benefits that come from this realignment are: they prevent gaming because when the individual pays the bill there is less interest in manipulating the service to a higher code; they sponsor diversity because while HSAs are restricted to health care use there are no other constraints—you can pay your dentist, eye doctor, massage therapist, acupuncturist, health food store, or even your gym if you are exercising for a health related reason. And knowledgeable patients are more able to bargain for a better price. If a physician's administrative cost is 27% of their gross income there is room to negotiate if you are paying on the spot.

But this realignment will only come if HSAs are promoted by the government and included in government funded entitlement programs—and that means subsidizing them for those in poverty. HSAs can reorient the system, but they will work well only if we are willing to make them universal and spend what is necessary to deal with the asymmetric information that exists in matters of health by educating the public. Underlying all of our healthcare decisions should be knowledgeable consumers making the most informed choices possible. They are the invisible hand that guides healthcare in a direction that brings value to society. A Public Health Service whose function is to keep people healthy by providing education and preventive screening examinations at no cost, or a cost based on income, would be the best remedy for our current profit oriented system. A healthy population is a public good, just as much as an educated one; and just as they do with education the state should play a bigger role in getting us there. Providing such information would also deal effectively with the last element of a marketplace—regulation and transparency.

Elements of the marketplace—regulation and transparency
There are many voices in a marketplace, some louder than others. In ours it seems that their strength is proportional to their money. Some voices argue against increasing transparency because it interferes with business—because it hampers their ability to increase profits. Providing corporate transparency means giving away company secrets;

and making less profit off more informed customers or stockholders. The strategy behind these loud voices is that of a defensive alignment with a profit orientation; it's the same as we saw with Social Darwinism where survival of the fittest was applied to the economy. It is the emphasis in our corporations where the function of the board of directors is to make sure that the corporate leaders' focus is fixed on making a profit for the shareholders. The strategy behind transparency, on the other hand, is the creative alignment that leads to systemic progress.

Increasing transparency in governments is a primary emphasis of the OECD, the Organization for Economic Cooperation and Development; it is at the foundation of our market system; it is what informs and empowers the invisible hand that brings value to the system. And it is the best way to counter the accumulation of power in our world's governments so that only two, Bosnia and Rwanda, made positive steps in improving transparency in the last ten years. While we can see the importance of transparency in making the marketplace more equitable a full appreciation of its power is apparent only when we see its role in enabling better adaptation, only when we see human and social systems as adaptive, as CASYs. Without seeing its power to inform adaptation we remain blind to the full value of transparency.

Adaptation in nature remains largely a hidden process of trying and testing mutations for survival value. Even though bacteria can speed up their rate of mutation their manipulation of their DNA remains experimentally random. Higher level CASYs adapting to their social and economic contexts should be able to see further than simpler agents that have only their DNA to play with, but they often remain blind to their own internal problems. We can build complicated simulation models of our systems and test them for accuracy so we should be able to better deal with our problems, but without seeing differently we are more likely to just perpetuate and expand them. Conventional wisdom is generally stuck in the old way of seeing;

in our case the solutions are based on mechanical regulations rather than addressing a system's context and allowing time for adaptation. We don't see our problems if we have slept with them for a few years. The sight of those looking at how to improve our system, according to John Kenneth Galbraith, is clouded by our social models or financial advantage, or by what is called in psychology, confirmation bias. It's the same with healthcare. Seeing the system differently, as a CASY, is the first step in identifying and correcting their problems.

The need for regulation is minimized when the beneficiaries of the system, those who are ill in the case of health care, are empowered to make choices, as they are with HSAs, and when transparency is maximized as it could be by an active PHS. Just as regulation, commodification, and third party insurers are primarily responsible for the defensive alignment that created our healthcare problems, HSA's and an active PHS can realign it in a healthier way.

This realigned marketplace has a chance if, and only if, we empower the invisible hand that guides the market to increased social value—and that means breaking down the asymmetric information present in the system. Empowering Public Health to do this education and to help the patients determine their need for 'illness care' is an essential part of HSA's. It's time to feed the Doctor Baker's.

CHAPTER 8
NO LAB-RAT LEFT BEHIND—EDUCATION

Almost all formal schooling and research is "a strenuous and devoted attempt to force nature into the conceptual boxes supplied by professional education."
Thomas Kuhn, *The Structure of Scientific Revolutions.*

The creation of something new is not accomplished by the intellect but by the play instinct acting from inner necessity. The creative mind plays with the objects it loves.
Carl Jung

Like our health care system our educational system is a social CASY made up of individual agents on lower levels—students, teachers, administrators—working in local, state and national levels of organizations that all qualify as adaptive agents and agencies. Any examination of the system needs to look at these agents, the part they play as CASYs in the larger system, and the environmental pressures that frame how they adapt. In looking at our healthcare system we saw how mechanical treatment of its agents compounded the problems by pushing them to a defensive alignment and disenfranchising the patients. The situation is similar in education.

There are educators and students as well as the system in which they function. In education there has been no marketplace because our ancestors saw it as a social good: it recognized and developed talented individuals, enabled social movement, and, for good or ill, it socialized the children. But, as we all know, this system also has its problems.

Some argue for adding marketplace elements in order to improve our schools with vouchers that pay for private education. Privatizing healthcare, as we have experienced, unleashed the shadow side of capitalism and the cycle of regulation, gaming, and realignment that has crippled our system. Do we want to risk that with our children? In healthcare we proposed a solution that included public health services for keeping people healthy and private services in an illness care sector for when they get sick. We will see how the same mix would be helpful in education. Schools should focus on education and the private sector should assist those who have significant need of special services. Since many of the factors leading to problems learning have their roots in our bodies or our brains not working optimally these problems often come under the rubric of illness care.

The problems

Our educational systems have been criticized by the state for not providing us with people able to carry on our complex society and for not being fair and equitable in treating the students. They have been criticized by business for not teaching the students how to function in their real world. They have been criticized by parents for teaching material which conflicts with their family values. And they have been criticized by educators for selecting out, not those who are innovative and creative, but those who excel at conditioned learning and test taking ability, and for socializing our children to operate under acceptable norms for group behavior rather than promoting the individualism and the adaptability that have been our roots. Higher education has been faulted for being partial to the wealthy, as well as dumbing down entrance and curriculum requirements in gaming for government grant money.

Solutions for our educational problems have been sought in better teachers, class room size, increased financing, parent, community and religious involvement, and business models that test frequently for quality assurance. Of all these the only consistent improvement has been with smaller classes that enable more contact between teacher and student.

The CASY paradigm enables us to see that most efforts to change our educational system have been based on the mechanical model. Like our approach to healthcare we have treated the agents in the system as if they were objects. We have focused on input (the curriculum) and output (the test) and built factory schools to house the assembly line. But again, just as we saw with healthcare, objectifying adaptive agents shifts their alignment to the defensive, both decreasing creative novelty and increasing hostility. It pulls up the most available reaction to this threat, the reptilian brain's flight or fight response, and our zero tolerance for violence responds tit for tat with our increasingly militaristic and restrictive alternative education programs. They are seen as the only recourse to the violent student. Over a century ago when there was still a frontier fleeing was a real option, but our crowded world and compulsory education have eliminated this avenue, regulated the activity of the agents, and increased the potential for violence as the agents are objectified and abused. This same stuck paradigm plagues all of the agents involved with our schools: the students, teachers, administrators, as well as the social systems—local, state and national—that we have established to do this work.

There is another part to the flight or fight reaction that also plays a part in this context. Peter Levine, in his book *Waking the Tiger*, tells of the impala that suddenly falls to the ground uninjured when it realizes it is losing the race with the cheetah. The animal suddenly dissociates, it shuts down mentally and physically, so that it doesn't feel being torn apart by the cheetah, or, more hopefully, that it may awaken later and escape after the cheetah, mistakenly thinking it dead, had dragged it off for later eating. The impala's dissociation is a helpful adaptation in both cases. Bruce Perry is an expert in child abuse and with how children cope with their abuse. He points out that dissociation in humans is a continuum that extends from day-dreaming to coma, and that it is just as successful an escape for a human agent being abused as it is for the impala. We must ask ourselves if the dissociation we see in our schools on the part of both the teachers and the students may result from some type of abuse.

CASYs adapt by playing with the elements available to them in response to changes that they sense in their contexts. They adapt defensively or creatively according to their alignment; and alignment is influenced by the agent's perception of their environmental context. Optimizing the context—the number and diversity of elements with which to play, the perception of safety, and the level of cooperation and camaraderie among the agents with whom they work and play—will optimize the alignment and growth of any CASY, including our children and the system established to educate them.

The context for the student is their physical and family environment, the network of relationships in the community, and the mental development that is made up of the informal education they bring with them from their home and community, the richness of their neural connections that reflects their past experience, and the mental states and stages of development they were in as they processed these experiences.

Most of the teachers and other adults in the system share the physical and social environment of the student. The mental environment is made up of the regulations with which they must work, the friendliness of the work environment, and the conventional wisdom or the paradigm of the society. Here as elsewhere a CASY's alignment is critical; and more than any other factor it is based on the sense of emotional safety present in their environment.

The elements of the systems are what the agents play with in adapting and in the educational system they vary at each level. For the student they are the concepts and tools they learn and master to the point that they can play with them. For the teacher they are the curriculum and the materials used in teaching it, the local system and its facilities, and the students. For the local system they are the state's rules and regulations, the curriculum, the buildings, the financing, the teachers, and again the students. The state seems to play virtually with all of these elements often forgetting, like higher level CASYs are wont to do, that many of the elements they manipulate and play with are CASYs in their own right.

In the mechanical paradigm these elements are objectified and regulated, but just as in healthcare, this leads to gaming the system. And not only are the agents objectified in our educational systems but the process as well. Learning theorists divide learning into classical conditioning, like Pavlov's salivating dogs, and operant conditioning, responding to Skinner's rewards or punishment. The learner is analyzed in this process; he is dissected to find out how he learns. But the researchers focused on the learner as a receptacle and ignored the type of learning we see in children before they enter school, the most rapid learning in all of human development. We need another way to look at this.

In the following we look at each of the agents in our educational system beginning with the system itself. We look at its history, at its response to mechanical treatment, at its context; and we propose ways to honor and support the agent's ability to adapt. We look at how individual CASY agents, both teachers and children respond to being treated as objects and propose better ways to honor their agency and enhance the outcome of our educational systems.

The system

As in all social systems the evolution into a CASY was gradual and involved many adaptations to changes in our social environment. Primitive societies relied on informal education and it was sufficient to socialize the children and teach them the tasks needed to live in the group. Even when societies became stationary, giving up hunting and gathering, education done by families was sufficient to teach the family centered skills that increasingly went beyond informal learning to include the training necessary for the family trade. Informal learning is largely prior to learning language, it molds who we are and how we think, and it comes directly from one's culture through the parents and community. It comes, as it were, covertly, without our awareness as we, as infant and young children, learned by mimicking the behaviors modeled for us by parents, siblings and others. This modeled learning is an integral part of the initial conditions to which CASYs are so sensitive. Informal education leads to enculturation and it was only when communication was established between different cultures, with their different ways of seeing the world, that the next level was needed. Formal education, what is called explicit learning, came later when cultures and languages had developed, and critically, when they were exposed to each other. Formal education is conscious and cognitive, but it too is openly shaped and controlled by the society.

One of the earliest formal schools in the western tradition was in Athens, a secure and safe trading center. But even here, as we have seen, Socrates was condemned for teaching about other cultures and raising the inevitable and uncomfortable questions about the relative values in the various cultures. Bringing to the surface and raising questions about the unconscious enculturation of his students condemned him in the eyes of his fellow citizens.

Formal education has balanced on this edge ever since. With increased social complexity the need increased and with the Industrial Revolution society became complex enough that schooling was considered necessary for everyone; it became a function of society. But it still maintains a cultural identity because those introducing novelty that questions social constructs, like Socrates did, are still often sacrificed to cultural values.

Education in America

Coming from the context of the early Industrial Revolution our founding fathers read the works of the 18th Century social philosophers who saw, pondered, and considered the social, cultural and political changes of the time, and generally proposed increasing the role of education to deal with them. Our country's founders had a lot of faith that an educated *man, with property*, would make good decisions in their governance. Property was important because a man with property had an interest in maintaining and improving its value, and in that day this was not done by speculation but by labor. From the time of the Magna Carta English property holders had a voice in government. Property defined a responsible agent. Women were left out in the property area, just as they were in church but, because they could be expected to pass it on to their own children, they were educated.

Schooling in early America, particularly in Puritan New England, where it was organized and socially promoted as a means to extend Biblical literacy, was carried out by the communities and small enough that it had only two manageable agents: the teacher and the students. Boards made up of a variety of the local ministry and members of their congregations insured as much as was possible a non partisan yet moral focus. Religiously oriented colleges were available in most of the larger cities for those interested in teaching or the ministry. Schooling was simple in its organization. Primary education's alignment was providing the student with the tools to figure costs, make change, and to read and study the Bible, which was considered by the Puritans the foundation of moral action.

Much of the north was populated by the Scotch-Irish who brought with them their values on education. As this group followed the frontier and migrated south and west those values were carried with them. Whether schooling was community or family based it maintained the simplicity found with a limited number of elements; it was focused on providing the individual student the reading, writing and math skills needed to further their own education, and a moral foundation for doing so; and it didn't threaten the culture.

This alignment promoted the individuality that was already strong in those who chose to immigrate. The frontier tended to strengthen it even further. By the mid 19th century, however, our country was changing from agrarian to industrial. Towns were turning into cities, the frontier was rapidly disappearing; and schooling was also evolving, getting larger and more complex with both more students and more subjects.

Responding to these changes professional educators became enchanted with the Prussian education system. The children in this system were organized by age, it was universal, and it appeared to do well at "socializing" them. In the early days of industrialization the mechanical paradigm was unquestioned—focusing on input and output was just the way things were done—and the Prussian system was its application to education.

John Taylor Gatto, a New York State "Teacher of the Year" in 1991 argues that these mid and late 19th Century changes in our educational system were designed to subvert our democracy. He argues that the changes introduced during this restructuring impaired independent thinking among the students, a change opposite to that needed in a democratic society. While accepting the fact that they did and do, the changes were hardly a conspiracy; they were just part of the mechanical paradigm. Like the rationale behind the changes following the Flexner Report that tried to eliminate diversity in health care, the dominant paradigm in both areas was the mechanical one that valued order and predictability; the school systems we built were just stuck in that framework.

Prussian education and its problems

Gatto selects William Torrey Harris who was the U. S. Commissioner of Education from 1889 to 1906 as instrumental in the conspiracy. Prior to becoming Commissioner, Harris was the Superintendent of Schools in St. Louis where he started the first kindergarten on the Prussian model. Harris was inspired by many of the industrial leaders of his day, especially Andrew Carnegie, whose funding of the Flexner Report we have already looked at. Just as the Flexner Report led to the standardization of medical education and the virtual elimination of diversity in healthcare, educational policies followed the same track; standardization is much more valuable in the mechanical framework so there was little place for diversity or individuality. Reflecting these values Harris presented a series of lectures at Johns Hopkins in 1893 that outlined his educational philosophy. In the first he discussed the differences in educational goals for several cultures and pointed out that:

Ninety-nine out of a hundred people in every civilized nation are automata, careful to walk in prescribed paths, careful to follow the prescribed custom. This is the result of substantial education, which scientifically defined, is the subsumption of the individual under his species.

Subsuming CASYs

Harris's comment is a blunt condemnation of 'substantial' education as it stands and has been used as such by Gatto and other critics of our system; we don't like to think of *our* children as included in his 99%, nor the sound of "the subsumption of the individual" that education is mostly all about. But Harris's role in this is more subtle. His critics have seen his 'substantial education' that leads to the subsumption of the individual as applying to what we have called formal education—what Harris was developing in his expansion of public education—but if you read his lecture further it is clear that Harris was referring to informal education as doing this subsuming; and he is right on the mark in this. Informal education creates ones cultural blinders and subsumes the child's individuality into the culture. Formal education in Harris's philosophy went along with Socrates and was the "emancipation from this subsumption." One problem Harris had with this was that he limited those able to learn formally and get out of their cultural boxes to 1%, condemning the rest to remain automata. But his major problem was the mechanical model in which he framed the solution.

Just as it did and does in healthcare, mechanical analysis and regulation of adaptive agents puts them on the defense and promotes gaming or defensive adaptations and the unintended consequences that normally follow. Structure and function change together in natural selection and the structure of our educational system shifted from locally controlled districts that produced individuals, to top down federally controlled state systems that, despite Harris' understanding, increasingly produced automata. In education as in so many other higher order CASYs that have accepted the mechanical model the system tends to forget that the elements it plays with are CASYs on their own levels.

The pattern seen with other mechanically managed CASYs began here in the educational system. Children, as the archetype of CASY can adapt to almost any situation. Most adapt to this mechanical learning system and become willing workers. They become proficient test takers, good at memorization and learning tasks; they become a significant part of Harris' 99%. Some resent such treatment and learn to game it. They alter their alignment toward the defensive pole and start thinking about self preservation, about ways to game the system to improve their position; or they disassociate, day-dream, or drop out. For those who can't adapt gangs and cliques are always present for flocking.

When the cohesion rule becomes operative in a threatening environment the agents flock. Children do this by seeking protection with mother, or, as they get older and shift their identity from family to peer group, by identifying with that group. They became, in David Riesman's publisher's terms, a part of the *Lonely Crowd,* where one takes his or her cues for proper behavior, not from their inner voice, but from other agents in the flock. These children become, in Riesman's metaphor, like small radar sets; constantly sending out signals to see what others are doing, and acting accordingly. They have not developed the inner gyroscopes that are self orienting. Riesman associated this behavior with corporate pressures and ethics, but it's more fundamental than that—it's a normal mid-brain defensive flocking response to the perception of threat. It is the central force behind enculturation and it was augmented in the Prussian school system.

In a democratic society, as our Declaration of Independence points out, power resides in the individual and it is individuals whose collective judgment determines the best government or the best course of action. As Gatto points out the value of this individual choice is greatly weakened when children lack the inner gyroscopes, the self-respect, and sense of inner authority that is more associated with independent learning.

Children, raised in the Prussian educational system, are much more likely to see society's political leaders as authority figures; and children educated in religious schools are more likely to flock behind their 'authorities,' be they Ayatollahs, gurus, Rabbis, or charismatic leaders. Flocking—following the leader, sensing the behavior of others and acting in concert—is a mid-brain response to the perception of external threat, and if the perception of threat increases it may stimulate even more primitive responses.

This shadow side of such a mechanically oriented system has not been well recognized, but it brings into play the same pressures we have seen with defensive measures in all CASYs. What Gatto sees now in how our educational system destroys individual initiative and subverts democracy is the same thing the German theologian Dietrich Bonhöffer saw in retrospect in how the German school system allowed for the Holocaust. It is what Alice Miller, the Swiss psychologist who looked at the mechanically oriented and abusive child rearing practices popular in Germany prior to World War II, saw as the reason for the repressed hostility that allowed the German people to blindly follow their abused and abusing but charismatic leader. These practices continued through both informal and formal education so they were compounded; social propriety in Germany was following those in authority, first in the schools, then in the state. The subsumption of the individual under his species meant not arguing with those representing a higher authority, and not seeing oneself as a creator or participant of that order. That was a disaster for Germany, but what we don't stop to realize, except for largely ignored people like Gatto, is that with Harris and his colleagues we incorporated the same system in the United States. Its emphasis on uniformity is what Gatto looks at in his claim that our schools systems were designed to subvert democracy, but, just as with the Flexner report that led to the standardization of medical education, uniformity and standardization are at the root of the mechanical model.

Those wishing to control CASYs rely heavily on promoting the flocking behavior that identifies the group; and promoting fear is the easiest way. Advertisers point out that you will not be accepted as well, or as appealing, or as sexy if you don't have their particular product. Hitler and Goebbels showed the Germanic people how they were manipulated by the evil and wealthy Jews, establishing them as a group to fear. Flocking behavior is easy to control, as Karl Rove well demonstrates, by just raising the perception of threat in your targeted group. It is this kind of abuse of supposedly independent agents that subverts democracy. It is based on seeing agents as objects to be manipulated, but this mechanical view was just how we saw the world a century ago; and it remains dominant today because, as we saw with the AMA after the Flexner Report, flocking behavior is more predictable than individual behavior, and mechanically minded policy makers need predictability. A democracy, like other CASYs, is healthier, however, with a diversity of *individual agents* who participate in a larger system but are not subsumed into it. The proper way to treat the group is to care for the one.

Funding and accountability—Testing and conditioned learning

Other factors than Harris's scientific education played a role in this shift in alignment. How the system is fed has an impact, so the shift from local, to state, and then to federal funding played a part as the feeding of the system shifted from the community to the state.

Government funding requires accountability and the measure for this in our mechanically oriented system is outcome; and outcome is measured by the test. Test performance, rather than learning how to work and play with concepts, tools, and ideas became the measure for the system, so increasingly, as these measures became an established part of the system, well studied "scientific" conditioned learning techniques were used to maximize the child's test performance. Conditioned learning techniques are well studied because they are the methods used on lab rats learning to run a maze.

In conditioned learning the agent is manipulated by rewarding proper behavior, and not rewarding, and sometimes punishing, bad behavior. It is the result of analyzing the learning process and of seeing the agents as objects to be manipulated—and according to Kant's definition it's abuse. Conditioned learning is an example of the problems associated with using rewards to control behavior—a defensive alignment is fostered any time a CASY agent senses they are being used or manipulated, *even by rewards*.

Moving education to state control also subjected it to more social pressures. So the orbiting of Sputnik in 1957 prompted both a flurry of analytical studies showing that our schools were not keeping up with the rest of the world in science and technology, and to pumping more money into that part of education—both the studies and the money being mechanical responses. So too, analyses today see our current problems in education in terms of easily measurable mechanical factors: dropouts, poor test results when compared to those of other nations, and graduates that still can't read or make proper change. And we continue to respond mechanically by focusing on these elements as we analyze and attempt to tune up the system. We improve test scores by teaching to the test, or even the test, if we can get it. We decrease dropouts by providing highly structured alternative education settings that look even more like the conditioned learning techniques used on rats. The output of our factory schools is a student proficient at memorizing, but with little ability to use the material stored in his brain in the real world. Rats do learn the task when taught in this way, but it is a *task* and it is easily forgotten. The forgetting is due to the fact that conditioned learning is mostly done in the lower parts of the brain; it does not get to the cortex where it is networked and permanent. A phenomenon called fatigue, known to all those doing conditioned learning, shows that such learning is both superficial and easily forgotten.

Such solutions are based on the mechanical analytical approach that looks at cause and effect, or supply and demand. We measure output and think we can fix our problem by better regulating the process; it's like treating the symptoms in medicine. In this case it means regulating our children. This has been our pattern for over a century. But linear thinking such as this doesn't work with networked CASYs like our ecosystems and our healthcare system; nor does it work with our children.

Under Harris's leadership schools in America moved from the mixed age model of the one-room schoolhouse, where a child was not grouped at all, to flocked schools with age based grades that ignored underlying differences and facilitated both the use of conditioned learning techniques and defensive flocking. In short children are treated mechanically, 99% of them are identified as automata, and flocking is supported by age based grades. Our schools were turned into factories, and industry was assured that they would have workers willing and able to do assembly line tasks without getting dissatisfied with meaningless work. But, as Gatto and many others point out, that is not what we need today.

As in every CASY the novelty and diversity associated with a creative alignment are more beneficial for the system than the size and efficiency associated with a defensive one. Novelty and diversity come from creatively aligned agents in the system playing with the elements available to them in a safe environment and allowing for time to adapt. This setting maximizes the opportunities to use the plasmid model; the role of the larger system becomes that of bacterial colony, and the process becomes that of natural selection—of identifying, sharing, and promoting what works. As in health care the role of the larger system is also to provide a safe and emotionally warm environment that promotes creative play of the elements of the system by the agents—as long as those elements are not CASYs on a different level that would feel manipulated. The most important area for this action in the educational system is at the school level where it is done by the teachers and their principal.

Agents of the system—Teachers

Teachers today are maligned from all sides—unfair in itself, but perhaps one of the reasons we have escaped some of dangers accompanying the system in Germany where the teacher is more of an authority figure. Parents blame teachers when their children have problems, the system blames them when the children don't test well, and, reflected in their pay scale, society doesn't think too highly of them either. Few students today plan to be teachers and the conventional wisdom seems to correspond to the old university joke: 'those that can, do; those that can't, teach; those who can't teach, teach teachers.' Yet fifty years ago teaching was one of the more honorable professions and even today there are few professions with as many idealists and socially responsive individuals—at least at the beginning. How did we get from one to the other?

As education moved into larger systems that required administrators, teachers found themselves more and more in the middle, between parents and administrators, and blamed by both sides when children didn't measure up. Their position was similar to that of the physicians threatened with the loss of their licenses after the Flexner Report. Indeed in 1981, following the ideas of H. Ross Perot, who mistakenly thought that improving the teachers would improve education, the Texas Legislature took away all the teacher's credentials in the state and made them take a literacy test before they could be reinstated. Threatened physicians grouped together to form the AMA, but Texas was and is a "right to work" state where the business counts for more than the individual, and unions were without any power to help the disenfranchised teachers. Those lost were almost exclusively minority, but frequently very good at relating to their students; often education is better done by role models than by what most commonly refer to as teaching, and the Texas system was the loser in this process. Teachers became increasingly defensive. Just as in health care a defensive alignment led to shifting the focus from the real purpose behind the profession, helping the student, to the defensive one of insuring your own survival and place in the system—teachers too began to join in the gaming.

Teachers are as adept at gaming as any other CASY that feels manipulated and threatened. In healthcare problem patients are "turfed" to someone else service; in education problem students are passed on to next year's teacher, turfed to special education or to affirmative action schools that are often military based and at best a broad experiment.

Since test results are what count teachers teach to the test, often relating, when able, the answers to specific questions known to be on the test. Racial profiles can sometimes be used to exclude a student's test scores from those used to judge the school. If the stakes are high enough, as Steven Levitt relates in his book, *Freakonomics*, teachers will sometimes game the results by answering test questions themselves. California stopped its teacher merit pay because it promoted this kind of gaming. Texas teachers were so good at performing the 'good teacher dog and pony show' to impress their outside evaluators that the state had to discontinue its bonus program for those good teachers within ten years.

Just as in health care these programs are based on a mechanical model where the agent is treated as an object, evaluated or measured, and rewarded, or not, based on a test. And, just as with healthcare, this mechanical treatment leads to increases in the gaming rather than improvement in the system.

On the other hand good things happen when teachers are treated and respected as the complex adaptive agents that they are. Jerry once worked at a local elementary school and participated in a make-over that turned the teachers and the school around within three short years. In our community, elementary school principals were usually taken from the ranks of old coaches, which assured a stable situation with few changes. A new state law, however, mandated that new principals have experience teaching at the age level they were going to administer. So the new principal for one of our elementary schools was a teacher who had some different ideas about how to educate children. Her teachers initially saw this as a threat, but with a little time she won most of their trust and cooperation. Others could not adapt and transferred to other schools. The changes that she incorporated made it harder to turf children to out of classroom activities; she wanted the teachers to be responsible for teaching their children. All of the teachers were eventually trained in Special Education *and* in working with the Gifted and Talented, so every student had a teacher better able to address more of their particular needs—turfing was not an option.

The teachers had regular sessions where they shared ideas and brainstormed for new ones. They wrote grants and used the money for teaching supplies, innovative parenting programs and paying the salary for a full time counselor. Recognized and honored as teachers, they became excited about teaching—their alignment shifted to the creative. Within three years the ranking of this school on Texas' Achievement Test went from a bit above average to becoming a mentor school, looked to as an example by other schools throughout the state. And unlike some other mentor schools, like the Wesley School in Houston upon which the No Child Left Behind program is based, the learning advances of these children persisted and were not based on teachers cheating. Three years is not a long time and this experience shows what happens when teachers are recognized as complex adaptive agents and given the opportunity, support, and the challenge to do their job. It also shows the importance of the administrators. The principal soon was enticed away to a better position and other administrative leaders also left. Within two years the school test performance was back to average.

The response of these teachers to the real challenges of teaching shows the difference between gaming and productive play. Gaming is generally playing with elements of the system to increase one's own survival and interest while the goal of productive play is to help the system to work and function better at its task. Gaming is selfish play. In productive play these teachers got grants when they needed money, they played with the curriculum, or what is supposed to be taught. And playing caught on with the students; learning became a fun activity. A proper alignment doesn't stop gaming; it just makes it more creative and changes the beneficiary from the agent to the system. The curriculum, what teachers deal with and society has decreed that they impart to the children, is a proper element to game.

The curriculum

Current schooling differs across the world reflecting the variety and values of our different cultures and it is these elements that make up the curriculum—it is culturally determined. A typical public school has an emphasis on the secular and scientific approach to learning about the world. Religious schools, from the Christian or Hebrew based education of the west and the comparable madrassas of Islam, to the monasteries of the Orient, teach secular material within the framework of their own culture and belief system. A fundamental part of the Palestinian curriculum centers on the evils of Zionism and its expression in Israel, just as much of ours included information on the evils of Communism and their expression in Soviet Russia, and vice versa with theirs showing the evils of Capitalism and their expression in the U.S. The emphasis in these systems, secular and religious, is on their particular world view and they all tend to see their view as superior to others. They also tend to see in analytical terms where the agent, or student, is a cog in the cultural machine, and all seem equally willing to subsume the child for the good of the culture—but the religious ones more so, and the curriculum can be modified to promote this.

A different aspect is represented by the vision of people like Maria Montessori, the founder of Montessori Schools, Rudolph Steiner, whose ideas are the basis of the Waldorf Schools, and the Sudbury Schools that began in the '60s and have since spread around the world. These leaders and their followers felt that children should be the focus; that children are usually excited enough about exploring their world that they don't need a stimulus, and that the best teacher is a facilitator on this path. Their curriculum is based more on the needs of the developing child.

While we have both options in most of the western world, our public educational systems have developed primarily around Harris's social model—to serve society more than the child. Currently in the United States we are following the ideas of H. Ross Perot, which were accepted in Texas and are now being implemented nationally. Perot felt that to help students live in the world they needed to be taught how to fill roles in industry and business. This meant focusing on the basics of math and language with frequent testing to assure both accountability and competence; such testing is now done regularly so that "no child is left behind." It also meant that the curriculum came to be more important than the CASYs in the system—both teachers and students.

In most schools the curriculum is determined on a different level than where it is used. It comes down from above; often from state groups with an agenda of their own. In public schools it has tended to become more dogma than guideline. The same process in healthcare, where commodification shifted the focus from the adaptive patient to practice guidelines and the fixed and mechanical procedure code, is seen in education with the shift from the student to the test result. In child centered schools control is maintained at the level of the teacher, or even the student, and the curriculum remains a guideline that can be played with.

In the mechanical paradigm the elements are regulated or manipulated to procure the desired output, but the elements played with here are the students and the teachers. And again, such treatment is perceived as a threat and promotes a defensive alignment. In education as with all other CASYs we believe it is better to maintain a context conducive to creative alignment and let life unfold as informed agents continue to adapt.

Adaptation is not a part of the mechanical paradigm—it's invisible in that mental framework. So the powerful forces of adaptation are ignored and not seen in our search for solutions. Our prevailing model remains mechanical so problems are addressed by analyzing to find cause, and regulating to control effect. Just as in healthcare and all other social CASYs this mechanical approach ignores the adaptability of the system; and just as in healthcare, it doesn't work.

Curriculum becomes 'content driven education'

When emphasis in education is determined by the analysis of particular social needs the goal of the system shifts to meeting those needs by focusing on the particular subject material. After Sputnik analysts demanded a stronger scientific and engineering curriculum. In such situations the material becomes the focus rather than the child, and it is taught using the accepted teaching methods that are the same as the conditioned learning tools we use to teach rats in a laboratory. Learning in such situations, with both rats and students, is by repetition, monitoring or testing, a treat or a smiley face when done correctly, and no treat, and more of the task, when not done right.

A good example of the results of this kind of learning is that related by Nobel Prize winning physicist Richard Feynman in his story of teaching physics students in Brazil. Feynman spent a year teaching physics to graduate students in Brazil who had been taught in this conditioned, repetitive manner. Feynman, in contrast, played with everything. He began as a child building and fixing radios and ended up freezing "O" rings to show how they contributed to the Challenger disaster. He played bongo drums and wrote a score for a ballet with bongos. He painted, and at one time had his own art show. His editor gave almost as much space to his learning how to play the tin-pan-like frigideira for Brazil's Carnavale as he did to their educational problem.

The graduate students did very well with direct questions on theoretical matters, but were at a complete loss when it came to applying the information they had neatly stored away in their brains to the real world. What Feynman shows us with this is what he lived: only by playing with the elements can we master them; only by playing with them can we make them a part of us; only by playing with them can we get to know what they mean and be comfortable enough with them to use them in a new area—and conditioned learning is not play.

There are awards annually in the U.S. for excellent teachers, and teachers getting these awards have uniformly shown the ability to get their students involved in projects that stimulate learning—they play with the subject. The greatest teachers in our western tradition, Socrates and Jesus, both used situations, stories, and questions to get their followers to think in new ways, encouraging them to play with the concepts they were trying to teach. Thinking in new ways is often not in the interest of the culture and it got both of them killed, but the method they used, of playfully using elements familiar to their followers to bring out different ways of seeing their world is the same method used by our excellent teachers today.

This method is described by the Greek word, *meiutic,* describing what a midwife does—it draws thought out of the student bringing new ideas to the surface. The root of our word for educate is the Latin *educare*, similarly meaning to draw out of someone or something. Child Centered Play therapy and many other forms of psychotherapy that are client centered are similarly meiutic in their ability to draw out of the troubled client different ways of seeing the situation that they are in, and in the process making them more able to deal with it. The best education builds a network of connections between the student and his or her world; and it's best done by play. And it's best facilitated in small classes where the teacher has more interaction with the student, the only change that consistently works to improve outcome.

It works most consistently because more than any other part of the context of education it enables and empowers the emotional part of the learning environment: the safe, secure and nurturing environment that promotes a creative alignment. Peter Senge described the creative environment in the workplace as loving. Arthur Zajonc points to the established connection between learning best from those we love, and Resa Steindel Brown, in her memorable odyssey *A Call to Brilliance,* applies this to our schools:

But without love in our schools, teachers wither, children remain unengaged, and learning is a chore. Teachers wonder why they chose this profession and students look for excitement elsewhere. Without love in our schools to rekindle the inner spirit, everyone in the system is transformed from a blossoming human being into a management problem.

Content driven education and the conditioned learning behind it, helps us pass tests, especially when class time is devoted to teaching to the test. But it doesn't build neural connections and it fails completely to convey any kind of love or to provide any environment conducive to creative alignment. It also suffers, as does all conditioned learning, from what some researchers call fatigue.

Planarian worms, with only a small collection of nerve cells for a brain—that the worm can regrow in six days should the head be accidentally, or experimentally, cut off—can be taught to choose a particular path in a branching tube. Planaria need water to live so drying their environment provided the stimulus to move and flooding it the reward, and they learn it rapidly, usually in about three sessions. But after they learned it they all stopped trying. Experimenters have labeled this fatigue, but it is more than just being tired. They disassociated, they curled up and refused to try—and refusing to try means no water so they would even die. The experimenters were able to resolve this rebellion by either giving the worms more space in the reward area or by making the experimental learning more complicated. Animal researchers working with higher level animals like rats and cats are more familiar with this problem and associate it with an overabundance of negatives in the training process. Is this what is happening to our children as they grow up in our schools and our "NO" and "DON'T DO THAT" environments? Is this contributing to the number of children who are copping out, doing drugs, and opting for gangs rather than education?

Conditioned learning creates artificial connections in the brain that are more easily forgotten when they are not reinforced; and the factory-like environment of conditioned learning is seen as threatening by many. Lasting learning, like Feynman's, is associative and networked, with neurons connected by repeated use during play-like activities.

Expanding the curriculum to fit society's complexity

We argued previously for seeing a role of Public Health in educating our population about health care issues in order to overcome the asymmetric information that is present in our system. Such education informs the 'invisible hand' and allows for the more creative adaptation that brings value to society. People with more information are able to make better choices. This is how education enhances social mobility; it gives us the tools to function better in society so we can adapt easier to new challenges.

Formal schooling with teachers began and continues to be the primary means of dealing with the increasing complexity of society. It enables the students to get out of their inherited "boxes" and improve their place in society by moving to a different social or economic level, or on the other hand, by choosing a life style that brings them more personal satisfaction. It gives them the tools needed to work and live in a different environment than that provided by their informal education. But it can go further than that. Overcoming asymmetric information empowers the invisible hand so that agents can adapt in ways that are more likely to improve any system, at any level.

But addressing the asymmetric information that exists in our complex society today goes beyond helping the student to become familiar with the elements of their environment and giving them the tools needed to play with them. It can actually look at our use of models, the mental structures we make that help us understand our world. More than any other aspect of their teachings their looking at and questioning of models is what got Jesus and Socrates killed—this disturbs our foundations. The absence of this aspect of education also defines the 99% that are Harris' automata who are comfortable living in the boxes they were placed in by their education. But Jesus and Socrates demonstrated information about our models can be taught.

Expanding the curriculum to teach models

As Kuhn observed in our opening reference most education is a concerted attempt to put the world into the conceptual boxes of the current paradigm. This is a substantial limitation on the vast interrelationships found in the real world, but this limitation allows for our differing cultures. Most of us, including our educators, have a hard time seeing the boxes, let alone seeing outside of them—they are the mental atmosphere in which we live and breathe. Instead we see the box as the real thing—we mistake the constructed maps in our brains for the territory itself.

The boxes are not just our conceptual models of the world that we learn in our science classes, but include most of the informal learning we gained from family and culture: how we see others, what we value, whether we see the world as friendly or hostile, how we see our place in the world, and now, whether we see other agents as objects or CASYs—these views form our cultures. They are the conventional wisdom, and as Arne Dietrich points out in his neuroanatomical view of creative thought, being stuck in the conventional wisdom is a major block to creative thinking. These are only conceptual models, and are just as much models as was Ptolemaic astronomy or evolution and quantum mechanics. They have also escaped our educational system and the questioning and evaluating that goes with it. They are formed in our early childhood and most of us go through our lives without examining the constructs we made that determine in large part our decisions and how we see and interact with the world.

This blindness puts us in with Harris' 99% that were considered automata. Most of us act on reflexes and there is no intelligence in a reflex.

This aspect of education was addressed by Paolo Freire in Brazil in the early '60s. In his book, *The Pedagogy of the Oppressed,* Freire shows how oppression is linked to these conceptual boxes and how it is often supported by the conventional wisdom and the political powers that rely on this 'wisdom' to control the society. It is very much like the pre-Copernican world view where people were assigned inherited tasks because that was their destiny. Our social classes today represent this same kind of thinking. Freire, in working with oppressed workers in Brazil, found that the best way to help them overcome their oppression was by group education. He could teach these illiterate adults to read and write in about four weeks, giving them the major tools needed to deal with their environment. But he also taught them about the foundations of their second class citizenship; about the ways that the language they used and the culture they were born into, raised in, and saw as their own, established their inferior social status and oppression—simple things like our not too distant practice of calling a black man "boy."

Ruby Payne opened a similar program in the United States with her explanation of the differing world views associated with the poor, the middle class and the wealthy. The *oppression* of the poor, both Payne and Freire agree, is often aided significantly by the way the poor see their situation; it is their conventional wisdom that they accept as just the way things are that is a major handicap to their progress.

When Freire taught his adults to read and write he gave them the tools of social mobility, but when he taught them about models he inspired and empowered them to function on another level. He broke down the asymmetric information that had been used to keep them in their places and gave them direction. This allowed these Brazilian workers to deal more effectively with their oppression. In the language of CASYs the concepts gained in this education added to their mental context enabling these people to see more clearly how they fit into the CASY of their society; and it enabled them to play more effectively with the elements in their environment. This is what Socrates and Jesus taught too, but unlike them Freire was just jailed and deported. Despite this the Brazilian Workers Party was organized in part because of his work and in 2002 they won Brazil's national elections, putting the populist Lula da Silva in as Brazil's president. Education can work to overcome asymmetric information and bring value to society, as it appears to be doing in Brazil, but it is not something that a privileged power base has much interest in supporting.

The cultural blinders that Freire removed with his teaching are a subtle means of maintaining the asymmetric information that hobbles the invisible hand, empowers the privileged, and prevents many societies from progressing. Removing these blinders is a critically important part of education if we want to bring value to society, particularly for the older students like those Freire taught. Older students are more likely to have progressed beyond the stage of concrete thinking to the stage of formal thinking that enables them to better understand the nature of these conceptual boxes. One of the most common descriptors of Freire's work is translated as consciousness-raising; it is this step that moves one from Harris' 99% that are automata, and shows how short sighted Harris was. Freire showed that people could be taught in this way about their cultural boxes; with this education Harris' 99% automata can become conscious agents.

The student

In our current mechanical view we don't see students as CASYs; we seldom see the child as more than a mechanical receptacle whose inner processes are less important than their outward conformity and test taking proficiency. In this approach we overlook, and likely contribute to, why the student is not learning in the first place.

One of the major unspoken problems in our educational systems is reflected in the flattening of the learning curve when a child enters school. Learning curves plot learning over time. The learning curve of an infant is almost vertical as they learn, all at the same time, how to work their bodies, how to interact with and exert some control over their environment, and the beginnings of language. But at age six or seven this curve rapidly flattens—children essentially stop learning. Were it not for this one fact we would have more scientists and engineers, and our young people would be better able to deal with challenges in a variety of situations.

Many early childhood education programs hint at such benefits. Addressing children with home environments considered at risk, these programs focus mostly on enriching their environment and have resulted in higher IQs, higher levels of education and income, as well as less problems with the law and illegal drugs. This early environment and the flattening of the learning curve are problems we need to examine in order to help our educational systems; and in order to understand them we need to know how infants and preschool children learn.

Adaptation in children

The growth and development of children as they grow from infants to toddlers, and from tots to teens, is just as evolutionary as the adaptive changes we see in nature, but it's also faster because the elements are different. The environmental elements of the adaptive process in children are not the genes that build the proteins that affect our form and function, but the neural constructs we make as we build our brains: we learn which neurons to use to work our bodies; we learn language that enables us to think in particular ways. We learn, in short, our own peculiar culture's model of the world—models that influence our behavior for the rest of our lives. But there is also some structure here—it is not a blank slate. Part of the brain is hard-wired.

The part of our brain lowest down near the top of the spine is called the brain stem. Injuries to this part of the brain mean that we die because this is the part that keeps us breathing and helps regulate our heartbeat. It is also the oldest in evolutionary terms and is called by many the reptilian brain because reptiles have this degree of organization in their central nervous systems. This part of the brain also includes many defensive adaptations that are easy to access, like the flight or fight response, that helps us better deal with danger and live for another day. This primitive part of the brain has been tested by natural selection for over a hundred million years and there are no changes here during child development—it's hard-wired. Every animal having this level of brain has these reflexes.

On top of this primitive brain is the emotional, limbic, or mid-brain that acts very much like the operating system of a computer. It controls the input to the system as it builds its world. This part too has been tested, found effective by natural selection, and is less amenable to change. It has been called the relational or limbic brain since it builds relationships and establishes bonds in those relationships. Many higher animals have emotional bonds with others of their specie, and even, as our dog and cat, Julie and Flo, showed, between species—to say nothing of the bond between us and our pets. These emotional bonds aid survival because the community they foster acts as a defense—it's the beginning of the cohesion rule which comes from this part of the brain.

This bonded community plays a much stronger role in human society because, as well as providing for the defense, it also plays a dominant role in forming the incomplete parts of the infant's brain—it's the source of informal learning. Like the duckling bonding with the first moving thing it sees on hatching, the principles of the emotional brain are hard-wired, but the particulars are added by the cultural environment. Cues from this community tell the emotional part of the infant's brain whether or not an activity or a situation is safe, so its influence on the adaptable infant is profound. In this way the emotional based operating system governs the input to the third level brain, the cortex—the part that allows for the development of the self-consciousness that makes us *Homo sapiens*.

Again, adaptation has two sides: survival and diversity, and the direction a CASY takes is largely determined by their perception of threat. Children are vulnerable in every culture and will adapt to increase the level of safety in the system; they rapidly learn cultural lessons and behaviors allowing them to be part of the group and not a threat. This is what happens on a different level when bacteria and parasites adapt to live with a host without causing them distress. Culture is a defensive adaptation to the environment of the child; so in seeking safety children adapt to and identify with the culture—they are subsumed. Rather than being different and seen as a threat they are one with the family and culture, and these largely defensive constructs, which form the framework of the emotional brain, become the operating system that controls the input to the cortex—they are the paradigms through which we all see and build our worlds. In the language of complex mathematics they are the attractors that show the limits in the field of play for the agents in the system. Going beyond them, like Jesus and Socrates did, gets you killed—they are the limits of the culture.

Formal education can open a person to the presence of these cultural determinants and enable them to see more objectively. Harris thought only 1% able to do this. Freire showed him to be wrong. But the task is not for children; this is an act of transcendence and the agent needs an established sense of self before he can go beyond it to see a larger picture. That doesn't usually happen before the late teens or the onset of formal thinking. At the same time we need to be aware always that this transcendence is a goal that makes the culture less concrete and the process less traumatic.

Children, as the archetype of CASYs, are particularly sensitive to their early environments as they form themselves and, like the citizens of ancient Athens, we go to great lengths to protect them from the meddlesome Socratic midwives like Freire as they grow. Most of how we treat our children reflects the conventional wisdom of the culture in which we are subsumed, and may not be in their, or our own, best interest.

If we agree with H. Ross Perot and our first priority in education is to condition our children so that they can fill positions in the marketplace and work in little boxes, then content education and test scores may be the way to go. If, however, we have a primary interest in the self-actualization of our children, if we want them able to take an active and conscious role in playing out their own lives, if we want them flexible enough to deal with changes in their environment, if we want them to be able to see and solve society's problems with creative novelty rather than violent defenses, then there has to be a better way. It involves changing our paradigm to see our educational system as a CASY made up of complex adaptive teachers and complex adaptive students—and honoring their adaptability. With this view we may be able to deal with our problems in a more effective way and perhaps even maintain a higher learning curve through all of education.

How children learn best

The greatest learning in infancy and early childhood is done informally by observation, experimentation, mimicking, and even mirror learning, where the appropriate neurons are activated just by watching some one else operate. It is not done in a classroom, with a teacher, or in a conditioning, 'lab rat' environment. It's done best in a caring environment that promotes the state of safety that allows for creativity as discussed earlier. This state—zone, flow, or play—is one of optimal performance, optimal adaptability, and optimal learning; and it's impossible to maintain when threatened. The first step in promoting more effective schools is to make sure that they are safe for the children, and that they encourage creative play. This is not "safety" in the usual sense of the word that we think of in the aftermath of 9/11, but of safety from threats that a child perceives, threats to their familial or social environment like unstable, or divorcing parents, or parents with no time to be role models. A safe place for learning is best created by a stable group of caring adults. Threats for the child do not usually come from the physical world which they are exploring, but from the emotional realm which is already wired in their mid-brain. As the child gets older roadblocks to self expression play a larger role.

Threats to this emotional safety for the older child can be anything that threatens their self image. In the world of education that even includes an evaluation, or a test. Benjamin Zander, conductor of the Boston Philharmonic and Professor of Music at the New England Conservatory, began giving his students A's and grading on other than performance when he saw that they were so anxious over their grade that their performances were hurt. The wide-spread use among performing musicians of anxiety modifying drugs argues the same point. Alfie Kohn, similarly, has written extensively about the problems created *in the child* by our judgment and evaluation of their school performance. The Sudbury Schools don't test, but use feedback and coaching to guide students and a consensus between students and their teachers for evaluation. These leaders have come to realize that a fearful and defensive alignment blocks creative expression.

Given a safe environment children play; and their play is recursive—they do the same thing over and over. Repetition increases the efficiency of the neural networks that play with the elements in the child's environment. It leads to the laying down of myelin around the used neurons, a process facilitating that particular set of connections that also saves them from the periodic pruning that cleans away unused synapses.

Some educators see the pruning that normally occurs at around age six as an explanation for the flattening of the learning curve that occurs when a child enters school. But neuro-scientists teach us that myelination substantially speeds up processing time; impulse transmission in myelinated nerves is much faster so learning should be even faster and more efficient if it uses these trusted and well used learning networks. This fact emphasizes the importance of enriching a child's early environment and explains why programs with this focus result in long-term benefits for the individual and society. Children play at different things as they grow up and increasing the variety of elements in their environments also increases the number and variety of myelinated neurons and this translates into the enhanced abilities these individuals carry into adulthood. Increasing the number of elements in their environment also increases the challenge. The planarians, whose learning was discussed earlier, that gave up on the task after they had learned it, never got bored, never disassociated, and never gave up when more elements were added to their experimental environment.

The problem of course is that schools don't use these pathways in teaching children. The creative play of a child before they enter school is about as far different an approach to the regimented conditioned learning that takes place in our schools as one can get. Only when our school administrators, our teachers, and even parents realize this will our schools be able to utilize the optimal pathways that allow our children to maintain their high learning curve.

Infants play with their bodies and their families. Teenagers expand this by playing and gaming their relationships; working people game the rules at work. Einstein's games were filled with the elements of the world and the laws of physics that governed them. How well we play and what we play with is dependent on our genetic endowment and our neural constructs from early childhood.

Unlike Einstein most of us are not consciously aware of our playing processes so we tend to discount their importance. And our authorities, more often upset with our gaming of the systems they have established, foster such concepts as 'an idle mind is the devil's workshop' and limit the definition of learning to what we observe in lab animals. In places like the 'Skunk works' the adaptive nature and success of such play in adults is honored and supported, but most often the value of the creative alignment is overlooked and people are encouraged to just do their job; and in children it is considered a waste of time—they should be doing their homework.

Creative play with the elements of ones environment is the most effective and efficient learning state we have ever found. Ever building on what it has already learned our brains continually adapt to new challenges by playing with the elements available to them and are able to handle more elements faster and better. Creative play accounts for an estimated 95% of our knowledge base. This learning is horizontal, networked, and more often myelinated. The 5% learned in the conditioning processes of the classroom is hierarchical, artificial, and less often myelinated. Only 3% of this memorized material stays with us for any length of time.

These figures come from Dr. Fred Donaldson, who has based his career on how children learn best. "Authentic play," the phrase Donaldson uses, is the primary learning mode of children. Like Richard Feynman teaching in Brazil, Donaldson realized the ineffectiveness of formal education while teaching physics at a major California university. He also knew that infants and children, with their almost vertical learning curve, were the archetypal learners. In every part of the world the early years of childhood are the peak of learning. Donaldson wanted to find out how children learned best and wound up working in a day care where the children taught him to play. He has been playing and learning ever since. Play, he is careful to point out, is not about winning or losing—it's about building connections.

Children absorb their world through all of their senses and integrate it into their developing brain through play—play is the brain's major integrator. We have seen how repetitive behavior leads to the myelination that makes those pathways more efficient. This is true not only for tasks like walking or opening a door, but the behaviors we learn by modeling others, and the model is imperative—children generally only do things they have seen. A distraught family once sought Jerry's help when their two year old son began urinating in the corner of their living room. Resolution was easy when Dad realized that his son was only mimicking his own behavior of occasionally urinating in the corner of the stable—their horse's living room.

Neural connections are built and reinforced by repetitive behavior, but there are also other factors. Children go through developmental stages as they grow where there are optimal windows for learning in particular areas. The developmental stage for the optimal learning of language, for example, is from about the 6th month of gestation to about two years. We have already discussed this window in connection with ear infections. The overlap of the windows for both language learning and ear infections are why they are such a problem and why we need to focus on preventing them.

Other stages are just as important and even less open to later fixing. The window for vision closes in infancy and children born blind with conditions that can be surgically corrected need to be operated on within that window or they remain unable to see even though they have properly functioning eyes. Stages reflect patterns in the way the neurons in the brain are connected. Over relatively short windows many neurons become hard-wired.

Besides the importance of these windows of development, or stages, the emotional *state* of the child also controls their ability to play. As in all CASYs perceived threats lead to defensive responses; in the defenseless child's case they stop playing and look to the mother for safety.

In many cases a problem arises when the source of safety is compromised. We can see, for example, the acting out of children in the classroom whose parents are divorcing, and the futility of trying to control their behavior by telling him to sit down, be quiet, and pay attention. The child is acting out on an emotional state of fear and anxiety while the adult response is more often mechanical—aimed at outward behavior. It's a mechanical response to an emotional problem, and it doesn't work. You may get the desired behavior, but, by not recognizing and honoring his emotional state as a CASY trying to deal with his own inner turmoil, the child is damaged in the process—and their ability to learn in this environment is negligible. Objectifying and regulating a child's behavior is still treating them as an object and is abuse. Effective learning is stopped in the presence of threats that negatively alter the emotional state of the child.

All parties, parents and teachers, seem oblivious to the ability of the child to learn from their environment. A common problem in elementary school shows up with children whose parents are divorcing, as in the example above. But when parents are called in to the school for conference a frequent response is that the children don't know about the divorce. On the contrary children learn from all of their senses and respond to changes in their physical, social, and mental environments; their learning is wholistic.

The efficacy of wholistic learning depends on the emotional state that a child or person is in, and that depends on their perception of threat in their environment. Serious threats call on the fight or flight response that is hard-wired and easily accessible in the most primitive part of our brain, but it's not well developed in vulnerable children who must rely on others. Threats to the ego and our relationships call on limbic defenses like flocking behavior that similarly limit cognitive functioning and play. This level of response is much more common in children entering the school years since they are also transferring patterns learned in the family to their peers. Just as the functioning of the immune system is trumped by the more serious threat of blood loss, cortical functioning is trumped by fear and anxiety. Some elementary school administrators are realizing the importance of school counselors to address and deal with these problems, and addressing them enhances the child's ability to learn.

In a safe, secure, loving environment creative play and exploration are natural. Donaldson points out that this kind of play is also outside of the ego. It's the ego that is most often threatened, it gets stronger and more developed as a child grows, and increasingly it plays a major role in identifying dangers as whatever threatens it stature.

Michael Mendizza talks about when the worlds top golfers were asked about their early experience learning the game. They related that their mentors asked only: "What did you learn?" and "Did you have fun?" This teaching approach produced a safe and non threatening environment where *play* could work to integrate information from all of their senses to make them masters of the game.

They were never asked about their score. Like testing at school the score is a measurement, it's mechanical; it supports the ego if it's good and threatens it if it's bad, but either way it becomes the focus of the game and prevents creative play. A wise golf pro trying to encourage us suggested that we alternate hitting each others' ball as a means of enjoying and learning the game. This does make the game more fun because it obliterates the ability to focus on the score. Yet what we focus on, and use to evaluate today's students, is the score. And just like the golf score the test score is a very real threat to the developing ego, to say nothing of the anxiety put onto the teachers and administrators whose livelihood may be affected.

Achievement tests have been around for a long time, but in the past there was no preparation for them and neither the student, the teacher, nor the system was rewarded or punished based on their results. It is 180 degrees different with today's tests that are the center of focus for the whole years' curriculum as well as the measure of the system and the basis of its reward or punishment. The pressure on the student to perform is tremendous—and it's the score that is important, not the process, and not the child.

Japanese education was subject to these same types of pressures in the 1950s when opportunities in higher education were limited and based on test performance. It led to one of the highest teen-age suicide rates in the world, which declined as they made higher education more available. Such treatment produces anxiety and fear, and it shuts down creative play, the most effective learning tool known.

Yet testing remains the only way in our conventional wisdom to evaluate the process of education. It is the only way we know how to evaluate the marketability of students. But it focuses on the output and mechanizes learning, a process that is resisted by all complex adaptive agents. The response of CASYs to mechanical treatment is defensive alignment. In children this means flattened learning curves and more automata, increased cohesion and more gangs—and more violence. In Japan the culture leans to self violence so suicides were increased. In America the pressure is to act out so school shootings are increased.

As much as we would like to think so optimal learning is not a conditioning process where information is presented to the student verbally, visually, or in a text, incorporated by them, regurgitated on a test, and maintained for life. It's an experiential process that incorporates data from all of the senses and integrates it with all prior learning; and it is constrained by the developmental *stage* and the emotional *state* of the student as well as the paradigm of the familial and social environment.

The importance of stage and state are relatively straight forward in the process of learning, but the importance of one's paradigm is equally important. Conformity to the cultural paradigm assures the developing child the most secure environment where they can play. In a very real way there is evolutionary pressure to adapt to these values. As long as a particular characteristic provides a survival benefit there will be evolutionary pressures for its expression.

We are sometimes puzzled by the appearance of animal behaviors that are seemingly altruistic and do not appear to be in the animals self interest. This confusion arises because we have tended to overly focus on the defensive alignment of adapting for individual survival, but there is just as much creative evolutionary pressure for the development of diversity where these 'altruistic' behaviors have a clear survival benefit. The same pressures are also present in class values, which accentuate the need for education about these unconscious constructs along the lines developed by Freire.

Educating about paradigms

Ruby Payne hinted at how people in different classes explain their position in life—it has to do with the model or paradigm present in these classes and it is learned informally from family and environment. Those in the upper classes tend to see their position as a right, those in the middle tend to see it as a result of their own work, and those in the lower classes tend to see it as a matter of luck. Many of our fundamental stories carry these differing messages. The stories justifying the divine right of kings carries over into the rights of the upper class and is aided by the Judeo Christian tradition where nobility is commonly portrayed as a genetic trait. There are also stories about the rain falling on both the just and the unjust so whether it falls on you or not is just a matter of luck. In different traditions stories like *The Mahabharata* and the *Book of Job* tell of the gods playing dice and how ones circumstances can depend on the Gods playing with us. These are the kind of foundational stories that affect our thought processes without us knowing it; and Payne and Freire dealt with them by bringing them into a person's awareness and so changing the way people see themselves.

Each of these class associated views comes with values regarding education. In the upper class, where one has a right to position, property and prestige, you can be a slouch in your private prep school and university and still be assured of a position that allows you to continue your life style, or even be elected president of the United States. In the lower classes education cannot compensate for luck and the best way to get ahead is to play the lottery. Only in the middle class is work and education valued for how it can help one progress. In the upper classes it's unnecessary and in the lower classes it's meaningless.

These class values exert pressure on their members to adapt to them because adherence to the particular paradigm establishes the greatest level of emotional safety for those in the group. While such adaptations are not likely in the DNA they are definitely in the neural connections.

Consider, for example, the decreases in literacy in our Hispanic population. From 1992 to 2003 prose and document literacy dropped by 7.4 and 6% in our Hispanic population. The reason for this is credited to immigration, but there may be other factors as well. The Hispanic community in this country remains predominantly in the lower economic class where luck matters more than education. When this value is perceived as the way things are it becomes part of the context to which CASY agents adapt and the result is a decline in the value and need for education in the population. Is it this value we see manifest in these literacy trends?

With the polarization we are experiencing where the rich are getting richer and the poor poorer, and both extremes increasing at the expense of the middle class, educational values, a work ethic, and democracy in general are the losers. Freire showed that this trend can be reversed with education about ones paradigm.

Paradigms also limit learning because information outside of, or contrary to, our cultural paradigms often remains invisible to us. Compared to other developed countries we have a very violent society and our prison population is the highest in the developed world, but we have accepted it as normal. The World Bank has published evaluations of many of the world's governments in *Governance Matters*, which compares the nations in several areas relative to governing. In most areas the United States is in the higher percentiles, but in the area of 'political stability,' that looks at violence, we are in the 60% percentile. We have lived with this problem long enough that it is invisible; so we miss out on the valuable perspective of others, we deal with the problem using regulatory fixes that perpetuate inbred ideas, and reduce the cross-pollination that comes from the mix of ideas on the margins. We tend to rely on experts who, just as in health care, are in the center of the field where there is little cross-pollination and most of the ideas are inbred and incestuous. In this and all other areas we need to guard against the limitations that Kuhn points out in the opening paragraph—of focusing our education and research on nothing more than confirming the inbred status quo of the current paradigm.

A few needed changes

In our current social paradigm powerful wealthy people are honored for the things that they have done and can do, and children are mostly invisible. The pay scale of those working with children reflects these values, as does our absence of a standard maternity leave.

Pediatricians consider six months enough time to get the infant past the stage where their poorly developed immune systems are more vulnerable to infection, but new mothers in the U. S. are lucky if they can get a leave of absence, usually with no compensation, for six weeks. And child psychologists are now telling us that the second half of the first year is just as critical as the first half. If the first six months are needed for the development of internal defenses and immunity the second six months are when infants develop their model for exploring their external world and their attachment patterns are formed. This is when they lay the foundation of their interaction with others, and the stable and safe mother bond is critical in this process. A normal 6 month old child in beginning to explore his world will always look to mother for facial cues of safety or danger when confronted with something new. When she is not there this exploration is delayed.

Our primary goal in addressing the context of early childhood and early childhood education should be to foster the playful state by creating safe places. This is the primary role of the family and without it children are handicapped. Parental education on these elements of child development is generally scant, and the social support needed to help mothers foster this process is absent. The best person to evaluate and promote the development of an infant and pre-school child is an *informed* mother.

Similarly the way to evaluate a student's abilities and how well they have mastered the tools needed to deal with the outside world is not by testing, but by the observations of a well trained teacher. This is also the person in the best position to resolve any shortcomings. As mentioned previously, children with problems are easily turfed into special education or automatically moved to the next grade level and to a new teacher every year. Being identified and treated as a "problem" is not likely the best solution for a student with learning problems. There may be many successful solutions to this problem, from team teaching, to open classrooms, to the one room schoolhouse, but it is not likely found in objectifying the child which is what we do when we define them as a problem and put them into behavior modification programs.

Such treatment focuses on the problem rather than the child. It's like our clinics where a laceration is in one room and abdominal pain in another—problems are abstracted out of the individual and are objectified. In both education and healthcare the student and patient are abused when they are treated as objects whose learning assets or liabilities, or physical or mental disabilities, are gamed for the financial benefit of the local system. Again such treatment elicits a defensive posture in the child that is incompatible with authentic play. The flattening of the learning curve as children enter school naturally follows from such treatment; all CASYs respond to perceived threat by increasing the primitive defensive adaptations of both flocking and flight or fight where violence is a ready option.

The roots of violence

Formal schooling and outward orientation to authority mean that children in the system lack a strong inner direction and are more willing to make those who don't share their particular "authorities" into *others*—less than us—the beginning step of Zimbardo's evil. So we have 'the white man's burden,' that justifies destroying other cultures and educating them in ours; or we see others as different enough that they can more easily be sacrificed for the good of one's own society. We went through this with the Indian "savages," Germany did it with the Jewish "vermin," Stalin did it with the independent peasants that Communism turned into the greedy and rapacious "kulaks," Islamic extremists do it with the American "Great Satan," and the Hutu with the Tutsi "cockroaches." Today we sanitize the estimated 655,000 Iraqi dead by turning most of them into 'collateral damage,' but each one creates a hostile environment conducive to breeding a new terrorist. Few on either side doubt the others willingness to use nuclear force. This ability to turn others into objects is often an extension of one's belief system.

Gregory Paul shows a direct correlation between religiosity (measured by belief in biblical literalism, frequency of prayer, and church attendance) and decreased societal health (measured by rates of homicide, life expectancy, childhood mortality, teen abortions and pregnancies, and sexually transmitted diseases). While not denying a correlation his critics question a cause-effect relationship since other factors may be at play as well. While the issue is complex the dynamic of allegiance to an authority, whether it be political or religious, tends to decrease the value of those outside the family of believers—and makes violence to them less of a problem. Old Testament history provides example enough of this dynamic and of its religious justification. Fundamental religions foster the me/us versus the other, but the view is selfish and ignores the teachings on who is a neighbor, and the even broader view of living as part of the world's family.

There is of course a sizeable body of evidence on the other side of this argument; religious training does teach the value of the other and compassion for the less fortunate: The bishops of Denmark refused to help isolate and mark the country's Jews; the French village of Le Chambon lined up in solidarity behind their pacifist and anti-Nazi minister in refusing both Nazi rituals and celebrations as well as hiding the Jews; Dietrich Bonhöffer criticized the 'cheap grace' that allowed people to compartmentalize out the evils present in their systems. Those acting out against depersonalizing another have a strong inner direction and more self-respect—they are among Harris' 1%—and are less likely to accept the authority or the conventional wisdom that is arguing for the abuse. We believe this is an alignment problem, that it is influenced by ones religion, but that it goes beyond it. Religions and cultures with a rigid code of behavior tend to instill a defensive alignment in its members and agents with a defensive alignment are more likely to accept and act on the principles of Social Darwinism and its accompanying lack of compassion for those less fit. James Prescott showed how this works.

Prescott was the director of the Child Development section of the National Institutes of Health from 1966 to 1980. During that time he carried out a study on the origins of violence in which he looked at violence and child rearing practices in various cultures. He found that there was a strong correlation between violence within the culture and restrictions placed on childhood behavior, the same conclusions reached by Alice Miller in her looking at Germany.

In the cultures he looked at where the children were allowed more freedom in their experimentation with their world there was less violence. In those where childhood activity was restricted or structured there was more violence. But it went deeper than that. The differences he saw in the respective treatment of the children reflected a fundamental difference in how these societies saw children. In the peaceful permissive cultures children were seen as a part of the community and were given enough space to develop on their own. In the more violent cultures they are more often seen as assets or extensions of the family. In one they tend more to be treated as agents; in the other the tendency is to treat them as objects. Bonhöffer argued that an authoritarian school system made the Holocaust possible. Prescott and Miller show that treating the child as an object may have been the particular aspect of the German culture and school system that enabled this violence. As we saw with bacteria increased levels of violence follow when we abuse CASY agents by treating them as objects; and the same dynamic carries over into our treatment of children.

Unfortunately one of the primary behaviors Prescott used in rating the degree of freedom was sexual play. His conclusions presaged much of what primatologists looking at chimpanzee and bonobo behavior found twenty years later: restrictive sex is associated with more violence. They were also confirmed by Dr. Miller who tells of Dr Schreber, the 19th Century German equivalent of Dr. Spock in our time, who paid particular attention to preventing masturbation, even to the point of developing a device that supposedly prevented such activity. It is also one of the more common findings in jihadist suicide bombers. These men are generally raised in fundamentalist Islamic families, where young men are kept separate from the females, and in poorer Arab countries, where they have little chance of earning the money needed to pay for a wife.

Intimacy is one of the pathways humans travel in gaining adulthood. Arbitrarily closing the door on this path by condemning sexual play and open association with the opposite gender may have unintended consequences elsewhere.

Prescott's conclusions did not sit well with our puritanical leaning leaders, so the messenger got fired and the study was buried—an example of how hard it is to get anomalous information into a system and of how difficult it is to see beyond the red flags that one's culture raises in the face of threats to its conventional wisdom. Sure, we are interested in the causes of violent behavior—unless they are shown to be elements of our own culture.

This is not saying that children in these peaceful cultures had no restrictions. Unsafe activities were out of bounds—only when they are can children play creatively. Children in the peaceful cultures were mostly kept within the community of the women, where they were safe, and they were counseled on the risks that accompany behaviors, but the risky behaviors were not forbidden—and sexuality then did not have the risks it does today. They also honored the results of their children's experimentation as the resulting infants were accepted into the community without stigma. And sometimes there were even fewer children.

Margaret Mead tells of the 'children's house' where the children in the Trobriand Islands, one of Prescott's peaceful cultures, would go to play with their sexuality; but where, despite the high levels of sexual activity, pregnancy was unheard of. It wasn't until the children paired off in a union that was ritualized and blessed that pregnancy occurred. Several years ago I met a young woman from this culture who had had repeated early miscarriages. She had married an American military man against her father's wishes and outside of the culture. Her father's words to her when she did this were, "your marriage will be barren." It was only after she resolved the issue with her father, and had him bless her marriage, that she was able to carry her fetus to term. Voodoo works in the same way.

When contrasting such societies with ours it is also apparent that the more simple and peaceful ones have not developed the idea of property, especially when the property is another person. In primate societies the peaceful and free-loving bonobo are far less territorial than the more aggressive chimpanzee where the alpha male dominates over a fixed territory with the periphery regularly and viciously patrolled by the younger males. While men and women have different roles in Prescott's peaceful cultures there is no ownership of either wife or children—something we in the west have gone through and not entirely escaped. Chattel laws, where women and children were legally the property of the husband, were not repealed until the latter part of the 19th century and remain there spiritually for many of our patriarchal leaning religions. Women in many states could neither borrow money nor vote until the middle of the last century; and the glass ceiling remains in place in most large corporations. In western cultures a child's behavior reflects on the parents so there is more pressure to conform to social and cultural norms.

If we want to address the root causes of violence and do something about its prevention then we must be able to look at these factors without our current cultural blinders. We need also to recognize that these blinders define the paradigm operative in our educational systems which we work hard to perpetuate.

Current education's box

Over the last Century our schools have adapted to the mechanical model; they have been changed into laboratories where students are taught using conditioning methods proven to work on lab animals and constantly pressured into a defensive alignment by the ever present test. This shift to a defensive mode has been accompanied by a shift in student goals. Fifty years ago top students were choosing professional careers, or work in areas that enabled a high degree of self fulfillment. Today their defensive alignment pressures them into finance because that is where they can make lots of money quickly and be assured of some security. The abuse of treating children mechanically has pushed their responses toward the chaotic end of the systems spectrum evidenced by flattened learning curves when children enter school, decreasing performance, dropouts, and school shootings. This isn't evolution it's devolution. Rather than seeing the root of the problem in the abuse of CASYs, solutions have heaped on more abuse by trying to make the system more mechanical.

As it does in healthcare, the solution lies in the other direction. Health is enhanced when people learn to be hardier—where they have a sense of control, coherence, and challenge. And the neighborhoods and communities that work to incorporate these qualities through what is called 'collective efficacy', are cleaner, more peaceful, and more progressive; their populations are healthier and their children get more education. Stimulating such an environment in our schools allows for the authentic play that Donaldson points to as the most effective learning state we know. Even our well meaning efforts to give our children opportunities to expand their world may not be best for our children if it detracts from their ability to play with and integrate the world they know. The American Academy of Pediatricians supports Donaldson in pointing out the importance for the child of *self directed* play.

How to get effective learning

As in healthcare there is a chasm between what we pay for and what we are getting in our educational systems. As in healthcare there is a long unknown path that will get us where we want to be. And just as in healthcare seeing the system and its agents as CASYs and promoting the plasmid model will likely get us better results faster than any other tools we have. Progress with CASYs is not through regulating them or their elements but in changing their contexts.

The mentor schools in Texas, like the one Jerry worked in, apply this model as best they can within the current context of our Public School Systems. Private schools have an edge if they are oriented on the Montessori or Sudbury patterns where the alignment is already in place. Providing a safe and secure environment where children can engage and play with the elements they are learning about is the best way to help them learn. We cannot forget that our children are the CASY archetype and that treating them mechanically does them and society a great disservice. As benign and as necessary as they may appear activities such as testing for outcome, rewarding good behavior, and punishing bad behavior treat the child in a mechanical way and are not in the child's nor our collective future's best interest. Neither reward nor punishment for any agent at any level should ever be based on a test. Happy, active, playing, involved students are learning and they are not difficult to spot. Such a model best removes the perception of outside threat and interference that blocks free expression and play within a system. Such a model is the best way to maximize the learning curve.

Both education and health are social goods and should be funded by the society. High Schools were established and state funded when the complexities of industrialization demanded more training. Even more training and education are needed now to deal effectively with all of the social CASYs in our environment. This higher level of education likewise should be publicly funded; and it should include looking at our paradigms.

When illness is acute and people need help dealing with it private care is needed. When there are acute problems the flexibility and innovative aspects of a well functioning and properly aligned marketplace is the best place to find solutions. The same principle holds for education. When children have learning problems private help should be available to parents to help them cope. Mental health services should be available through both the public and private health sectors, and should be used liberally when children are threatened.

Another large problem is the lack of respect for teachers. Those who choose education for a career are looked down upon by others choosing more financially rewarding occupations. It is likely that education will never be as financially rewarding as being a lawyer, or doctor, or engineer, or even an investment counselor. But the sheer joy of seeing the flash of understanding in a student, of personally gaining the insight on how to reach a problem student, or of watching and helping children grow into responsible adults, is unmatched in any other profession. Returning our schools to smaller groups of mixed age students would allow the older ones to mentor or tutor some of the younger ones and share some of these experiences. An Education Corp similar to the Peace Corp could provide invaluable opportunities for both the educators and students. Combining such mentoring with adequate pay would likely make the teacher problem evaporate.

The physicist Heinz Pagels is "convinced that the nations and people who master the new science of complexity will become the superpowers of the next century." A key to accomplishing this is recognizing the child as the archetype of CASY, learning more about how they adapt and develop, and applying that understanding to other CASYs. Whether it be athletic prowess, scientific discovery, the much overlooked childhood task of building one's own world by making the right neural connections—or its counterpart of building a peaceful world—or even mastering the issue of complexity itself, increasing the well trained mother's time with her infant and fostering authentic play is the place to start. As Einstein said, "If you want your children to be intelligent read them fairy tales. If you want them to be geniuses, read them more fairy tales."

CHAPTER 9
A "Boids" Eye View of Society

Non-equilibrium systems, like society, are not comprised of single formulae, they are fractal and have diverse structure on many scales. They are composed of many autonomous elements, each operating with many different values. In the dynamics of these situations we get strange attractors, **not** *point or cyclic ones—a society existing in such a* limited *attractor would be a '***dead***' or '***dying***' society! In real societies we cannot predict 'exactly', solutions are nonlinear, there is a sensitivity to initial conditions, i.e., to history. There exists heterogeneity, multiple interacting dynamics, these systems are often non-deterministic—dependent upon 'random' events (like the recent tsunami). For such systems a new type of science is required, needing a new set of valuation techniques, a metascience of interconnected reality and values...*

Chris Lucas

Conventional wisdom: "the ideas which are esteemed at any time for their acceptability."

John Kenneth Galbraith. *The Affluent Society.*

It's hard to get a boids eye view of society because there are so many areas with differing variables to look at. Our healthcare and education systems are complex, but have a unifying focus; society encompasses them along with all the rest. Chris Lucas sees a society as a *strange attractor,* where there are so many variables that any predictability is lost, and hopes that someone will come up with a scientific way to handle all of the variables.

Analyses of society that dissect out just one or a few of its many elements run into the same problem as the pharmaceutical companies as they try to dissect out elements of our complex and networked physiology; they promote mechanical responses based on an incomplete assessment of a complex system. And the result is just as often the unintended consequences that we see so often in new pharmaceuticals. This is the problem with ideas like that of Natan Sharansky, the Russian dissident turned Israeli policy maker, whose book, *The Case for Democracy*, was a favorite of President George W. Bush as he tried to understand the middle east and its problems. Sharansky contrasts Communist Russia and democratic Israel and sees the differences as mainly due to democracy, basically to the idea that a free society is more progressive than a fearful one. While the idea is right the viewpoint is over simplified. He neglects the unifying aspect of religion, the cohesion promoted by external threat, the developmental stage of the differing peoples, together with a host of other variables. Without these missing elements the solution seemed simple: replace a tyrant with a democratic government. So the idea led us into a war with long-term, and largely unintended, consequences which we cannot begin to fathom. Seeing our societies and cultures as CASYs reduces the risks of multiplying the unintended consequences that commonly follow our mechanical analytically based actions.

Democracy, as pointed out earlier, is associated with a middle class paradigm. It is a *development* in a culture that has such a group; it grows from the stage of *autonomy*, where people have a sense of control over themselves and their environment, and it cannot be imposed on a group in the *power* stage where one has been controlled by an autocratic leader with no place for autonomy. It is not a part of the context, at least in the beginning.

Lucas's quote above gives us a taste a society's complexity, but as complex as all societies are they still have a context; and it is to its context that a CASY adapts. As our societies differ so do their contexts, but there is some common ground. A context has aspects that are physical, social, and mental, and agents adapt in each area. We will in the following look at how we have adapted in all three areas, at the contexts to which we have adapted—especially the areas more amenable to change—and suggest ways to use the tools of adaptation to guide our societies in a healthier direction.

Context of society

Physical elements, like geography, climate, and natural resources, are hard to change so humans have had to adapt to them. These adaptations are in our genes and are hard to change so this part has taken a long time. Then there is a social environment made up of the other people, along with strangers and foreigners, the government that regulates their interactions, the roles of men and women, and the culture that has resulted. Adaptations here are in our memes, the neural connections we make as we adapt to our cultures as children—they are difficult to modify. Finally there is the way the society sees, its paradigm. It is their peculiar way of describing and thinking about the world; it comes from their history and religion, and the storytellers that spread the particular way of seeing. The context here even includes more subtle elements like the language we use to communicate. Stories frame our paradigms—the way we see the world—and they are the variable in the context of culture with the most room for play. Economic and political systems are well down the trail.

We discussed earlier the value of using biological metaphors when describing complex adaptive systems and the closest parallel to a complex society is an ecosystem. Looking with one eye on history and the other on biology we can see that societies are relatively short lived when compared to ecosystems. At least this was true until mankind began interfering with ecosystems on an industrial scale. While there are some obvious differences we may be able to learn from ecosystems things that may be able to help us make our societies last longer.

Historians and social anthropologists agree that societies crash when they ignore the imbalances they create as they adapt. These adaptations are to the fixed geography (slow), the interpersonal social (faster), and the mental paradigm (fastest). The dangerous adaptations are those that lead to the structural imbalances in the overall system and most often they are defensively aligned.

Physical context—Geography

Geography is not subtle. It includes the physical world with its resources and limitations—it's made up of concrete, relatively fixed elements in the environment that frame many of our physical adaptations. An Inuit would have a hard time surviving in the Serengeti because of his physical adaptations to the climate and food of the Arctic. More difficult would be the survival of his culture where its art, ceremonies, sports, and rules have adapted to the Arctic environment; geography applies pressure to more than just physical adaptations.

Karl Wittfogel pointed out the connection between geography associated with regular floods or irrigation and authoritarian governments. Determining property lines after the floods or building irrigation systems and sharing scarce water rights for agriculture requires a higher authority, and societies from Egypt, to China, to the Utah Mormons, are ready examples.

A corollary to Wittfogel's argument is the risk of necessitating that kind of control by our continued pillaging of our own natural resources. This pillaging was allowed by the philosophy of the Renaissance that objectified nature—that allowed us, in the words of Sir Francis Bacon, to put nature on the rack and torture her secrets from her. It also results from the shadow side of capitalism with its defensive alignment that promotes the moral hazard of profiting from someone else's loss. This led to what Garrett Hardin called the *Tragedy of the Commons:* people acting with only self interest in mind tend to overuse and destroy resources held in common. Our commons today, the air that we breathe, the water that we drink, the oceans that we fish, even the land that we farm—the renewables that we over consume and tend to abuse—and all of the other non-renewable materials that we mine or pump from the earth, are a part of the geographical context of our systems. Our abuse of them puts us at risk because they are the hardest part of our context to change. Learning to live in the world without fouling our nest and destroying the resources that make our lives possible is one of our greatest challenges. Doing this cooperatively without introducing the despotism Wittfogel saw as necessary can be done; in many places such as community and regional cooperative water management boards it is being done. Seeing these elements as a critical part of the context of a CASY will facilitate this as we continue to move from the stage of *autonomy* into the stage associated with conservation.

Physical context—Energy

Healthy and balanced ecosystems are remarkably stable on a millennial time scale while our own social CASYs crash regularly. Social anthropologists, like Joseph Tainter and Jared Diamond, look at why civilizations fail, but seldom use the complex ecological parallels and limit the elements they deal with to make them more manageable. Tainter focuses on energy and shows how societies grow until the lack of energy available to them causes them to crash. With our market economies we support this argument because the focus is always on the most economical resource until it runs out. Both their analyses mostly continue the mechanical approach that looks at how the respective societies are balanced.

Diamond does look at the variety of elements that he sees as the contexts of the societies. As such his approach is more ecological and includes the geographical elements of resources and climate, the relational context of hostile neighbors and trade partners, and the ideational aspects of how the society in question deals with the challenges created by these interactions. He even credits the ideational response of the society as a primary factor in whether or not it survives, but he doesn't seem to see this process as adaptation and he is unable to describe it well because most of the stories are not there; most of his collapsed societies left little in the form of written records. In those societies that survived a crisis and continued the stories were critical to the success because they framed and supported a creative adaptation.

Both Tainter and Diamond show that collapsed societies tended to increase in size to the point where the costs of supporting them were no longer sustainable. Diamond's geological resources were a fundamental limit that included the use of energy. Energy comes from the geology, either in the form of trees to burn or the more concentrated carbon sources of gas, oil, or coal that have allowed us a longer period of growth than other cultures with less efficient or concentrated energy sources.

The use of energy is a characteristic of life and all CASYs. Nature has reached a balance relying only on solar energy; we should strive for the same.

Other factors enter as well; our crops pull nutrients from the soil to grow and repeatedly planting the same crops depletes them from the soil—some societies crash with soil depletion. In others, such as Easter Island centuries ago and Haiti in our day, deforestation led to agricultural and social collapse. Ours appears more sustainable because it is built on fossil fuels that have lasted longer, but in all the societies that Tainter looked at the hierarchy eventually outweighed the available energy and the system crashed. As the Chilean planner Gilberto Gallopín points out, "There is no question that the contradiction between the modern world's imperative toward growth and the Earth's finite resources will ultimately be resolved in some way. The only question is how that will unfold."

If we can learn from these cycles, let alone from nature, we should realize that a complex hierarchy that is built on a diminishing base is unsound both ecologically and socially. We need to find a sustainable balance, as is done with all long-lasting ecosystems, and not rely on continued use of fossil fuels that are rapidly becoming economically unavailable. Finding and using an economically sustainable energy source—solar, wind, hydrogen, or a combination, or even utilizing and colonizing bacteria that can produce fuels, or even those that create an electric potential as they recycle our waste—is learning from ecosystems that are stable over much longer time periods. Threatened bacteria, as pointed out earlier, do not all begin mutating to find a way of coping with the threat. Random mutation in bacteria is far more likely to be disruptive to the organism than creative so for all to participate would be suicidal. In comparison our actions as we uniformly use up our most available and economical resources, or live off profits from our appreciating home values, or any other bubble in our speculative driven economy, can be seen as a form of societal suicide. A healthy system is diverse, a goal we should be reaching for in all areas of our social systems—even energy.

Social context

The social context has to do with how the agents in the system relate to and interact with each other and their neighbors. There are too many elements in this area to deal with, or to even be aware of, but on a broad level we include gender differences and roles, how the society deals with inequalities both real and created, how and in what direction it grows, the role of government, and the problem of outside threats. We look at the easy one first.

Social context—Outside threats

Not only do societies collapse from abuse of their physical resources, like Easter Island and Haiti when they ran out of trees, but they can be challenged in other ways. People get infected, ecosystems get weeds, and societies can be invaded. But in all these systems the degree of the threat is proportional, not only to the strength of the invader, but to the health of the host. Our properly working defenses, as we have seen, give us major advantages as we cope with infecting organisms. A primary defense is limiting the playing field and doing this as a society turns invaders into immigrants and reduces the problem. Strong and well balanced ecosystems are more likely to incorporate new species and use them to increase diversity rather than succumbing to them as weeds. Teachers in California, for example, credit the cross-pollination of educationally aligned and motivated Oriental immigrants with saving their test scores from significant drops. Healthy and diverse societies are better able to handle immigrants and the opportunities for cross-pollination that they provide are an asset to the host.

In unhealthy systems invaders are more likely to grow unchecked to the point of being defined as weeds in ecosystems, and infections, abscesses or tumors in human hosts. Or they just take over as did the European immigrants to the Americas in the 17th and 18th centuries after the Native Americans had been decimated by small pox. To an unhealthy host invaders are a significant danger.

On a cultural level this is the problem that many developed countries are now discussing in regard to their immigration policies—how to preserve your own culture/society/ecosystem while introducing new members. Seeing this from the CASY point of view, with its understanding of flocking behavior and the importance of alignment, allows for action based on an understanding of CASY fundamentals rather than fear and the emotional reactions more often associated with the perceived threat from the stranger. And seeing our system's complexities allows for decisions that will make them stronger and in a position to benefit more from cross-pollination. The CASY perspective of maintaining the health and creative alignment of the adopting culture while incorporating cross-pollination from immigrants, adds insight to a very complex problem.

This ecological analogy also clearly shows the importance of a proper alignment in the maintenance of a healthy society. Defensively aligned societies are threatened by foreigners. Vibrant healthy networked societies welcome new ideas and are much more able to accommodate immigrants without them being a threat to their system.

Defensively aligned societies tend to promote the mechanical paradigm where their stories look for cause and effect, for the how and why behind events. They are linear and connect the dots. They analyze situations to find the faulty part or the responsible party—they find something to fix or someone to blame. This view, exemplified by Social Darwinism, applies pressures for defensive, competitive adaptation that increases violence. Social Darwinism led to the eugenics movement that was a central part of Nazi Germany, the justification for their and subsequent genocides, and even for the pressure on birth control in developing nations that we in the U.S. promoted during the cold war. As we eventually found out with the global backlash to our birth control—seen as eugenics—programs such analysis ignores the networks that make up a complex system.

Social context—Gender influences

In the complex mix of elements that make up societies one that we may be ready to play with is the balance of male and female. Almost all of the ancient cultures that left a written record were patriarchal and aligned on the vision of their founding fathers that were defensive, competitive, more violent, and usually included building memorials to oneself as the leader. The poet Shelley shows the futility of this in his poem *Ozymandius*, the Greek name for the ancient Egyptian pharaoh Ramses II. The poem tells of finding a giant statue of Ozymandius, buried in the sand, and shows how transient and ephemeral is our life on earth and how fruitless is the, usually masculine, desire to build monuments to ourselves—but we still do it.

Male interests are usually outward from the family; the dominant male is the protector of the family, tribe, clan ... nation. His alignment is defensive toward the accumulation of power and importance, toward building such monuments that will demonstrate those attributes, frighten away competitors, and outlive the builder. There is genetic pressure in this direction because powerful males are more attractive to many females, who see them as better protectors. The monuments can be made of stone or money, they can be corporate or political; they demonstrate what Marcus Borg calls the three 'A's of success in western society: attractiveness, achievement, and affluence. But they are mostly a male effort. Even with an Equal Rights amendment guaranteeing women equal treatment in the workplace, the workplace has maintained its male orientation. There is little in our world that honors women's work with children that, both traditionally and biologically, has been their major concern. So the alpha male dominated hierarchy, defensively aligned on accumulating, expanding, and defending their own particular niche, has adopted similarly aligned women and continues growing without much to counter it.

Carol Gilligan has studied the differences between how men and women frame their worlds. Male hierarchies in both the animal and human worlds tend to be oriented vertically; they stress the individual and competition. Female structures are more lateral networks that favor cooperation. In our workplace we expect women to behave like men and reward them for doing so, but we need to empower the yin, not try to make it more yang. While there are social systems in nature and alpha males who get first serving at dinner, everyone in the group gets fed when the system and nature are in balance; and when chimp alphas get to feeling extra special they are usually put in their place by a cohort of the females. Similarly the "grandmothers" of the Iroquois League had impeachment power over the chiefs—something our founding fathers failed to include among the many federalist ideas they adopted from the League in crafting our Constitution. This likely seemed a small and negligible item to them, if their patriarchal blinders allowed them to see it at all. We know from his correspondence with his wife Abigail that John Adams knew women were being left out of constitutionally established power, but she could not persuade him otherwise.

From the CASY point of view a feminine power of impeachment for the incestuous abuse of masculine power that we see in most governments would have an enormous effect; and this solution comes, as do all remedies for inbred weaknesses, from our own healthy root stock. The interest of most alpha male chiefs, on obtaining and maintaining power, or on building a memorial to themselves, was significantly balanced by the watchfulness of the Iroquois grandmothers, whose interests were generally on sustainability—on what would be best for the children seven generations down the road. Grandmother's values would obviously benefit us today and switching from expensive special investigating commissions to a cohort of grandmothers would not be a bad start. Cross breeding in this manner with our own ideologically healthy root stock is the best way to deal with all inbred weaknesses.

Social context—Special elements

Cross breeding may also help resolve another problem. The observation that institutions are eventually destroyed by an excess of their first principles has been credited to Acton. It's an idea that is clarified when we see the system as a CASY and their first principles as special elements in their beginnings. Again CASYs are very sensitive to their initial conditions so these founding principles need to be refined and as efficient and strong as possible. We have also seen that the way to make these characteristics stronger is by inbreeding. So as the society grows these traits are inbred and integrated into all the elements of the system. But the inbreeding eventually introduces the weaknesses that bring the system down.

Growth in the direction of ones orientation is initially viewed as desirable and is therefore largely unrestrained. Originating in the vision of their founders such growth has few outside controls because it expresses their vision for the future. But such a vision often lacks the ecological balance of nature because it most often represents the paradigm of their respective founding *fathers* and is not balanced by *female* interests—the *yang* dominates. Male interests are more in resonance with a defensive alignment, with the building of monuments, with the concentration of power and prestige. But as this view is further refined over time the hierarchy of the structure gets larger, and the inbred weaknesses more of a problem—they combine to make it unstable and the system crashes.

A first principle of the ancient Romans was the maintenance of the Empire for the benefit of Rome, so the inbreeding strengthened and empowered the military, but led to inbred weaknesses as the military took over, was farmed out to non-Romans, and what Romans there were had lost much of their allegiance to their corrupt and autocratic government.

The Soviet Union was founded on the idea of countering the shadow side of capitalism with a planned economy; and the inbred weaknesses of their planned economy played a dominant role in its collapse. While military expenses in response to Reagan's military initiatives and our back door support of the Afghan *mujahedin* may have played some role, most of the credit for the fall of the Soviet system properly goes to many other factors. Both Jonathan Schell and Richard Rhodes argue that we did not win the cold war by means of our military build-up. Indeed Reagan did an abrupt about face on his aggressive tactics in 1986 when it became clear that our military involvement in European maneuvers coupled with increasing our nuclear preparedness were being read by the Russians as steps leading toward a preemptive strike, to which they responded by likewise alerting and preparing for a military response. Chernobyl, the loss of oil revenue—the price of which Saudi Arabia had dropped to $5.00 a barrel—and the inefficiency of their oversized planning hierarchy were all factors in the Soviet Union withdrawing from the "Cold War" and its subsequent crash as a system.

The growth of foundational institutions and the inbred weaknesses that eventually bring those institutions down should prompt our consideration of our legal and military systems which appear to be our first principles. Our burden of attorneys guarantees our liberties, but winds up clogging our courts and often abusing justice; and our military both projects and protects our global power, but often creates more hostility than it resolves.

Just how and with what these various inbred institutions should be cross-pollinated we leave to those more familiar with them, but some suggestions for the military are presented in the following chapter.

Social context—Governance

Governments, in the age of autonomy, take the form of social contracts between the people and the government. The people give up some of their rights as individuals to the society 'in order to form a more perfect union, establish justice, insure domestic tranquility, provide for the common defense, promote the general welfare,' in order to secure the 'blessings of liberty' for themselves and their posterity.

But governments are also CASYs that adapt to their differing contexts and have their own alignment. Agents in defensively aligned governments are under pressure to increase their own survival or power, and to get their own agendas passed. To achieve these goals they most often resort to gaming the system, using whatever methods they can get away with. The burning of the Reichstag in 1933 gave Hitler's National Socialist Party opportunity to blame the Communists and consolidate their power. They later blamed the Jews for other societal evils. Those on either side of the aisle in the U. S. blame the other side for our social problems, and as the Reichstag was used to blame the Communists, 9/11 was used to blame Iraq.

Governments are able to do this mostly by maintaining a defensive alignment in the population; by promoting the fear that Sharansky shows handicaps democracy. Fear promotes both flocking and the use of primitive responses that are more predictable, more easily manipulated, but also more violent. Alignment will be discussed further in a later section, but is should be clear, even from this brief introduction to this viewpoint, that such governments are not likely to secure the blessings of liberty for their people, whatever the form of government.

Sharansky argues and Bush accepts that democracy provides some protection from war, but The Peloponnesian War was started by democratic Athens, the Wars of the Republic were carried out before Caesar crossed the Rubicon, the wars of Colonization were fought by states with representative governments, and we in the United States have a long series of invasions, into Canada in 1775 as the first action of our Revolution, later in 1812, and again after the Civil War, to Mexico in 1848, the Philippines in 1898, up to Iraq in our own time. We've even done it secretly in Iran and Guatemala when their democratic actions were seen as threats to elements of our society, and in Afghanistan when it could frustrate our enemy.

Democracy is not an immunization against violence. Indeed Amy Chua, in *World on Fire,* warns us of the dangers ahead in democratic societies by showing how the disparity of wealth that emerges when the defensive alignment of capitalism is unrestrained leads to conflict when a people's democratic ideals cry for equality. Democratic societies were built by a middle class and they work best when that section of society is strong and well informed. Alan Greenspan showed how our present situation reflects that of a century ago in reporting to a Congressional economics committee in 2005: "The income gap between the rich and the rest of the US population has become so wide, and is growing so fast, that it might eventually threaten the stability of democratic capitalism itself." Our current administration, however, has built an ever larger governmental hierarchy and put in place policies that have tended to polarize Americans both economically and politically; and it has done so at the expense of the middle class where our democratic roots are formed and nourished.

Actions in international relations have not helped either as they also continue with the mechanical analytical model. We try to balance elements in the rest of the world just like we do at home, but we know it doesn't work when we try to help ailing ecosystems by analysis and regulation; it doesn't work with CASYs in general. The networked diversity found in an ecosystem is what makes it work.

Seeing our systems differently is the first step in helping them improve. We can with this new understanding maintain a more creative alignment in our governments. There are groups that evaluate governments and their evaluations help. The EEU evaluates the governments of those states wishing to join and points out areas that need attention. The publication *Governance Matters* that was discussed earlier grew out of the World Bank's evaluative section. It evaluates governments in the areas of: Voice and Accountability; Political Instability and Violence; Government Effectiveness; Regulatory Quality; Rule of Law and; Control of Corruption. The Iraq Study Group also gives a hint about how to avoid partisan politics and become focused more on creative solution. This group attempted to deal with the very complex issue of our actions in Iraq. It did this with a group of political partisans and came up with a consensus report. Despite the consensus those in power decided to ignore their recommendations, but the group itself may provide a model for how to maintain more of a creative alignment in government. Giving such groups more respect in the media, more time to explain their conclusions, and more of the bully pulpit now dominated by the executive would help to spread their consensus to a broader base among the people. While such a body cannot make laws they can influence public opinion.

Social context—Inequality

There is a long history of trying to deal with inequality. In our earliest societies it wasn't much of a problem because indigenous peoples generally had poorly developed concepts of private property and labor was divided on a natural basis—the men did the hunting and the women the gathering. With the dangers of predators and childbirth life expectancy was short and children were more reliably raised by the community. Networked societies such as these had less inequality, but ownership of property and the classes that followed was an ancient adaptation that led to material progress and most of our past cultures had already refined it to the point that indigenous equality was not an option.

With the establishment of private property the threat of its loss applied pressure to the defensive side of adaptation that was guided by the social context towards the two of Borg's three "A's" that are masculine—affluence and achievement. So the societies were increasingly patriarchal, hierarchical and aligned defensively on increasing power, and the female, egalitarian, networked way of seeing lost out; other means were needed to deal with the resulting inequality.

In the Biblical Hebrew tradition the people were stewards of the land, and the land was periodically redistributed in the Jubilee year. But the concept of ownership and private property was too powerful an idea—stewardship and Jubilee didn't last long. The Romans developed the idea of usufruct where a person was allowed to reap the benefits of a property held by another as long as the property was maintained; it was a take what you need and leave the rest for others approach, but even this lost out to private ownership.

The reward of initiative when property rights are established is an unparalleled force for action because the reward goes to the individual with the initiative. It also, as the Peruvian economist Hernando de Soto points out, gives the individual a source of capital to invest. But at the same time it shifts the focus away from the community toward the individual and undermines the sense of community equality. Indigenous egalitarianism is easily overcome by the material progress associated with well defined individual property rights. Land reform becomes a real threat in such situations.

In the 1950s, global corporations from the developed nations with interests in developing nations, such as the United Fruit Company in Guatemala or British and American oil interests in Iran, were threatened when those developing nations talked of land reform or nationalization of resources. Private property is a founding principle of developed capitalist-oriented nations and efforts by these nations to cope with the resulting inequities could easily be identified with communism so the threat was manipulated by stories that led eventually to the CIA's clandestine overthrow of the democratically elected governments in both Guatemala and Iran. Yet agrarian societies may benefit from land reform, which levels their playing field, just as developed nations, with their information economies, can benefit by reducing asymmetric information, which levels theirs.

All people are not created equal, but when inequality is institutionalized and fostered in a system it grows, and soon enough the imbalance in the resulting classes threatens the whole. It is an element in society; often it is associated with a first principle such as the free-market base that grounds our economic system. We have accepted the ideas of the Social Darwinists, portrayed in our day by Ayn Rand, who argue that wealthy people have risen to the top by virtue of their superiority; wealthy and powerful people, in this view, should be supported and their self-interest relied upon to guide the system. Alan Greenspan was one of Rand's followers and demonstrated allegiance to her principles in his support of deregulation during his entire tenure at the Federal Reserve. It was only after the crash of that system in 2008 that Greenspan apologized for his role in it explaining that there was a "flaw" in his philosophy. Such a view focuses on power and competition, and lacks the ecological balance of a more networked female perspective, Rand's gender notwithstanding. It ignores the significant role of cooperation in nature which has more of a female alignment. Much of our world, reflecting this defensive alignment, is centered on supporting the wealthy and powerful, and their monuments. This is Rand's masculine alignment and it is unhampered by the demands of children who are invisible in her writings and count for little; most developed nations show this in their declining birthrates.

We should be more familiar with this dynamic in America where our past flirtation with the survival of the fittest ideas of Social Darwinism in the late 1800s led to a class structure reflecting the power of dominant males, but also to a populist revolt because it was not consistent with our democratic values. Marx tried to show how this shadow side of capitalism leads, without some kind of outside control working to maintain fair practices, to a class of owners with all the wealth and a class of powerless workers in poverty; and that appeared to be where we were headed. Masculine monuments extended from Mt. Rushmore (mostly Calvin Coolidge) to the more useful, but none the less monumental, Public Libraries (Andrew Carnegie), National Parks (John D. Rockefeller Jr.), and the many corporate behemoths of that day; it continues today in our many large philanthropic foundations. But the disparity led then to populist revolts manifest in large and violent strikes that raised the fear of increased social unrest and the specter of communism. In our day we have the populist demonstrations against the World Trade Organization in Seattle and other cities.

As discussed earlier we resolved this problem a century ago by promoting and funding secondary education with its social climbing tools, which raised the person's awareness and level of consciousness so they could better deal with these challenges. We also perpetuated the problem by taking the mechanical approach of balancing the powers: limiting the size and power of large corporations on the one hand while empowering labor on the other. Mechanical solutions generally lead to a power struggle and this was no exception.

Those measures took care of Social Darwinism in the first part of the last century. But that was then, and we have problems learning from history, so we are going down this same road today with our "ownership society," where the owners are rewarded by a 15% tax on capital gains while the workers can pay close to double that on their labor. With little to no effort to promote the middle class and raise the lower class we are retracing our path in Social Darwinism and creating the classes today that Marx predicted, as well as increasing the gulf between the rich and poor that our great grandparents saw a century ago as both unjust and a great potential for civic unrest. And Alan Greenspan sees the solution in the same place our ancestors chose a century ago—education. With Communism no longer a threat, however, there appears to be less concern today about social inequality than there was then, and with our mechanically oriented educational systems it likely wouldn't help anyway.

Unfettered growth to power is a characteristic based on competition that resonates with the defensive alignment in evolution. It's powerful, and it's useful, and it is always going to be there. It's a view that has dominated our world since we became civilized, but if we are going to understand it and use it we need to be aware of the inbred weaknesses that go along with it. A defensive alignment, where the emphasis is on the power and scale needed to keep one safe, is refined by inbreeding, so it brings with it the potential for inbred weaknesses; and it increases the division between the wealthy and empowered, and those not—between those who are building the monuments to themselves and those actually doing the construction. It unleashes the shadow side of capitalism, the defensive side that focuses on increasing scale, efficiency, and profits, which can now be seen as an inbred weakness.

These monuments to capitalism continue to grow; and this growth is largely supported today by the democratic governments of the developed world who see such growth as a first principle of progress without a clear view of its inbred nature. Both democracy and capitalism are expressions of the autonomous stage of human development and they both share a masculine orientation. Women were second class citizens throughout the industrial and political revolutions that created our modern world, and have only recently gained political and economic independence; male interests and alignment continue to dominate.

The best way to deal with these forces is to make them transparent; women know when men are abusing each other—give them a pulpit. And for those at the bottom of the social scale Freire's primary function in educating Brazil's working underclass was in making their station more transparent. The social playing field is leveled by educating the underclass in the nature of the paradigms with which they live; it builds a more ecological society.

Seeing society as a CASY enables us to understand why mechanical or regulatory methods have not worked to control its excesses. The view helps us to understand why governments emphasize defense and fear when they want to control the populace; and it helps us to understand growth in a new way—as a powerful defensive adaptation. We have looked at the role of women, inequality, government, first principles, and immigrants—all elements influencing our relationships with others. While there are many more elements that do this, such as kin, these give an idea for the power behind seeing the system as an adaptive one—and for the need to stimulate a more creative alignment. While the above examples show why this is important they only hint at how to change it. That requires looking at our paradigms.

Social paradigms

Paradigms, we have seen, are how we explain our worlds. They are formed largely in our preconscious stages before we reach the age of eleven or twelve. Mostly they are formed by the language we speak and the stories we hear.

Language is the part of the context that provides the tools to communicate with others in our culture; in and of itself it does much to frame how we think. Our organization, for example, of language into subject and predicate—the actor and the action—contributes greatly to our ability to think in terms of causation and see the world as a big machine. There is no way, other than the unwieldy concatenation of elements, to show networked or complex systems in our language structure. This concept of literary determinism, where language is connected to one's paradigm, was originally proposed by Edward Sapir and Benjamin Whorf. It is generally accepted in modified form today—how we think is affected by the language we speak and vice versa. Orwell, in *1984*, recognized that language can be manipulated to influence thought. One of Israel's steps in building a national identity was to resurrect Hebrew. Ireland and Wales are trying the same thing with their original languages, and the creation of a written language is a common step for many indigenous societies as they move into the modern world while trying to maintain their own identity and culture. The policy makers in these countries are addressing the context; time will tell how the people adapt.

But written language is not alone in its subtle influence; there are also now other media that appear as influential as the written word in creating our perceptions. Unless a person is trained in using the media, where they see and learn how the particular medium itself is used to manipulate the story and persuade the audience, they are much more credible than the printed word; and the media have become a highly manipulable part of our language context. Media expertise is used mostly for advertising and influencing our perception of needs and wants, which gives us but a glimpse of its ability to shape how we think.

The paradigm part of the social context is influenced by these unconscious media effects and the variety of stories we tell with them. As we saw in the section on education these stories create the paradigm that acts as the operating system for our informal education. They do the same for our societies as they create the paradigm that determines how the society sees and responds to outside stimuli—and it is all mostly unconscious. And different stories can promote fear and hostility. The stories told to the children in ancient Sparta fostered fear in the Athenians just as those told the children in today's Palestine bring fear to the Israelis. Stories also help determine whether or not a society survives. In all of the societies Diamond looked at that survived a crisis the reason was found in the stories they told.

Social paradigms—Storytellers

With our continued mechanical viewpoint it is easy to elicit fear by stories that separate out the *others* and make them into hostile and powerful threats. Fear promotes the flocking that makes a society more manageable and predictable; it's how Karl Rove manipulated the American people to win elections. But it also draws on the fight or flight response that increases the potential for violence when fleeing is not an option. On the other hand stories showing the similarities that go beyond our superficial differences increase our tolerance and allay our fears.

Every society has its storytellers—they are an integral part of the complex system and its adaptation. Stories come from parents, hoping to stimulate their child's development, educators, trying to increase neuronal connections, and from those in the society given our respect as leaders.

Local storytellers generally have the parental stamp of approval; less credible should be those more distant, especially those in a position of power. It is difficult to know the value or verity of a story without searching a story-teller's real agenda and this is as difficult to discern for private industry as it is for the government—both should boost our skepticism. "The function of the government is to lie," said the Rev. William Sloan Coffin, who spent years in the CIA prior to going into the ministry. "Lies require violence to support them and violence requires lies to support it." The burning of the Reichstag and the association of Iraq with 9/11 were examples of this presented earlier. They were not presented to equate our leadership with that of Nazi Germany, but only to show how easy it is for powerful agents to step in this direction when the steps increase their power and can be taken in secret. Noam Chomsky's, *Managing Consensus* details much more of the same.

Blaming another agent satisfies our sense of justice, gives us a focus and increases the power of the storyteller. Blaming another allows us to focus on them as the one responsible instead of realizing and accepting the complex nature of our systems, with the likely possibility that we may share some of the responsibility. But it is also the first step in dehumanizing the other—Zimbardo's main point.

On the other side we can tell stories that heal, like those told by the group *Search for Common Ground*, that bring people together rather than divide them. Beginning in South Africa this group writes and produces soap operas that focus on the commonalities shared by all humans rather than our ethnic differences. They are now produced in many African, Asian, and even European countries where ethnic conflict had been a recent problem.

The stories that we hear, the language we hear them in, and the medium we hear or see them in help to create our social paradigms. In a complex society such as ours in the United States they are multiple; seldom if ever do we meet someone whose paradigm is totally congruent with our own. Often however we share areas that make up Galbraith's *conventional wisdom.*

Social paradigm—Conventional wisdom

The phrase was coined by Galbraith to describe the viewpoint that becomes accepted and common because it benefits some segment of the population, most often financially. It's an adaptation in the social paradigm, but all too often it leads us in the wrong direction—a direction that benefits the segment but harms the whole. The conventional wisdom in healthcare is that we are stuck with high tech expensive diagnostic tools and equally expensive therapies; a viewpoint that spares an examination of the industry that both profits from and promotes the particular viewpoint while ignoring inexpensive and unrewarding therapies. Similar industrial supported obfuscation is present in the tobacco industry with their denial and outright manipulation of tobacco's habituation potential, the chemical industry with the problems of bisphenol A and other toxins, the beef industry and hormones, and others. Where ever there is a place for someone to gain there is pressure to create conventional wisdom to support it.

Governmental policy where there is a representative government is not that different. When governmental action or inaction results in disaster the common practice is to "fuzzy it up" with denials of the obvious, conflicting statements, numerous investigations of limited aspects of the disaster, and a deluge of paper that make the real issue invisible. Katrina and Abu Ghraib are two recent examples of governmental culpability that were fuzzed up in this way.

In a different area John Perkins explained some of the behind the scenes adaptations leading to the conventional wisdom and acceptance of globalization in his recent book, *Confessions of and Economic Hit Man*. His job was to go into developing countries and evaluate their potential to pay back loans from funding agencies like the International Monetary Fund or the World Bank. But his hidden agenda was to inflate that potential to create debtor nations. This gave our country, who financed many of them, leverage that we used for political support internationally.

One of the things most lamentable to him was the change he saw over the 15 to 20 years of his activity. While he started out as a clandestine operator, careful to keep the purposes of his calculations hidden, it didn't take long for the agents he was working with to understand what was going on and to join in the plunder. By the time he retired it was openly just the way things were done and agents around the world were in collusion with him and profiting greatly by ripping off their own people. It doesn't take long for conventional wisdom to overcome our sense of right and wrong, especially when it is profitable or increases ones power.

Perkins experienced and recorded a particular adaptation for a society. The adaptation was defensive; it was designed to increase the power of a particular agent, the U.S., in the larger system of world politics. It also facilitated the survival of the many foreign agents who bought into it, but it hurt a lot more. In contrast, an alignment on creative novelty will increase a system's diversity and complexity, result in a more level playing field, and increase the health and success of the system. A generation is the time it took for the adaptation Perkins records, and other social realignments are comparable.

Habermas records another: the transition in the western world beginning the last of the nineteenth century from a society based on open informed discussion of policy and politics to one based on consumerism, where the individual agent is manipulated more than informed, and where power resides with those having a more unequal share of the information. Here too he describes, like Perkins, the transition to a defensively aligned system.

The defensive alignment behind conventional wisdom should make us more aware of the fact that the benefit of these stories is limited. This alignment is promoted most often by the powers that control our societies. All cultures have storytellers who create the conventional wisdom. In the Moslem world they are often powerful and respected Imams, or religious teachers. In the west they are more often politicians or those with the most power. Politicians have a 'bully pulpit' that comes with the job and those with the most power have no trouble paying so the stories that dominate tend to be the ones that help these agents keep their power. Storytellers are usually expert at repeating the spin that benefits their spiritual or financial patrons and retelling the stories eventually results in public credibility and conventional wisdom regardless of their underlying truth or falsity.

All of these social and conceptual elements are applying pressure to adapt; and the alignment of our systems is mostly defensive so the adaptations are centered at getting larger and more powerful. The nations that have the largest gross domestic product, economic growth rate, and are the most powerful dominate in our world and are emulated. This is our conventional wisdom, but it is leading us away from the systemic benefits to be found in a cooperative and creative alignment. The question now is how to change our social alignment.

The first step in this direction, just as it was for Freire's students, is the realization that there is another direction. When this realization is in place other elements can be played with: transparency overcomes asymmetric information and levels the playing field; compassion for all of the players is a human element; and a smaller unit empowers and helps the agents in the way seen by E. F. Schumacher, in his *Small is Beautiful,* but it also empowers the plasmid model.

Honoring adaptability

Our conventional mechanical paradigm doesn't see adaptation as desirable. It tries to regulate adaptation and control it, which pushes the system toward the defensive side. Defensive adaptations benefit the individual with the desirable characteristic and tend to polarize the system into the haves and have-nots. When threats are removed agents are more likely to adapt creatively. This is the difference Sharansky sees when he talks about the progress of democratic systems as opposed to fearful ones, but it's not democracy that is the difference, it's the fear.

This realization and the paradigm that sees and honors creative adaptation is possibly the only change needed to help our systems improve. We have seen what it can do with the 'skunk works,' and sensed what it could do to health care in earlier chapters, but until we see it and practice it we will continue to argue about the ethics of giving placebos to people, which encourages and enables their bodies to adapt in beneficial ways, because they don't pass our mechanical tests. We have seen the vision of what it could do for our educational systems to change the lab-rat model to one that honors the adaptability of our children and their teachers. The same potential is present for all of our societal problems when we see the agents in our systems as adaptable rather than as cogs in a machine.

Stimulating transparency

Transparency levels the playing field, handicaps the abuse of power, and facilitates the invisible hand that is adaptation—and those with the most vision in the areas that would help are again likely to be the grandmothers. The traditional means of maintaining transparency in the United States has relied on what is called the fourth estate, a free press with the freedom of speech. But there are different levels in society and transparency is valuable at all levels.

Social transparency

With consolidated ownership, the media, like our major parties, increasingly represents corporate power and money. Even without consolidation financial influence via sponsors limits the expression of contrary viewpoints, as is clearly the case with commercial television, but also extends increasingly into our national public radio and television stations. Public radio and television, and independent programming like C-SPAN (paid for by cable networks), can provide balance and transparency to the corporate view; they should have public sponsorship. While this is our traditional and most powerful tool for maintaining and promoting transparency we should not stop there.

Our social forms of entertainment can also play a role. Documentary films are increasing as the technology for making them becomes less expensive. Increasingly they tell stories that counter conventional wisdom and stimulate much public discourse. In ancient Greece the popular form of entertainment was the theater. The playwrights were the storytellers for the society and an integral part of most plays was the chorus, which often reflected the conventional wisdom. With the chorus being only a part, the rest of the play could show the weaknesses as well as the strong points of the conventional wisdom—and often the gods were called in to counter it. The plays stimulated public discourse and were seen as a valuable part of civic society—and because of this viewpoint the citizens were paid to attend. While we may not need to go to that extent CSPAN channels and possibly some others showing this type of documentary should be available on all standard cable services without associated advertising. This should be entertainment that questions, ridicules, and shows the ethical fallacies of our conventional wisdom—something like "The Axis of Evil" comedy show should be a part of it. It needs public support because it could never get sponsorship from the financial powers that benefit from our skewed thinking. This is the kind of cross pollination needed to help creative societies thrive. If such entertainment was developed locally it could also, as it did in ancient Greece, provide an interesting focus for community life. Activities that stimulate public discourse and add to the society's transparency will increase its complexity and empower its agents; and when fear is minimized and the alignment is creative it will increase its health. Gibbon, in his monumental *Decline and Fall of the Roman Empire*, is adamantly clear on the role of bread and circuses in the fall of that civilization, and thought provoking entertainment would do well to replace our current circuses.

Individual transparency

As helpful as the fourth estate is at providing social transparency it often does not see our problems in a helpful way because it shares the male paradigm. Power and its partner corruption are mostly male issues and they tend to escape notice when males are looking. Zimbardo's prison experiment lasted for almost five days and its problems were felt, but were not identified until a woman was asked to look at it—and the experiment was terminated. Women seem to have an uncanny ability to sense a male's abuse of power; and corruption is best countered by measures that limit or reduce an agent's power. Such a perspective adds transparency in this critical area.

This does not necessarily mean putting more women in government. Women, as Ayn Rand, Margaret Thatcher, and the feuding women leaders of Bangladesh amply demonstrate, are just as easily seduced by power as are males. It means honoring women's roles that center on the family and around the children, and empowering those elements. Those familiar with the powers of those that govern smile or laugh when I propose such a system of monitoring, but it worked for the Iroquois, for Zimbardo's prison experiment, and the overly dominant alpha male chimps. We believe it's worth a trial.

Passing an Iroquois Amendment to replace our congressional oversight and investigative committees, as well as our special prosecutors, with a standing committee of grandmothers with the power to remove the official from public office would be a much more effective method of policing congress—to say nothing of what it could do with the executive branch. Honoring older women for their experience, their values, and their ability to sense male abuses carries those values into the system. This would be a major step toward an ecologically based society and one that limited the abuse of power.

The use and abuse of power is the norm when the population is in the *power and authority* stage with an autocratic leader. As societies move to the later stages of *law and order* or *autonomy* those in power wishing to increase that power must operate secretly, making incestuous deals with their ideological brothers and sisters to increase their power; this is mostly the how and why behind Acton's aphorism—it's not necessarily the power that corrupts but the secrecy and the incest behind it. The hidden agenda revealed in the Downing Street memo that led us into the war with Iraq is a likely example of this process. Power over another requires asymmetric information and some degree of secrecy; it leads to its own brand of problems like those seen at Abu Ghraib and Guantanamo.

Sometimes the abuse of power is hidden by how we see because our paradigm limits our understanding of other cultures. Even when we try and are conscious of the problem, as was Margaret Mead in Samoa, we are not able to completely stop reframing the other culture into our own model. And if a part doesn't fit we are far more likely to ignore it than we are to change our model.

A similar problem occurs in research. Since most research is funded by institutions embedded in and profiting from the conventional wisdom there is significant pressure to make the data fit the model.

As long as this persists our perception of the world frames our behavior and influences what we see. We make decisions based on our perceptions of how the world is rather than on the facts and, depending on our status, we can even verify our perceptions. Thor Heyerdahl of *Kon Tiki* fame went into the Polynesian Islands and told the people there that he was looking for certain types of artifacts that would demonstrate a connection with South America—and the Polynesians were more than happy to find them for him. American leaders were similarly looking for a reason to get rid of Saddam Hussein and after 9/11 found such reason in manufactured links to terrorism, like an Iraqi connection with Al Qaeda, and weapons of mass destruction in the form of yellow cake from Niger. According to the Downing Street memo, both "intelligence and facts were being fixed around the policy" in order to justify invasion. Some believe there was a conspiracy among the neocons to get us involved in Iraq, but it is just as likely an error of authority. When an authority figure asks for information in support of their particular idea or point of view, they are likely to get it. Neither Heyerdahl's nor Bush's conclusions accurately reflected the truth; they resulted from the erroneous mental models and biased alignment of the 'authorities,' and the attempts of their staffs and associates to support them. In both cases perceptions, rather than facts, led to erroneous conclusions. The Tonkin Bay incident that led to our open warfare with North Vietnam was similarly manufactured, demanded by the perceptions of the military who were trying to justify their own positions.

Perceptions are thus important for defining our reality, but sometimes they can even create our reality. When a pregnant woman perceives a threat her body responds by releasing epinephrine which crosses the placenta and increases muscle mass in the developing fetus at the expense of brain mass. Epinephrine in this case is a signaling molecule that determines which genetic elements are read. The real world of protein structure, function, and our behavior is affected not only by the environment, but by how the environment is *perceived.*

Governmental transparency

An area of our nation that has a particular problem with the lack of transparency is our centers of government. They were established in the days before rapid transportation, in the days of the horse and buggy—in the days when people met in small groups to discuss politics and policy. Such centers were necessary in that they allowed our governing agents to communicate with each other. But that reason is gone today with communication immediately available across the globe and travel time cut to hours. Concentrating our governments makes the agents accessible to each other, but it also makes them more accessible to both lobbyists and terrorists. And it facilitates inbreeding and the unethical kind of communication that requires the absence of a record. Washington D.C. has been correctly labeled the most inbred town in the country. That's a polite term for what is more properly called incest.

What would happen to our governments if legislative agents stayed home and worked out of open offices with no doors, where they could be monitored better by the grandmothers as well as those that know and elected them? They could participate in governmental processes by email, fax, or phone, or even video, but not behind closed doors where there is no record or transparency. The lobbyists would have to travel more, the terrorist would lose a target, and the agent would be on the margins and more open to the benefits of cross-pollination.

Another means of limiting the power of our elected officials and making their actions more transparent would be opening their financial accounts. We already do this with their campaign funds, but since so many leave Washington much better off financially than when they arrived perhaps their personal accounts should be open as well. Instead of just opinion, bloggers could then share *information* on how much so-and-so congressman deposited from such-and-such corporation. Early in 2007 Governor Perry of Texas came under fire when a direct correlation was shown between a substantial campaign contribution from the drug company providing the vaccine for the human papilloma virus and his signing a mandate that all young women be immunized with this vaccine. The mandate was reversed. Transparency in this case unveiled an incestuous relationship and aborted its products.

Transparency in government is a stated goal of developed nations, and America, under our current administration, has taken some well deserved hits. In our war with terrorism we describe the terrorist organizations as hiding under a cloak of secrecy and fail completely to see the incongruity of doing this while increasing secrecy in our government by ten times that of previous administrations. Toward the end of WW II, after it was clear that Germany was losing, Hitler's propaganda chief, Josef Goebbels, observed that, "Even if we lose, we shall win, for our ideals will have penetrated the hearts of our enemies." That seems to be the case with us in regards to the secrecy that nourishes the roots for corruption. It does us no good in a country striving for openness and less corruption in government to adopt the level of secrecy seen in clandestine terrorist cells.

The whole system tends toward secrecy and because the resulting asymmetric information can be used to consolidate ones own power; it is unlikely to police itself. The mechanical and defensive orientation of the 'checks and balances' that attempt to control our government by a balance of power tends to build up agencies that compete for power. Examples of this process were seen in the analysis of the various intelligence agencies following 9/11.

But there are movements such as "clean elections" where campaign funds come from tax money rather than corporations. If, as seems likely, politicians are bought, then it is better that the owners be the taxpayers rather than special interests. Clean elections also enable candidates from middle class America to run for office, where they represent middle class democratic values and compete against those traditionally in the upper class who represent entitled values.

Corporate boards are in place to assure as much as possible the same kind of transparency in our companies, but in many cases the boards are nothing more than 'good old boys' who collect their fees, ignore the business, and too often fill each others pockets. John Thompson is a coach at Georgetown University; he also sits on the board of the Nike Corporation. In 1998 he approved a salary increase to $1.7 million for Nike CEO Phil Knight. Shortly thereafter his team received a $400,000 endorsement from Nike. Helping out in this way is just taking care of a friend, but it's also incest when we see the system as a CASY. Assuring the information needed to guarantee transparency should be the role of government. Doing so increases transparency, limits the abuse of power, and strengthens the "invisible hand."

Compassion

There is a glaring difference between ecosystems and societies: inefficient or unproductive elements are allowed to die off in ecosystems while inefficient or unproductive elements in human societies are supported. The element behind this difference is that of compassion, a distinctly human characteristic. Animals are said to have compassion, but while there are numerous examples of animals acting compassionately such actions are more likely to be instinctive; they reflect the fact that there is indeed a survival value associated with the altruistic behavior that comes from the creative and diverse alignment of evolution. Compassion is based on the ability to put oneself into another person's situation, of acting with empathy, and is a hallmark of human functioning.

Primitive responses like fight or flight reside in the reptilian brain and are shared by all species having that level of brain. Flocking behavior came with the limbic system and is similarly shared by animals having that level of brain. But compassion is a cortical response that is best and most fully expressed in humans. Caring for others and building a compassionate society is common ground for all our great religions. It was built into the Mosaic Law; it was one of Jesus' primary messages; it is the stated purpose of the zakat given to charity in the Islamic world; and it is fundamental to Buddhism. But in order to respond as our spiritual leaders teach we need to function in the cortex of our brains. And fear, that stimulates our defenses and draws on our ever present and easily accessible primitive responses, makes that very hard.

Compassion also pulls the heart into this mix. We are finding that the heart has a plethora of connections—chemical or hormonal, neuronal and electrical—with the rest of the body, and that the heart receives a direct and profound benefit from compassionate activity—one reason why pets are such a benefit for people with heart and vascular diseases. A compassionate act strengthens the connection between the cortex and the heart. The strength of this connection, and our ability to think and play compassionately, is indirectly correlated with our incidence of heart disease, high blood pressure, and strokes.

In his work with people having coronary artery disease one of the major, but largely unpublicized, parts of *Dean Ornish's Program for Reversing Heart Disease* is group therapy that focuses on removing the barriers that we build around ourselves in order to protect our egos. Opening your heart to others by removing these barriers is a very real metaphor, says Dr. Ornish, for what actually happens in the blood vessels that supply the heart and whose closing is the primary cause of the problem. It is also the essence of compassion. Our challenge then is to build a society that incorporates more compassion, one that tries to address the class issues that Greenspan and Chua see as major problems in our not too distant future.

The best way to move in this direction is to provide the context of safety that creates a playful environment in which to deal with the challenges we face and to promote respect for other agents. This is fundamentally true for all CASYs at all levels—provide a safe context and let the system evolve. This perception of safety stimulates the creative adaptations that benefit all of the agents in the system. We have already discussed this in the context of healthcare and education. It's also true in how to best help other nations develop as well as save ourselves.

William Easterly, retired from the World Bank, shows how little has really been accomplished by the millions of dollars spent on foreign aid programs built around our analysis and providing of critical needs. We use the same model trying to repair ecosystems, and it doesn't work. Providing goods and services undercuts the ability of the recipient to develop their own capacity. The Southwest Industrial Areas Foundation says the same thing about domestic charity: The mechanical analysis and supply of needs is not an effective way of helping others. Our analytical and mechanical view sees these elements as the major lack, but providing them robs the developing society of growing their own means of coping. Instead they become dependent on outsiders. As Easterly points out, providing goods and services from outside tends to push the developing nation toward dependency rather than self sufficiency. Understanding this concept, a fundamental rule of the Industrial Areas Foundation is never do for someone what they can do for themselves. Better is to empower agents to adapt, to support their context in areas where it is deficient, and try to make that context a safe place in which to play.

The approach Easterly and the Industrial Areas Foundation criticize continues the analytical/mechanical mistake of treating a system by providing something to balance a perceived deficit, the same approach that we now know doesn't work with imperiled ecosystems. We get caught up in giving the hungry person a fish instead of the equipment and information needed for him to catch his own.

Social perceptions

A safe environment allows for play and creativity, while a fearful one leads to defenses, cohesion, and giving more power to those in position to protect us. Since the lower brain's defensive responses are so much more accessible, having been tested and refined over millions of years, promoting fear is the most common avenue for governments seeking to increase their power. In 1967 the New York Times published a story about a leaked governmental report that looked at the prospect of switching to a peace oriented economy. *The Report from Iron Mountain* was not in favor of such a transition; it pointed to the benefits of the defensive alignment—economic growth, social cohesion, and an increase in central power—and concluded that they were more beneficial that the unknown social adaptations that would follow changing to a peacetime alignment. *The Report from Iron Mountain* turned out to be a satirical parody, but parody or not its accuracy was verified by the dissolution of the Soviet Union almost a quarter of a century later, a scant two years after they switched from a defensive alignment. The cohesion that was manufactured by focusing on outside threat held it together in a defensive alignment. Perceptions are important and from a governmental perspective maintaining a defensive alignment is the way to go. As Chomsky and Herman portray with numerous examples in *Manufacturing Consent*, social alignment results almost entirely from defensive messages from the government accepted at face value by the media. Without resolving this the policies of the future are likely to turn defensively on the perceptions of those in charge, and lead to more of the Kon-Tiki or Iraqi WMD type errors.

It is an unfortunate truth that a diverse society, such as ours in the United States, needs a crisis, an outside threat, in order to pull together. It is mostly unstated yet common wisdom that Franklin Roosevelt knew that the Japanese fleet was planning on attacking us in the Pacific and that he soft pedaled the options of monitoring their fleet closer, or taking other steps toward more effective preparation or deterrence, in order to pull us together in fighting the War. Nafeez Mosaddeq Ahmed convincingly argues similarly for 9/11 in *The War on Freedom*, a book that is the equivalent of *The 9/11 Commission Report* for the rest of the world. Political leaders in a diverse society will always have to create a critical sense of threat before the cohesion rule pulls society together so it is often not in their interest to prevent catastrophes that can serve their long term goals.

The alignment that promotes this activity is defensive; we see solutions in making us stronger or larger so that we can better survive in our competitive world. Until we can see our systems as CASYs and alter our alignment to one including more creativity we will continue getting larger and more unstable as we follow the course of the dinosaurs. Continuing our current path there will come a time when the empire we know as the U.S.A. will fall, and the bigger and more unequal it is at that time the harder that fall will be on the people living in that system.

Understanding the often deceptive nature of our perceptions encourages one to search for ways to address these problems and teaches us to honor those that see things in a different way even more than those in bed with us—even when they are an opposition party or an enemy. The ancient Roman historian Plutarch tells how his people were convinced of the wisdom of the Greeks when Carneades, a Greek diplomat, argued convincingly one day for the presence and importance of natural justice, and on the next day, equally convincingly, arguing for the opposite. Like Carneades school debate teams are not told which side of the argument they are going to represent prior to the debate. Would that our politicians could be similarly broad in their understanding and that those hearing political debates could appreciate issues as well as emotions and as easily understand the paradigm of the opposition. Lacking this ability to see, understand, and argue both sides of an issue, who today, more than the opposition, is going to hold up the mirror so that we can see our own weaknesses and the errors of our reasoning? Incorporating the other viewpoint brings a balance, an earlier synthesis, to ones' position that increases its value and wisdom. As pointed out earlier, Machiavelli's advice to keep your enemies close by was to allow for this information.

In an emotional argument speaking to the issues is seldom a convincing position, and those speaking truth to power seldom even have a pulpit, but they usually bring more light to the subject. Gingrich's comment on the failure of our third party payer system in healthcare was the truth and he had the fortitude to tell it as he saw it, but it was politically poisonous because it showed a fallacy of the conventional wisdom and the imbedded system. Unfortunately, while he added some clarity, his partisan view did not allow him to see that they would work only if they were general, i.e., supported by a government he wanted to downsize.

It takes both sides, both viewpoints, to see the whole picture. It takes the ability to translate the others paradigm into one's own language before it can be understood. A win-win solution demands at least two sides and the agreement of both in the solution—so all we need in

America are two sides. Corporate interests are well represented by both of our dominant political parties so all we need is a Populist Party to represent the people. We need to balance our political storytellers with the voice of the grandmothers and their interest in the children, and our business oriented agents with those of our prophets looking at sustainable ecological living and compassion. In all areas we need to look for and resolve asymmetric information where it is contributing to inequities and detracting from the informed adaptation of the invisible hand that brings value to society.

Adaptation and society

It has been our position throughout that CASYs resist analysis and regulation; that they are best managed by addressing their contexts and allowing time for adaptation. From the point of view provided by complex mathematics, described by Chris Lucas at the opening of the chapter, our different cultures represent the *basins*, or *centers of interest*, that become apparent when solutions to equations with many variables are plotted—they are the *attractors*. Our problem in finding solutions to our social problems is finding, in the context of the society, the critical variables *that can be played with* which will make a difference, or the elements that can be safely added that will turn the *attractors* into *strange attractors* that would allow our cultural systems to morph into something new, and hopefully both more stable and more friendly.

Ecosystems are far more diverse with many interacting species rather than just people that make up our societies; they involve the interplay of many species and inefficient or unproductive agents are ignored as they die off. Despite the famines, the epidemics, the scourges of ethnic cleansing, the tsunamis, and the Katrinas that we have experienced over the last few decades most do not seem willing to just let the inefficient parts of humanity die off. We appear to be moving toward an increase in compassion, of caring for the weaker agents in our respective societies, from a self-centered, survival of the fittest, orientation to one realizing the brotherhood of mankind. The humanism that dominates western culture has concluded that humanity itself is more important than continued evolution; or at least that the state that at times requires, and more often allows, the meaningless sacrifice of individual lives is not worthy of being the next level of evolution.

Dying for a higher level system seems the norm in nature: bacteria die in order to make biofilm, cells die in order to make organs and differentiate into fingers and toes, and social insects sacrifice themselves readily for the colony. On our level it was considered the greatest honor to die for the fatherland through most of recorded history. In Europe the shift away from this came with World War I when books like *All Quiet on the Western Front* portrayed the ignorant brutality of warfare and the human commonalities shared by those in the trenches. As John McCutcheon puts it in his song *Christmas In the Trenches,* about the shared celebration of Christmas in 1914 where both sides met in the middle of their now peaceful battlefield: "On each end of the rifle we're the same." In the United States it came with the ignorant and meaningless brutality seen in Viet Nam that fed the protests to that war. But while the Europeans moved toward political and economic measures that decreased hostility, the U.S. moved to a voluntary professional military where there is less room for dissent, and more flexibility for the Commander in Chief.

Self sacrifice for a higher purpose persists today in human societies, but has shifted from the state to religion. Today's *jihadists,* both Islamic and Christian, seem more than willing to sacrifice themselves to destroy the great Satan or the abortion clinic. Self sacrificing behavior is considered aberrant, but it's not. It's just that the associated rise of humanism in western thought has essentially concluded that the individual is a higher order than his institutions. In a way we have stopped evolution, or at least decided on a different pathway—a pathway that includes compassion for others of our species. That new pathway is strengthened when we see differently.

Our dominant stories that help us see, however, have been mechanical ones that reflect the precarious balance of powers. They tend to ignore adaptation and the value of play in the process of adapting. We need stories now that allow and help us to see differently. An example of their power hopefully comes from the genocide in Darfur.

It is easy to think of ways to stop the genocide in our traditional way of thinking: arm the victims, shoot down the planes, and send in military help. But such methods escalate the violence and cement the defensive alignment. China's close economic ties, their military presence in Sudan, where they protect their oil interests, and their veto power in the General Assembly made the issue one that the Sudanese government could ignore. But when someone realized where China's values lay and began calling the 2008 Olympics the "Genocide Olympics" China rapidly lined up with the rest of the world and the Sudanese government accepted additional UN observer and peacekeeping troops. This reframing changed history and saved lives. It's an example of what is possible when the alignment and adaptation are creative.

Society and the plasmid model

The most powerful tool that one gains with the CASY paradigm is likely the use of the plasmid model in adapting. This is the true bottom-up development and it requires lots of players. Billions of bacteria participate in adapting to our antibiotics and the effort would not succeed as well without both the numbers and the sharing. In our defensively aligned society we rely on central, organized, adaptation; the pharmaceutical companies handle the drugs, the curriculum department handles the education, and government handles the economy and society. But it doesn't work well; and perhaps now we can understand why. We have seen answers to our problems in going to a larger scale with more central control, but the solutions lay in the other direction. Central governments cope with individual needs with impersonal requirements and mechanical doles. Better would be local people making personal contact that allows aid to better fit the need. The World Bank does a very good job of spending a billion dollars on aid, but it has little idea on how to spend a million dollars in a thousand places, and no clue on how to spend a thousand dollars in a million places—but that is what we need. Local school districts, local health departments, local food supply, local corporations, and local governments can all be used to find out what works better for a specific challenge in a given situation. Conscious play with the elements of our environment implies that the agents are knowledgeable about both the elements and the system in which they are playing—imagine multiplying the skunk works. Such a system would require many changes from our current political and economic structure, but they need not be revolutionary. Shifting our emphasis from Gross Domestic Product to Gross Domestic Novelty, or, as Bhutan has already done, to Gross Domestic Happiness would be a small significant step. The role of the larger central agencies is to provide a transparent clearing house for what works locally.

These elements will evolve, but we can speed and influence the process by: encouraging the plasmid model; assuring a safe environment where agents can play with the elements and create novelty; improving their education to expand the elements with which the agents can play; and providing the transparency that counters asymmetric information. This is the context that we can play with today.

CHAPTER 10
As American as Apple Pie—The Military

We annually spend on military security more than the net income of all United States corporations. This conjunction of an immense military establishment and a large arms industry is new in the American experience. The total influence—economic, political, even spiritual—is felt in every city, every State house, every office of the Federal government. We recognize the imperative need for this development. Yet we must not fail to comprehend its grave implications. Our toil, resources and livelihood are all involved; so is the very structure of our society.

In the councils of government, we must guard against the acquisition of unwarranted influence, whether sought or unsought, by the military-industrial complex. The potential for the disastrous rise of misplaced power exists and will persist.

President Dwight Eisenhower, 1961.

For the child with the hammer everything looks like a nail; for the surgeon with the scalpel everything can be fixed with an operation; and for the man with a gun everything can be fixed by the threat of force. These are tools that we make and use. They are our extensions. They give us identity. They give us meaning. Sometimes, when we use them wrong, they can hurt others. As a general rule, when we use them on other agents that we objectify in the process, they satisfy Zimbardo's definition of evil and cause a great deal of harm. But the harm is not just to the other; as Gandhi and our psychologically traumatized and suicidal soldiers point out, it hurts us as well.

How we got here

After the Great Depression and its resolution with World War II both economists and politicians saw the world according to the mechanical Keynesian model where an economy could be kept in better balance by government spending. And the economists, politicians, and the generals, saw the potential of increased military spending as a means of both balancing the economy and preventing some of the problems that had led to two world wars. Many of the "New Deal" agencies were designed with the hope of channeling government money into the economy in order to stabilize it. But they were declared unconstitutional by the conservative Supreme Court. The military-industrial complex adroitly replaced these agencies and provided both access to balancing the economy and a powerful instrument for foreign policy.

We were the world's leading economic power and having a standing military would augment and safeguard that power and allow the government a means of balancing economic trends by increasing its spending. But by 1961, when Eisenhower left office, he warned us of its potential dangers—it had already grown too large and too powerful. It permeated our society then and continues to do so today—and its growth is virtually unopposed. Every state benefits from defense industry financing in some way; and as always fiscal gains lead to conventional wisdom. Attempting to control military spending in Congress reaps hostility both nationally and at home. The military has a broad root system and is a powerful tool for those that control it, but tools are to be used.

The writers of our Constitution feared a strong central government and had no standing military. In their Federalist system the central power was balanced by the military being under state control. In times of threat the central government would call upon the states for military support. But Federalism died in the Civil War and gradually state National Guard units, first by inspection and oversight and later by pay, were included under national control. Then in 1973, when the draft was ended, the military became a professional tool of the executive branch of the government—and just as tools define and give meaning to a carpenter or surgeon this tool often defines our nation.

With the expansion of the military seen by Eisenhower it rapidly became a CASY and took on a life of its own. Stimulated by the Cold War it has followed its World War II orientation to protect American interests around the world and help balance the economy—and it has become intertwined with that economy. The growth in healthcare is at least threatened by misguided, mechanically oriented, governmental regulators that make the healthcare system more cohesive and identifiable, even if they don't effectively control its growth. There is no comparable outside control to the military industrial complex so it spreads its roots everywhere and its extensions are not readily identifiable. Being at the top of the food chain the MIC is not cohesive; its agents do not flock and are dispersed throughout the society. The only thing bringing this flock together is feeding more effectively so they tend to congregate around Washington D.C. Their only potential predators reside in congress where members are mostly interested in maintaining their power and prestige, which is in turn enhanced by military contracts for home industry. Anyone against the military, or for limiting its power, is against "Mom and apple pie" and replaced. A strong military has become conventional wisdom and a source of pride in our country.

From a defensive point of view this growth is a win-win solution—every agent benefits. But this view ignores the fact that tools are to be used; and using this particular tool brings death and destruction to those at whom it is directed, as well as hostility and defensive alignments with allies that mostly serve to escalate the conflict—it increases the likelihood of an unstable system. Besides this, as we are seeing with the numbers of Iraqi veterans returning with *post traumatic stress disorder* and a suicide rate double the rest of the population, it brings significant psychological damage to a high percentage of the deliverers. Gandhi was right on target when he scolded the British for dehumanizing their troops by ordering them to kill unarmed civilians; and we blind ourselves and dehumanize our own troops when we gloss over the civilian lives lost in our wars as 'collateral damage'.

Like an ecosystem the MIC also tends to be self supporting because agents in the system feed each other. So the Carlyle Group, with its staff of highly positioned ex-politicians and military people profits off their investments in armament by exerting their significant interests to support the industry; but this is an incestuous relationship. Furthermore members of congress get recognition and votes when they bring employment opportunities and income to their home districts. These financial and political benefits assure a plentiful 'food supply' which traditionally eats up between 50 and 60% of our governments discretionary spending. Our military spending almost matches that of the rest of the world. We spend more than 6 times as much on defense as the next highest nation and more than the next 12 highest spending nations put together.

As responsible citizens, and followers of Eisenhower's advice, we need to ask what this industry is doing. Halliburton stock is up from $9.00 in mid 2002, before the Iraq war, to $69.00 in late 2005. Most other defense contractors have similar gains.

Despite legislation blocking private arms sales to countries engaged in conflict or with human rights abuses the United States government, not bound by this legislation, sold weapons to 18 of the 25 countries actively engaged in military conflict, including Angola, Chad, Colombia, and Pakistan, where they claim an estimated half-million lives each year. In 2003, 80 percent of the top 25 importers of U.S. arms, including Saudi Arabia and Uzbekistan, were identified as either "undemocratic" or human-rights violators by the U.S. State Department. Of nations said by the State Department to harbor terrorists, nearly 90 percent have purchased weapons from the U. S. Like others of our social CASYs, our weapons marketplace appears to have also become aligned on profits.

The Constitutional function of the military is to provide for our defense. But over 200 years, a Civil War, two World Wars, a Cold War, and numerous interventions, the military has evolved to become a powerful tool of the Executive branch for defending not just our country from attack, but our national interests. And defending our interests has been defined broadly enough to involve our military in preventing Guatemala's 1954 land reforms—which threatened the property of the United Fruit Company—to our strategic dependence of the middle east oil countries, the underlying reason, according to Alan Greenspan, for our preemptive war in Iraq. Tools are to be used and the big stick of the American Military has not been idle.

Initially the states were to provide and support soldiers when called upon to defend the Union. There was no other source of support so the power of the central government was severely handicapped. With the de facto demise of federalism in the Civil War the military became a standing army needed to fight first the Indians, then Spain, and then expand to fight in the World Wars of the last century. The federal government was in control. Again, its alignment shifted from homeland defense to protecting our interests around the globe as it became an arm of foreign policy. And doing so meant using the threat of force, because after all it is the military.

Our founding fathers argued against a standing army because it would overwhelm the power of the individual states. We've come a long way since then.

Violence and CASYs

History, the Cohesion Rule, child psychologists, and now even some military strategists are united in support of the fact that violence is not an effective tool when dealing with CASYs. The primary reasons behind this is that the punished CASY goes into defense mode, which builds hostility, increases the potential for violent responses, precludes cognitive measures, and blocks creative development.

Gregory Foster, at the U. S. National Defense University, discusses the efficacy of the different means of persuasion. He names three broad categories: coercion, persuasion, and inspiration. We have seen how the use of regulation or force in the mechanical paradigm increases hostility. Foster agrees. Coercion, the most commonly conceived form when one talks about the use of power, involves military, the threat of destruction, to get compliance. Laws and regulations, and the police power to back them up, are also coercive but more acceptable because, presumably, we, or our elected agents, established the laws to make our own community life more safe and orderly. We willingly give up some freedoms in the purchase of safety.

On a softer scale, but with much the same results, we add the use of moral coercion in the form of shame. But coercion on any scale limits the expression of a CASY and elicits a defensive alignment; if there is any lesson in the history of colonialism it is that the natives eventually get restless. Those coerced by force or shame are more likely to be resentful and eventually rebel. Those coerced by more friendly regulations and community laws are more likely to game them.

Persuasion uses a carrot to elicit a desired behavior, but this too leads to resentment at being treated as an object and manipulated. We don't know how long the grandmother in Kipling's story had to feed the wolf from a distance before it would not bite the hand that fed it, but likely it was around the point when grandma began to see the wolf as something closer and different than just the animal she was feeding to keep it away from her grandchildren. Relationships are not built when we see the other agent as an object to be manipulated and used. As long as the relationship remains oriented on using persuasive power on another as an object to be manipulated, it is likely that they will continue to bite the hand that feeds them. Rewards and awards are almost always associated with someone else judging performance or behavior, and attempting to manipulate it or exert some control. We easily recognize this feeling when we are the ones being evaluated, but we don't give it a second thought when we use it intentionally on our children.

Of the three types of power Foster discusses the only one with any lasting benefit is inspiration. This is where one agent elicits an A-Ha experience in the other that enables them to see in a different way; it changes the paradigm that controls how we see.

We commonly see inspiration as a manifestation of God's power and a reflection of His higher status, but it often comes from teachers, coaches, and even some political leaders like Gandhi and King. Therapists can inspire their clients and one of the understood rules of psychotherapy is that the therapist must be at a higher level of functioning than the client for it to be beneficial. In order for it to work with all CASYs the one promoting the new way of seeing must be on a higher level of functioning than the one inspired; and this level of functioning is moral, and has nothing to do with gross national product or any other measure of wealth or worldly power.

The same processes hold for all CASYs. If compliance follows the threat of force, the disciplined system—child, nation, or culture—will generally function on a more defensive and primitive level than that found in creative play, and the larger system is impoverished in the process.

Besides the defensive alignment a threat increases cohesion among those threatened. The threatened CASY looks for support: the child looks to the parent, the nation pulls together, and the culture looks to its people. This is the limbic, relational, response to outside threats, and the degree of cohesion is proportional to the threat. Reducing threat can act to disperse or open a system while increasing it constricts and closes it down. Responding to a threat mechanically, in a tit for tat, eye for an eye, aggressive manner pushes both threatening and threatened CASY toward primitive violent responses, unites the enemies, and often divides the friends. Yet this is what our system teaches. Both of our most recent "enemies," Osama Bin Laden and Saddam Hussein, learned their trade from American teachers, and the 'School of the America's' or its renamed successor 'the Western Hemisphere Institute for Security Cooperation' continues the process. We need to teach something different.

Peaceful leaders like Gandhi and King recognized the fallacy of the mechanical tit for tat approach and the value of treating oppressing systems in non-mechanical, and non-violent, ways. And spiritual leaders from Jesus and Mohammed to Buddha have taught us to value the "other"—the stranger, the enemy—not as an object, or in a mechanical way, but as human kin.

The distinctly human response that they propose draws on the cortex to creatively play with the elements of the situation to find a political compromise that has elements of winning for both sides—it has been called 'the third way.' This is what happened when someone, thinking out of the box, proposed renaming the 2008 summer Olympic games the 'Genocide Olympics' as a means of pressuring China in order to have Sudan change their policy in Darfur. It's what Jesus enjoined when he told his followers to turn the other cheek—a move that jujitsu-like turned the tables on the abuser prompting them to leave the non-cognitive state where abuse is more acceptable and enter the cognitive where one must think. As Walter Wink points out, ancient cultures reserved the left hand for dirty work so the right hand was the only one used for human interaction. Striking another on the right cheek was a backhand blow, which was proper when dealing with an underling. Turning the other cheek invited the oppressor to strike with the palm or the open hand, but this was how one dealt with insults from a social equal. What to do? The quandary puts the oppressor in the cortex where a human response is more likely.

Programs dealing with bullies at school also exemplify these principles. Approaches using all three of the boid rules are commonly recommended: children are advised to stay away from the bully (separation), or to join with another group since bullies generally pick on loners (cohesion). But the most direct and successful method of dealing with them goes beyond separation and defensive cohesion to stimulate a cognitive response in the bully. Children have been successfully taught to respond to bullying in ways that reframe what the bully is saying. If, for example, the bully taunts you by saying your lunch looks like vomit, your response could be appreciation that the bully cares about your health. Like turning the other cheek this response catches the bully off guard and demands that he think cognitively—it goes to the cortex, the part of the brain that makes us human. It's a response that can change the bully's alignment.

This reframing is what Gandhi and King taught with their non-violent approach to helping their particular oppressed people. There is little question that the approach works, but it works best when the 'oppressor' doesn't perceive anything that pushes him into the defensive state with its resources in the primitive brain. Gandhi's concern for the English oppressors, and for the harm that their perpetration of violence was doing to themselves, made him few friends at home, but was based on his knowledge that without *ahimsa*, non-violence to a sentient being, his whole plan wouldn't work. It required the unfettered and unthreatened use of the cerebral cortex in the oppressor as they try to make sense of their confusing and unexpected situation. The non-threatening nature of the situation creates a state *in the oppressor* where they can play with the elements of the environment. It is this kind of enabling on a variety of scales that can change a systems alignment and keep it aligned on creative novelty rather than on defenses. The Indian word for this, and a fundamental part of Gandhi's successful rebellion, is *satyagraha,* best defined, like

Freire's work discussed earlier, as consciousness raising.

If the purpose of our nation, as our Declaration of Independence and Statue of Liberty imply, is to hold its light up as an example to others—to show the world the benefits of democracy, freedom under law, and the wonders and bounties of a marketplace economy—then using a big stick has the opposite result. If, as the military strategist Foster points out, the best type of force to use is inspirational, and the worst is coercion, then we need to rethink our strategy. The use of overwhelming force consolidates the enemy and often divides friends; and it promotes primitive, reptilian brain, functioning that increases and promotes the violence and abuse that we now see practiced around the world. Such violent behavior stems from primitive reflexes that are far from those of which the complex human brain is capable, but they are readily accessible, tried and tested by natural selection for millions of years, and found successful. These reflexes are defenses that come with a survival benefit, but this doesn't mean that we should ignore our higher centers that make us human. If we wish to be light showing what is possible in human progress then we, as a nation need to change our alignment from defense and violence to the satyagraha that raises consciousness.

We have a son in the military who at one time referred to himself as just one of "the dogs of war." The phrase comes from Shakespeare's play "Julius Caesar" where Marc Anthony is foretelling the chaos introduced by Caesar's assassination. In the future, he said, rulers would, "cry havoc and let slip the dogs of war." As countless political historians have noted, crying havoc and letting the dogs out is altogether too easy when the dogs are professionals and a tool of the executive. It is even easier in the presence of an incestuous relationship between the military-industrial complex and a government that sees a need to stimulate the economy or assure us of needed commodities, whether they be bananas or oil.

Realigning our military

Our MIC needs realignment because protecting American interests in a global economy is an impossible task, especially with globalization shifting that control from nation states to international trade agreements. It is not likely that the MIC will be controlled or influenced by regulatory means because it is too much in control and too much an integral part of our communities. It's almost comparable to an ecosystem functioning in a social CASY. But its alignment can be changed if we have the vision and the political will. Senator Kucinich proposes changing the Department of Defense to the Department of Peace so the idea is not entirely foreign. But as Senator Kucinich has found out the idea is not well accepted. Before we can change the MIC we must change how we see; we must see our 'enemies' in terms of them being CASYs rather than objects. That change will allow us to see the value behind Foster's insights as well as the realignment that Sen. Kucinich is proposing. In addition, like Health Savings Accounts realigning health care, this change in viewpoint needs to be wide spread.

In 1792, a short four years after its ratification, the framers of our Constitution passed the Militia Act mandating that all young men participate in their respective local state militia. Our nation was still being threatened and wanted to be prepared. Most of our young people today feel no need to give any service to our country—paying taxes is considered sufficient, if not excessive, compensation for the benefits of our society.

Requiring such a commitment today would enable a program of universal service where every young person would be required to give some service to their country. This could be work related—rebuilding and serving at our National Parks, or the same with our inner cities, or other areas where our infrastructure is failing—or the Peace Corps, or the military, or volunteering for UN peace keeping. They could help staff day care centers, or help in education as teacher's aids, or even serve with religious NGO's such as the American Friends Service Committee, that are not missionary oriented. Missionary work, proselytizing for ones faith, as noble as it is, carries the message that one cultural story is better than another, and, in principle, amounts to the intent to commit cultural genocide.

National service should include education about alternatives to violence and how to have discussions among people with different backgrounds. It should teach us how to listen, rather than argue, and how to talk from our hearts—something on the order of communication proposed and taught by Carl Rogers and Eugene Gendlin. This is the beginning step in Kuhn's process of translation whereby one can understand another's paradigm.

As pointed out earlier the form of government is developed from the context of the society—their geography, stories and history. Democracy is built on the idea of personal responsibility, that an agent can have an effect on his future place in the world, and it's tied to a working middle class whose stories reflect the success of work—where people can succeed on their own merit and hard work and the development of novel ideas are rewarded. Our attempts at nation building need to move down a few notches from simply replacing the bad leaders with more bad leaders, to addressing the nature of the stories and other parts of the context that are amenable to change. Stories provide the context of our thinking and it is here that meaningful change can happen. It is here, and only here, that inspiration can happen. Tickle the context and let the CASY evolve.

An important lesson we can learn from the breakup of the Soviet Union, and the complete surprise of our intelligence community to that event, is that the easiest way to deal with totalitarian regimes is often to focus on changing their alignment. When the alignment is changed cohesion lessens; once the Soviet Union withdrew from the Cold War the glue holding that system together lasted only two years. If we had seen this connection we would have been better able to see what was happening in the Soviet Union. Rather than the safety and security that real community and a creative alignment foster, defensively aligned totalitarian systems show the weaknesses that result from that alignment. Tickle the context and let the system adapt.

In our attempts at nation building in Iraq we forget this critical process. Forcefully imposing a democracy is impossible. Democracies are grown in local soil from an empowered middle class. The use of force on another is mechanical thinking and always leads to a defensive alignment. Agents in the imposed government are put in the impossible position of trying to act cognitively and creatively, while at the same time they are being threatened by the occupying force for not performing, and by their own people for being pawns of the foreigners. It is most likely that the resulting strife will lead to another autocratic government. We have destroyed one only to foster a second. Defensive alignment doesn't facilitate creative cooperation. Tickle the context and let it evolve.

Teaching our young people how to influence others by sharing stories is the beginning of getting opposition parties to a table where differing views are heard and understood. It's the beginning of negotiating win-win solutions that honor the higher cortical functions that make us human. The success of this strategy depends on whether or not we can train our young people to actually function on this higher level, and we need more than Harris's 1% for it to work. Understanding ourselves and others as creatively adaptable CASY agents is the first step. Change the paradigm and let it evolve.

Sharing stories applies the plasmid model to this problem. Stories are information and they can provide the impetus for change. Changing the defensive alignment of our MIC will be difficult, but as Foster's position at our National Defense University suggests it is not impossible. The WW I story about the shared Christmas told of the midnight mass conducted by a British priest. Understandably it was one of the most meaningful experiences of his life, but it led to his essential ostracism from the chaplain's corp. The military is aligned to focus on the use of coercive force. Broadening the role of the military to include these other paths would also change its context. Tickle the context and let it evolve—it might even evolve into a Department of Peace.

Our defensively aligned military has not protected us from the 'smart bombs' of the terrorist willing to die while guiding them, nor the world from genocide. It has succeeded beyond our imagination at building an empire—just like Ozymandius. Is that what we want? We too need to change our context, or the way we see the world, so that we too can evolve in a more creative way.

In order to create an environment for evolution to occur we must see the other agent as more than an object to be manipulated—even when they are just bacteria. It means that we look at the environmental context of the other agent and do what we can to make it healthier for them, because as they adapt to these changes they are also more likely to be friendlier to us. It means that we do what we can to inspire others to maintain an alignment on creative novelty—and it's not done by coercion or persuasion. This is a fundamental principle in dealing with CASYs; it is equally true for bacteria, our children, our corporations, and our perceived enemies in other cultures.

CHAPTER 11
Religion—An Attractor That Needs To Be Stranger

...the thing is to find a truth that is true for me;
to find the idea for which I can live or die.
Sören Kierkegaard

As strong as is the drive for survival there is an equal evolutionary pressure toward increased complexity in all CASYs. We often see this, as Kierkegaard did, in finding something greater than ourselves for which we can live or die. Bacteria find it in sacrificing themselves to mutate or make biofilm for the good of the colony, or even giving up their independent existence to become mitochondria or protoplasts in the cells of higher life forms. Insects similarly sacrifice themselves for the good of their colony. For many years in our own history the tribe, the city, the state, commanded this kind of allegiance. We all want to create something bigger and better than ourselves; something, as Kierkegaard implies, that is transcendent—something for which we can live or die.

With the decline of the state as a moral center it can no longer command this dedication. In Kiekegaard's view, as well as that of many others today, the idea is found in religion.

How we think is heavily influenced by the context of our cultures, and the cores of our cultures are most often found in the stories telling about our religions. Judao-Christian stories tell of the partnership between God and his people. More particularly they tell of the partnership between the rulers and God so the 'divine right of kings' was a central concept of government until our revolution; and even today we don't argue the right of our president to impose religious decisions, such as that involving embryonic stem cell research, on the entire nation. Similarly the revelations of Mohammed tell us that Allah is God, the giver of the Law, and that all other laws are secondary to his law. So we have Sharia Law that rules Islam, with a leading place even in secular Islamic countries like Egypt and Turkey.

Judaism, Christianity, and Islam are sometimes referred to as the 'religions of the book' because God's word is in their sacred scriptures. Christianity and Islam explain that life is a test and that our future in the life hereafter is determined by how well we do on this test. If we do well we are rewarded in a paradise or heaven; if not the alternative is not so pleasant. We take this model into our own lives and similarly reward or punish our children for their behavior. B. F. Skinner made this reward-punishment model most immediate with his operant conditioning concept in psychology and his idea of a Skinner box where the subject could be constantly monitored and conditioning responses could be immediate. As we saw conditioning is the major learning tool in our schools; and as we have pointed out repeatedly, it treats the agent as an object where adaptation is one of those activities that more often leads to hell. One observant professor, seeing the connection, called heaven a big Skinner-box in the sky. As uncomfortable as this observation was for the fundamentalists in the class it is an accurate portrayal of the paradigm behind these religions.

Religion is often thus the basis of our differing paradigms. In the language of complexity a belief system is the closest thing we have to an attractor—it limits the field of solutions. For centuries the divine right of kings mandated that state and religion were closely tied together, and even though the tie is loosened in today's states we still generally recognize this connection and honor religions as the foundations for moral and social behavior. Even communist Russia realized this connection, and tried to substitute the religion of Marxism for the others represented in their many ethnic populations.

Religion plays a critical role in all societies because it provides the founding stories that are a fundamental part of the context of our lives. Because they are foundational, learned before we became consciously aware of our place in the world, these stories and the belief systems they foster influence behavior far more than does rational thought. They provide the ideas by which much of mankind live their lives, and for which many die. The belief system provides the cultural foundation for all growing and developing children in their own particular environments. Incorporated from the onset of life these belief systems screen, redefine, focus, and limit the input to the developing cortex. And because they are foundational, as we saw earlier with inbred weaknesses in general, there is a real risk of the founding principles being the seeds of their own destruction.

Religious beginnings

Our time honored explanation of religious movements has been rational man searching for explanations of natural phenomena in a higher power, so our ancestors had a pantheon of gods to cover each base. As they left the mystical stage of development and moved into that of power and authority the concept of one supreme god took over. But few have studied the nature of the "revelation" that is commonly at the foundation of an organized religion. The history of religion, mankind's relationship to God, extends far beyond our own written histories. Julian Jaynes points to the common nature of early peoples being led by the voice of God. Certainly this is the case with the *Iliad* where one can hardly turn a page without reading about one of the Gods talking to and giving direction to one of these early heroes. Sometimes the visit is personal, as when Lord Krishna visited Arjuna as his charioteer, or as the God of *The Old Testament* visited Moses on the mountain. The stories of these interactions are regarded as sacred by those in the culture, whether they be Hebrew with the *Torah*, Moslem with the *Koran*, Hindu with the *Bhagavad-*

Gita; or, since the process continues today, Mormons with the *Book of Mormon,* or followers of *The Urantia Book* or *A Course in Miracles*, to list but a few of the more prominent.

Religions generally begin with such a transcendent visit or voice, or the 'A-Ha'-like insight of a courageous leader like the Buddha under the Bo tree. Like the 'A-Ha' of the mathematicians discussed earlier the insight comes with the profound inner conviction that it is right. And, like the solutions 'given' to mathematicians that solve their problems, the religious insight too usually solves a social problem. And the solution goes on to become first a founding principle of the religion and, if the religion survives, to become the foundation of the culture. Moses brought the Law; Buddha, introspection and the inner life; Jesus, the transforming value of love; and Mohammed, the path of obedience. The particular insight for each was usually triggered by a cultural situation, so the religion originated in its own culture and grew, evolved, or faded depending on its fit with the context of the culture as it evolved—they were successful adaptations.

Jaynes proposes that earlier peoples, who experienced these voices more often, had a barrier that inhibited communication between the cerebral hemispheres in their brains. Speech, for example, is recognized in the auditory center in the *left* side of the brain. When the *right* side of the brain that corresponds to this center is stimulated the person hears someone speaking to them—but no one is there. Hammurabi received his Code, similar to and contemporary with Moses' Ten Commandments, from a God portrayed as sitting on his right shoulder and talking in his right ear. His perceived voice was made real in the form of a God. Neuroscientists today point out that the right hemisphere is the source of far more information and that the role of the left is to screen this information for that which is needed and appropriate.

Jaynes argues that human consciousness originated with the breakdown of this barrier between the two sides of the brain. After the breakdown the rational left hemisphere became aware of the irrational nature of the voices so they became less a force for behavior. Maybe Abraham would have hesitated more when commanded to sacrifice Isaac (or Ishmael in the Islamic rendition of the story), and Agamemnon, his daughter Iphigenia (which the gods demanded before they would send winds allowing him to sail to Troy) had their cerebral hemispheres been more open to each other. After this breakdown the rational left hemisphere became dominant and auditory hallucinations were made pathological, even though surveys today suggest that up to ten percent of a normal population have such experiences.

Jayne's argument however, requires a limited understanding of consciousness. Certainly self-consciousness predated his proposed breakdown because the presence of burial, art, totems, jewelry and story telling would not likely be there without some form of self reflection. What happened at the time of Jaynes's breakdown, and what dramatically changed the way we think, was the development of alphabets and the written word. Written language is almost always left hemisphere dominant so it tends to dampen the intuitive and creative right hemisphere; and as we saw earlier with Whorf and Vygotsky, how we think is greatly influenced by our languages. The breakdown in the bicameral mind more likely represents the ability that came with writing to use the left side of the brain to weed out the rational from all of the information presented by the right.

By the very nature of spiritual insight, however, the rational left hemisphere is overruled. Unlike the insight of Hadamard's mathematicians there is no way to verify spiritual insight except by its congruence with prior spiritual insight. But the revelation often overwhelms prior insight in its power so there is little room for compromise, which leads to a pathway fraught with defensive alignment and a reliance on force and violence.

As much as we like the idea of prophets communicating with one God and guiding us back to Him, there is altogether too much variety both in time and culture to support the idea of a single God—except the one described by Joseph Campbell that wears masks and tells stories designed to confuse. Yet the origin of these insights is still up for discussion and the parallel between the insights of the mathematicians and the prophets suggests an area for examination.

Srinivasa Ramanujan was a mostly self educated but gifted Indian who is responsible for several of today's more useful mathematical theorems. String theory in quantum mechanics and astrophysics, and the ability to determine the value of *pi* to an infinite number of decimal places depend of two of his theorems. Geniuses see things that others don't, but their insights are usually clear enough that others can understand them after the fact. Ramanujan has been called a "magical genius" because his insights are still unfathomable. While biographers in our mechanical/analytical system understandingly hesitate to ascribe his insights to the gods, that is what he claimed—he 'received' most of his theorems in dreams and said they came from the goddess Namagiri. He was unable to prove some of them in the traditional manner, but since they came from the goddess he had the confidence to put them out for others. G. H. Hardy was his mentor and sponsor at Cambridge. He pointed out that even with their divine source a number of Ramanujan's theorums were wrong, yet when Hardy was asked to rank the mathematicians of his day from 1 to 100 based on their genius he gave himself a 25, but Ramanujan got 100. Ramanujan, better than anyone else, shows us that the processes leading to mathematical insights are similar to those leading to religious revelation, and his error rate suggests that we must suspect that all information received in such manner has the same problem.

Religion's alignment

In religions as well as other CASYs there are both defensive and creative alignments. The creative is represented in the initial insights and the variety of the world's great religions that have come from them. But, as with most novelty, after the insight comes the defensive need to protect it. In all CASYs the defensive is most commonly seen in increased size and power and a decrease of creative play. In religion it is represented most commonly by a strong priesthood projecting both rigid dogma and intolerance to offenders.

This is a defensive alignment and it pulls up mostly primitive responses so there is a long history of violence associated with religion from the organized wars like the Crusades and the Crimean War to the less organized coercive conversions to Islam and Catholicism to the destruction of cathedrals and religious art by the Reformers and the Taliban. The most violent reaction was seen in the Inquisition in Spain and other parts of Europe dominated by the Catholic Church. Christian support of Fascism in Italy and National Socialism in Germany and the rise of Islamic jihad are only the latest examples.

This first-hand experience with religious violence has led Europeans to be more skeptical in religious matters—they are much less 'true believers' than are Americans. But as we have seen with Prescott's cultural studies, Miller's examination of German child-rearing practices, and primatologists' studies of the bonobo, there are other factors at play here in this tendency to violence.

How to raise a true believer

Foremost among the factors leading to the tendency to violence is abusing our children, the CASY archetype, by objectifying them. We ignore the critical tie to the mother by putting them in day care as soon as possible so Mom can return to work. We structure activities for them and teach them using the same conditioning tools we use on lab rats. We proscribe gender exploration and in some cultures separate them. In all of this we abuse them and abuse leads to a defensive alignment that is by its nature more prone to the primitive and violent responses that are hard-wired in our reptilian and limbic brains. We see this as the underlying difference between Prescott's peaceful cultures and those with more of a violent tendency. In order to counter this trend we need to see the agents as CASYs, play with their context in friendly ways, and let them adapt.

Allowing agents to evolve in this way underscores the importance of well adjusted children because they are the ones who will do the adapting—they really are our future. As pointed out in the chapters on complexity and education many of our social problems are rooted in our cultural view of children, a view oriented to seeing and treating them in a mechanical way.

Ours is a power centered culture and children handicap the quest for power so we have many ways to keep them occupied and out of our hair. Notably absent in our children's schedules is time for what Bertrand Russell called "fruitful monotony," or what the American Academy of Pediatricians calls child directed play, or what Fred Donaldson calls 'authentic play,' when children are given the time they need to organize their brains, explore their roots, formulate questions, and play with the elements in their environments. It is sacrificed to activities planned to broaden their world, stimulate their growth, and generally make them better able to work in the world, but in all of this planning the child is objectified. We are acting in the mechanical model, focusing on input to improve the result, and we are treating our children as if they were lab rats.

We have already discussed the role of the Prussian educational system and how it leads to the undue and dangerous acceptance of outward authority; as well as the state, this authority can come from fundamental religions—the violence that accompanied the Inquisition is rooted in the same processes as the bombing of an abortion clinic. And we have looked at Prescott's study showing the association of this kind of external control and orientation in early childhood with increased violence in the culture. This is just another example of how a mechanical alignment abuses CASYs and pushes them toward defensive alignment with its increased potential for violence and chaos. As long as agents are subsumed into something larger and more important that objectifies and dehumanizes another we increase the potential for violence.

Most religions support an atmosphere where parents and church play an active role in guiding the children. They do not support the idea of providing children the time and security needed for "fruitful monotony" or authentic play and thereby limit the child's exploration of the world and their alignment on creative novelty. Instead the children tend to be aligned defensively so they flock, identifying with the group, religion, or outside authority. Commonly, as they get older, they have a rebellious period where the "appropriate" behaviors demanded by the authority are trashed. With more time they frequently see themselves as lost. They become subject to the anxiety of *anomie*, where they feel rootless and disconnected. Raised with a rigid foundation of proper behaviors they are now floundering, directionless, and they tend to find control in their lives by a rebirth into the training of their youth. This is the 'born again' pattern followed by President George W. Bush as well as being common in many of our current jihadist suicide bombers.

The Islamic brand is a fundamentalism that has understandably become much more powerful because of the cohesion stimulated by both the Israeli-Palestinian conflict and our invasion of Iraq. Outside threat blocks creative play and pushes the agents together into a cohesive group that is aligned defensively toward the primitive fight or flight response. Just as our military presence in the Arab world has greatly fed the power of their fundamentalist factions, their suicide bombers have fed ours—and the level of violence escalates.

Puritanical, as opposed to pietistic, belief systems hold for the importance of building the City of God in the world and an individual's worth is defined by their conformity to this belief system. The pietist, on the other hand, is concerned with his or her relationship to God on an inner level, and not the outward evidence of that relationship. The more outward, behavioral, or mechanical the orientation the easier it is to justify killing the "evil" enemy. Our early Puritans killed the witches, and just as Islamic fundamentalist bin Laden called for war on "The Great Satan," Christian fundamentalist Pat Robertson called for the assassination of Hugo Chavez. "Bring 'em on," said our born again President.

Fundamentalism itself, in most of its forms, is a defensive adaptation to perceived threats. In Christian fundamentalism the threats came from Darwinism and the Biblical criticism made possible by developments in language analysis. In the latter part of the 19th Century church leaders met in many conferences and came to accept the defining principles for what it was to be a "Christian." These included the divine origin and literal accuracy of the Bible and the Biblical account of creation.

Similar arguments within Islam in the early 19th Century led to the establishment of Wahhabism, the "Enforcers of the Law," in Saudi Arabia, commonly seen as the most fundamental of the varieties of Islam. Religious fundamentalism, both Christian and Islamic brands, is grounded in the fear of having a false foundation, a fear that leads to a defensive alignment that restricts the ability of the agent to play with their elements to find their own path.

Obedience to church authority, orthodoxy, becomes important and is measured by outward conformity to rigid rules as the alignment of the system becomes more rigid and defensive. Dancing is denied to Baptists, as coffee and tea are to Mormons, and for the Wahhabis, "Every innovation is a going astray." When confronted with the relatively harmless nature of these activities the answer is that obedience to God/Allah is the sign of the faithful.

As pointed out earlier, children raised in an authoritarian environment often go through a rebellious period that is usually followed by an awakened, *born again,* commitment to the religion of their youth. We are all familiar with this in Christianity and the situation is similar in obedience and rule dominated Islam. Jihad, the battle for Islam, is most often defined as the internal struggle that we all go through in trying to keep ourselves from 'sinning,' or from self defeating or self destructive behaviors. But in Wahhabism it is defined as an external battle for Islam against outside forces; and it is one of the pillars of the faith.

The fundamentalism of Nazi Germany is another prime example of this dynamic and its association with violence. It was in many ways a religion with a charismatic leader, Hitler, a church that led to salvation, the Third Reich, and an evil opposition, the Jews. Fundamentalism originates from a defensive alignment where an enemy is of necessity created to promote cohesiveness in the community. The Third Reich needed and created an enemy on which to focus their problems, and the Jews filled the need. This is not to equate President Bush and his creation of an enemy by his "axis of evil" speech with the evils of Nazi Germany, but just to show that the dynamic is all too common and easily accessible to all of us in the primitive parts of our brains, especially when that brain is fundamentalistic and mechanical in its organization.

It is in the more primitive parts of our brains that these dynamics originated. Frans de Waal argues, after years of primate studies, that moral behavior originated as early primate bands grouped together for protection. It is unfortunate, he points out, that this 'good' social behavior is rooted in the defensive alignment that leads to a pronounced distinction between the *in* group and the *other*, and that such a distinction, while driving civilization also drives conflict.

As discussed in the chapter on education the defensive mindset is fostered even further in conditioned learning and content driven education. Bonhöffer and Miller argued that the holocaust was allowed by a society where a mechanical alignment required that our children be unquestioning in their obedience to authority. So citizens in Nazi Germany did not speak out when the sick and infirm were found missing—and communists and Jews followed. Opposition to authority in such circumstances is hesitant because, just as in our own McCarthy era, opposing authority was likely to get one included into one of these *other* groups.

As long as this dynamic is not consciously countered in our schools, churches, and media—in the stories we tell—we risk continued polarization, continued dehumanization of the other, and continued violence. Countering these forces with stories that share human values, foibles, and humor will go far in creating the increased number of variables that can push the attractors that are our various cultures into the strange attractor that better allows an expanded evolution.

Honoring creativity in religion

While a defensive alignment in religion leads to a strong priesthood, rigid dogma, fundamentalism, and violence, creating a safe place for religious exploration leads to creativity, openness, and tolerance. In the Reformation the power of the single church was overcome. The few hundred years that followed saw the origin of our major Protestant churches and many other independent churches as well. George Fox established the Quakers on a foundation of peacefully helping one's neighbor that has grown into one of the most widespread and effective non-governmental aid agencies in the world. In America Ellen White started the Adventists, Mary Baker Eddy, the Christian Scientists, and Joseph Smith, the Mormons. While many of these innovations were accompanied by some violence it has gotten less as the pot has become more diluted and the groups less cohesive.

Many of these early reformers also wrote books showing often profound wisdom. Apologists for Joseph Smith argue that this unschooled young man in his early 20s could not have written a work on the scale of *The Book of Mormon*. Claiming it to be a translated history of ancient Hebrew immigrants to America the apologists must deal, however, with their own archaeologists who find no corroboration of the story in the ground, with critics that show no such evidence of Hebrew culture, records, or language in America, and to literary critics that put it in 19th Century America. The most cogent argument for its origin puts it with channeled literature.

The spiritual insights that are often present in channeled literature call for an open minded view of their origins. The *Koran* was dictated by Allah and *A Course in Miracles* by Jesus. Both fit into this category, as do many of the interactions with God recorded in the Old Testament. *The Urantia Book* is another recent example of channeled work that, like the others, contains much information and insight, arguably beyond the abilities of their authors.

If not from the gods, and if greater than the person, then where do these insights originate? The *Urantia Book* and *The Book of Mormon* contain information that was talked about in relatively limited circles at the time of writing. Critics of Smith's work argue that he copied it from Solomon Spaulding who proposed the idea of near eastern migrations to Central American because of the similarity of their pyramids, but it is not likely that Smith had access to this work. Beyond the pyramids there is no similarity, but there are religious truths within *The Book of Mormon. The Urantia Book*, written in the 1920s and 30s, but not published until 1955, contains a reference to "enormous dark gravity bodies" that control much of the motion of the galaxies and other systems in our universe. Black holes had been theoretically possible even in Newtonian physics and had been proposed in the 18th Century; but totally ignored in the 19th. Einstein's 1915 general relativity theory reintroduced the possibility of their existence and the concept was refined by Schwarzchild and Chandrasekhar in the 20s and 30s, but few if any outside the inner circle had any understanding of the concept. It wasn't until the late 60s that interest in these astronomical bodies became more widespread, a decade or more after *The Urantia Book* was published. And it wasn't until much more recently and the use of X-ray astronomy that we determined 'black holes' to be at the centers of many of the observed galaxies, including our own, and that they do indeed have a profound effect on their motion.

All of these works fit within the context of the times they were published. *The Urantia Book* speaks much of evolution, the central issue of the early 20th Century, and *A Course in Miracles*, 'given' to a frustrated psychologist working at Columbia University in the 60s, is arguably one of the best self help psychology books available. If these works are from outside of the person of the author, and we rule out a unitary God because of the inconsistencies of His cultural expressions, then a likely source is what Carl Jung called the collective unconscious, or systems theorist Ervin Laszlo calls the Akashic Field.

The field proposes an Internet type of phenomenon that all humanity, and possibly all of life, is hooked into. Any thoughts are automatically deposited here for withdrawal by anyone having a key. And the wisdom seekers from all ages, as well as Hadamard's mathematicians, tell us how to find the key—look inward while in a non-ordinary state of consciousness.

Jerry is a Registered Play Therapist who is trained to give language to the play that is the voice of the child. *Authentic* play is not done at the level of the ego. It is performed in a non-ordinary state of consciousness. The dream healing done in the ancient Asklepiads was in a non-ordinary state of consciousness. Herb Benson's *Relaxation Response*, or what is called simply 'meditation,' is a non-ordinary state of consciousness that Ken Wilbur credits with being the most effective way to move to a higher stage of functioning. There are multitudes of ways to attain this non-ordinary state from the monastic fasting and prayer to the dervish whirling, and from practiced meditation to the controlled hyperventilation that people like Stan Grof call "Breathwork." Jerry calls it play therapy for adults.

This kind of activity amounts to the greatest kind of play that we can do with the elements of our environment because it hooks us in with the collective unconscious where the elements go far beyond our own capacities. This seems to be the kind of activity for which we as humans with our bicameral brains are peculiarly adapted. This is creative adaptation on its highest level that increases the elements in our systems so that they can become the strange attractors that can morph into something new. Through it all we need to remember the three basic rules of life: show up, play the game, and, particularly in consideration of Ramanujan's errors, the last one, don't get hooked on results.

And we also need to remember what life is all about. Perennial wisdom, prophets, and near death experiences point to the purpose of life as learning, and mostly, learning how to love. "Some day," says Pierre Teilhard de Chardin, "after we have mastered the winds, the waves, the tides and gravity, we will harness for God, the energies of love. And then, for the second time in the history of the world, man will have discovered fire." Seeing differently can help.

References and Notes

Preface

For a report of the FDA's announcement on the effects of cold medications on children see the New York Times for 29 September 2007.

Before his untimely death in a mountain climbing accident Dr. Pagels was a leader in the use and application of complexity principles in the sciences. Heinz R. Pagels. *The Dreams of Reason: The Computer and the Rise of the Sciences of Complexity*. Bantam. New York. 1989.

Introduction

Thomas Kuhn's *The Structure of Scientific Revolutions* (University of Chicago, 1962) is one of the most referenced books in the history of science and his use of 'paradigm' made the word almost common place.

Philip Zimbardo. *The Lucifer Effect: Understanding how Good People Turn Evil.* Random House: New York, 2007.

Ken Wilber's comments on the value of meditation in moving up the scale of spiritual development are from his *A Theory of Everything: An Integral Vision for Business, Politics, Science, and Spirituality.* Shambhala, 2001. Independent confirmation comes from Sara Lazar's Harvard study showing the benefits of meditation building the prefrontal cortex, the part of the brain that copes with emergencies if the individual rises above his reptilian brain. Lazar's work and results are available at https://nmr.mgh.harvard.edu/~lazar/

An overview of Reynolds's work is available on line at his web site: www.red3d.com/cwr/boids, but Reynolds doesn't talk much about the application of the rules in areas other than animal flocking behavior.

Chapter 1: Seeing with New Eyes

Franklin is the first American author D. H. Lawrence looks at in his *Studies in Classic American Literature* (Viking Press. New York: 1966). The quote is from page 15. Franklin's mechanical framework is clear, when one has eyes to see it, in J.A. Leo Lemay & P.M. Zall, eds., *Benjamin Franklin's Autobiography: A Norton Critical Edition,* (NY: Norton, 1986).

Information on the political rhetoric that justified our war with Iraq is told in a report prepared for Congressman Waxman in 2004 available at www.bushoniraq.com/iraq_on_the_record_rap.pdf. An in depth study of all the records collected by Charles Lewis and Mark Reading-Smith at The Center for Public Integrity, an organization funded by media interested in the validity of their information, is available at their web site: www.publicintegrity.org/WarCard (both accessed 23 Jan 2008).

The CBS report on veteran suicides was aired 13 November 2007. In looking at the age groups: "One age group stood out. Veterans aged 20 through 24, those who have served during the war on terror. They had the highest suicide rate among all veterans, estimated between two and four times higher than civilians the same age." (http://www.cbsnews.com/stories/2007/11/13/cbsnews_investigates/main3496471.shtml). The story of how they got the reports is of interest also because the government does not track this data. (http://www.cbsnews.com/stories/2007/11/13/cbsnews_investigates/main3498625.shtml).

Healthcare costs and productivity are the topics in *Measuring Efficiency in Health Care: Analytic Techniques and Health Policy,* by Rowena Jacobs, Peter C. Smith and Andrew Street (Cambridge University Press. 1996), and *Complexity, Problem Solving, and Sustainable Societies,* by Joseph Tainter (available online at www.dieoff.org/page134.htm). Tainter's work is from his book, *Getting Down to Earth,* (Island Press. 1996).

Tainter accepts the argument that the primary reason for the drop in productivity is that inexpensive illnesses have been cured with Public Health measures. I doubt this is the reason, or even part of the reason. In a recent conference call dealing with resistant bacterial infections I asked the experts why no one was looking at some low cost substances shown by Japanese studies to decrease the adherence of these deadly bacteria. The rapid and straight-from-the-hip answer was that there are many inexpensive materials out there that may help, but the funding is not available to study them. The reason the system is expensive is not that the cheap solutions have been exhausted, but that the system no longer looks at cheap solutions; the alignment of the system has shifted away from such a search to the defensive pole of assuring a profit. There is also no interest in the current system in looking with new eyes. We consider this a much more telling reason for the decline in productivity.

Alfred Korzybski coined the term "general semantics" and introduced the metaphor "the map is not the territory" in his book, *Science and Sanity* (1933). He had an interest in the error-prone ways we human beings see the world outside us and the problems that often occur when we take shortcuts based on our mental models that lead us down false pathways, i.e., when we confuse the "map" of reality that we carry around in our heads with the territory that is the real thing.

The use of the press and other information media to create the conventional wisdom and cultural consensus is best outlined in the book *Manufacturing Consent: The Political Economy and the Mass Media,* by Edward S. Herman and Noam Chomsky (Pantheon Books: New York, 2002)

Chapter 2: Elementary my Dear Watson—NOT!

While the idea of complex systems likely began with the application of biological concepts by Alfred Lotka in his Elements of Physical Biology, published in 1925, the major force behind the growth of the idea came from the conferences sponsored by the Josiah Macy Foundation in the late 40s and early 50s. Those involved with these conferences included the biologist Karl Ludwig von Bertalanffy, anthropologists Gregory Bateson and Margaret Mead, mathematicians John von Neumann, Norbert Weiner, economist Kenneth E. Boulding and many others. They were chaired by psychiatrist Warren McCulloch. A brief history of the interplay between the various disciplines of cybernetics, systems theory, and systems dynamics in the origin of complexity theory is "The Genesis of Complexity," by Ralph Abraham, available online at www.ralph-abraham.org/articles/MS%23108.Complex/complex.pdf.

An excellent definition of CASY comes from Kevin Dooley from Arizona State University, but notice the glaring, to us anyway, absence of any recognition that living things are included. (http://www.eas.asu.edu/~kdooley/casopdef.html Accessed 4/19/2006. Last updated 10/26/1996.)

Complex Adaptive Systems: A Nominal Definition. The complexity paradigm uses systemic inquiry to build fuzzy, multivalent, multi-level and multi-disciplinary representations of reality. Systems can be understood by looking for patterns within their complexity, patterns that describe potential evolutions of the system. Descriptions are indeterminate and complimentary, and observer dependent. Systems transition naturally between equilibrium points through environmental adaptation and self-organization; control and order is emergent rather than predetermined (Dooley, et al. 1995; Lewin, 1992; Waldrop, 1992).

The operational model of the complexity paradigm is a complex adaptive system (CAS). Example of CAS would include economies, ecologies, weather, traffic, social organizations, and cultures, to name but a few. While many writers and researchers have studied CAS, a concise nominal definition does not exist. I have forged theory from the works of [Murray] Gell-Mann (1994), [John] Holland

(1995), [Erich] Jantsch (1980), [Humberto] Matur[a]na and [Francisco] Varela (1992), and [Ilya] Prigogine and [Isabelle] Stengers (1984). The essential principles of CAS have been taken from each of these works and synthesized into a single description. The description is purposefully concise. A more lengthy description, with application to business organizations, is contained in the forthcoming paper "A Complex Adaptive Systems Model of Organizational Change," by myself, to appear in the new journal Nonlinear Dynamics, Psychology, & Life Science.

A CAS behaves/evolves according to three key principles: order is emergent as opposed to predetermined, the system's history is irreversible, and the system's future is often unpredictable. The basic building blocks of the CAS are agents. Agents are semi-autonomous units that seek to maximize some measure of goodness, or fitness, by evolving over time. Agents scan their environment and develop schema representing interpretive and action rules. These schema are often evolved from smaller, more basic schema. These schema are rational bounded: they are potentially indeterminate because of incomplete and/or biased information; [t]hey are observer dependent because it is often difficult to separate a phenomenon from its context, thereby identifying contingencies; and they can be contradictory. Schema exist in multitudes and compete for survival.

If all of this goes over your head then just think of a little child.

John Holland is one of the more notable figures in our early understanding of CASYs. He has built rudimentary adaptive systems using many variables and finds basins of interest (attractors), but nothing on the scale of living systems. See pages 229-31 in his *Emergence from chaos to order.* Perseus Press. Reading, MA. 1998.

The different stages of consciousness developed by Ken Wilber, Clare Graves, and their colleagues are explained in all of Wilber's more recent works as well as at his Integral Institute. It is the central theme of his, *A The-*

ory of Everything: An Integral Vision for Business, Politics, Science and Spirituality, (Shambhala, 2001). A simpler and shorter version is "Find your stage of consciousness," by John Lamy, published in the magazine *Spirituality and Health*, (2008, Jan-Feb;11(1):35-39,67).

One of the more interesting accounts of the Phocaeans knowledge of the world is in Peter Kingsley's *Reality*, (The Golden Sufi Center. 2003).

For a discussion of complexity from the viewpoint of combinatorial possibilities and computational abilities see Philip Anderson's presentation at the Second International Conference on Complex Systems, published in *Unifying Themes in Complex Systems*, Yaneer Bar-Yam and Ali A. Minai eds., (Westview Press. 2004). Elements in a system that network with each other have a number of possible combinations determined by the number of elements raised to the power of that number. A modest ten elements expands to millions of potential combinations. There is also a chess analogy that comes from M. Mitchell Waldrop, *Complexity: The Emerging Science at the Edge of Order and Chaos*. 1992: If one could program a computer to find the best of all possible moves in a chess game it would take something on the order of a billion years for it to decide on one move.

The effect of NAFTA on the Mexican farmer is portrayed by Monica Campbell and Tyche Hendricks in the *San Francisco Chronicle* in their report: "Mexico's corn farmers see their livelihoods wither away: Cheap U.S. produce pushes down prices under free-trade pact," Monday, July 31, 2006. An overview of this problem and how it effects current immigration is in Jeff Faux's article "What to Really do about Immigration", in *The American Prospect*, Jan/Feb 2008.

The importance of novelty and its utilization by the entrepreneur is the focus of Benjamin Powell's *Making Poor Nations Rich: Entrepreneurship and the Process of Economic Development* (Stanford Economics & Finance. 2007) which underscores the role of the entrepreneur in helping economies grow. In discussing the role of complex systems and novelty Peter Senge, of the MIT Sloan School of Management and the Society for Organizational Learning, said:

People as individuals do not create anything. Creation, or bringing something new into existence is always a product of human communities. The closest word that comes to mind on this is love. The real appreciation of the other. The appreciation of the quality of our relationship. As far as I am concerned, the quality of thinking in organizations is very, very strongly influenced by the quality of relationship. (In Yaneer Bar Yam and Ali A. Minai, eds., *Unifying Themes in* Complex Systems. Vol.2., Westview Press, Perseus Books, 2004, p.254).

The self sacrificing role of bacteria in making cellular life possible is part of what is called symbiosis and is the focus of Lynn Margulis's *Symbiosis As a Source of Evolutionary Innovation: Speciation*, (MIT Press, Boston. 1991). It also exemplifies their creative alignment. Their defensive alignment is represented by the fact that bacteria can speed up their rate of mutation and we don't know how or why. The mechanisms behind it are a focus of much current research. See, for just one example, the article by Ingegerd Gustafsson, Maria Sjölund, Erik Torell, Marie Johannesson, Lars Engstrand, Otto Cars and Dan I. Andersson in the *Journal of Antimicrobial Chemotherapy* ((2003) 52, 645-650), entitled, "Bacteria with increased mutation frequency and antibiotic resistance are enriched in the commensal flora of patients with high antibiotic usage".

The National Intelligence Estimate for 2004 is available at http://dni.gov/press_releases/20070717_release.pdf (accessed 26 March 2008).

Craig Reynolds came up with 'boids' in 1986. There are excellent programs on the Internet showing them in action that are found just by searching "boids".

Not much has been done to spread his model to promote a better understanding of CASYs but there is an excellent article to that effect in the Wikipedia.

The most notable commentator on the failures of the mechanical model in healthcare is likely to be Paul Plsek, who pointed out that all of the regulatory efforts aimed at fixing our health care system failed because the were mechanically based. See his Appendix B in the Institute of Medicine's *Crossing the Quality Chasm,* (National Academies Press. 2001). This is also where he discusses his 'rules' for working with complex systems.

"Man is a machine," comes from Jacques Monod. *Chance and Necessity: An Essay on the Natural Philosophy of Biology,* (New York. Knopf. 1974), page ix in the Introduction.

One of the more readable (most of the time) books giving broad coverage to the problems associated with the analytical approach to treating ecosystems is *Panarchy: Understanding transformations in human and natural systems,* edited by Lance Gunderson and C. S. Holling and published by the Center for Resource Economics of Washington D.C. through Island Press in 2002. The contributors look at a broad variety of ailing ecosystems and show how the analytical approach has not helped them. They call it the trap of the expert: ...much of our expertise loses a sense of the whole in the effort to understand the parts." (p. 7)

Books on creativity come from Mihalyi Csikszentmihalyi: *Creativity: Flow and the psychology of discovery and invention,* (Harper Collins. New York. 1996), *Flow: The Psychology of Optimal Experience,* (Harper Collins. New York. 1990); Graham Wallas, The Art of Thought, published in 1926, and from Jacques Hadamard, *The Psychology of Invention in the Mathematical Field,* (Princeton University Press. 1945). The discussion about Einstein's parietal lobes and the muscular play they controlled comes from Louis Cozolino, *The Neuroscience of Psychotherapy,* (W. W. Norton & Co. New York. 2002). Interestingly Resa

Steindel Brown in her memoir about education, *A Call to Brilliance*, tells of her mathematically gifted daughter whose orientation to mathematics was also centered on the movement and balance of the human body. One wonders how common this may be.

Ori Brafman and Rod A. Beckstrom in *The Starfish and the Spider: the Unstoppable Power of Leaderless Organizations,* (Portfolio Hardcover. 2006) show the differences between self-organizing and mechanical systems.

Health care sector lobbying is from the *Wall Street Journal of* July 10, 2006, in an article entitled "Lobbying Dollars:

Despite the wave of lobbying scandals, the money keeps rolling in to try influence the legislative and executive branches.

PoliticalMoneyLine.com reports that federal lobbying totaled $1.2 billion in the last half of 2005, the first time such expenses have exceeded $200 million a month. For the full year, federal lobbying topped $2.36 billion, according to the Internet tracking service.

Leading the biggest contributors in the second half of 2005 was Health care, at $183.3 million.

Sara Jo(sephine) Baker. *Fighting for Life,* (Robert Hale, Ltd. 1940). Her account of the epidemic is Chapters 4 and 5 (pages 76-123).

Chapter 3: Incest in the System

The two major books dealing with pharmaceutical-healthcare incest, without calling it that, are, Angell, M., *The Truth About the Drug Companies: How They Deceive Us and What to Do About It,* (Random House. 2004), and Kassirer, J. P., *On the Take: How Medicine's Complicity with Big Business Can Endanger Your Health,* (Oxford Univ. Press. 2004). These books look at the problem from the viewpoint of errors of commission; they look at errors that the incestuous relationship has caused. T. Colin Campbell's, *The China Study*, referenced earlier, discusses a few errors of omission, where the interests of the system closed off the introduction of contrary and potentially cross-pollinating information.

Dr. Graham's report on Vioxx and its increased risk for heart attack is available at: www.fda.gov/CDER/DRUG/infopage/vioxx/vioxxgraham.pdf, and his need to go outside the FDA is at: www.medicalnewstoday.com/medicalnews.php?newsid=16846, (both accessed 4 Dec 2006). The best estimates for the number of heart attacks varies from 88,000 to 139,000, and the mortality from those events from 30 to 40% (from the Government Accountability Project).

The budget for Health and Human Services is at http://www.hhs.gov/budget/ (accessed 5/25/07).

The WHO publication on malaria is at http://www.who.int/malaria/docs/TreatmentGuidelines2006.pdf. (Accessed 5/25/07).

Chapter 4: Of Germs and Men

The primary material for this chapter comes from Paul Ewald's *The Evolution of Infectious Disease,* (Oxford University Press, 1994.) and Henry Isenberg's "Pathogenicity and Virulence: Another View," (*Clinical Microbiology Reviews.* 1988 Jan;1(1):40-53.). Ewald shows with many examples how making it harder for bacteria to spread puts evolutionary pressure on them to adapt to being less pathogenic. The opening quote is from his concluding paragraph on page 215. Isenberg questions our traditional understanding of infection where the host and their defenses are not considered. Host responses, Isenberg's phrase for what we have been calling our defenses, play a critical part in who gets infected, how they respond to the infection, and the outcome of their infection.

General Yaalon's comment was reported in the *Washington Post.* Oct. 31, 2003, but a comparison of Israel's policy with Palestine and ours with bacteria is made possible only by realizing that both are CASY, operating on different levels, but following the same rules.

Information on the evolution of bacteria and the rest of advanced life forms comes from conversations with J. William Schopf and his book, *Life's Origins: The Beginnings of Biological Evolution* (University of California Press, 2002).

The shifting alignment of bacteria is portrayed in Assadian O, Daxboeck F, Aspoeck C, *et al.* in "National surveillance of methicillin-sensitive and methicillin-resistant Staphylococcus aureus in Austrian hospitals: 1994-1998" (*Journal of Hospital Infection.* (Nov. 2003);55(3):175-9), where they show that newly resistant bacteria are less virulent; and Adem PV, Montgomery CP, Husain AN, *et al.* in "Staphylococcus aureus sepsis and the Waterhouse-Friderichsen syndrome in children," (*New England Journal of Medicine.* (29 December 2005); 353(26)2820) which shows that the decreased virulence doesn't last very long.

In order for resistant bacteria to maintain their adaptation it needs to be genetically inexpensive, and often it is not. European researchers have been following the growth and spread of antibiotic resistance and find that it correlates with the use of antibiotics. When antibiotic use was decreased in Spain after the immunization for pneumonia was made available they found less antibiotic resistance in Streptococcus pneumoniae; resistance was genetically expensive in this case and when it wasn't needed it got dumped (Oteo J, Lázaro E, de Abajo FJ, Baquero F, Campos J; Spanish Members of the European Antimicrobial Resistance Surveillance System. "Trends in antimicrobial resistance in 1,968 invasive Streptococcus pneumoniae strains isolated in Spanish hospitals (2001 to 2003): decreasing penicillin resistance in children's isolates." *J Clin Microbiol.* 2004 Dec; 42(12): 5571-7).

Promoting the wise and cautious use of antibiotics is in our strategic interest. The problem of resistance is discussed further by D. Livermore in, "The zeitgeist of resistance." (*J Antimicrob Chemother.* 2007 Aug; 60 Suppl 1: i59-61).

Nathan Sharon and Halina Lis wrote an introduction to lectins in the January, 1993 *Scientific American,* entitled "Carbohydrates in Cell Recognition." A more technical and up to date discussion of lectins can be found on the Internet at: http://www.dadamo.com/wiki/wiki.pl/Lectins (accessed 25 Nov 2006). The specific role of lectins in bacterial adhesion and an extensive list of foods that interfere with this adhesion is covered in: Itzhak Ofek, David Hasty, and Ron Doyle. *Bacterial Adhesion to Animal Cells and Tissues.* (ASM Press (American Society for Microbiology), Washington D.C. 2003). This is also the reference listing the power of milk, and especially human breast milk, in interfering with bacterial adhesion.

Sheryl King's work with horses and mannose is in: King SS, Young DA, Nequin LG, Carnevale EM. "Use of specific sugars to inhibit bacterial adherence to equine endometrium in vitro," (*Am J Vet Res.* 2000 Apr; 61(4): 446-9), and King SS, Speiser SA, Jones KL *et al.*, "Equine spermatozoal motility and fertility associated with the incorporation of d-(+)-mannose into semen extender," (*Theriogenology* 2006 Apr 1; 65(6): 1171-9. Epub 2005 Sep 8). The role of the mannose lectin/acrosome is discussed in Gamzu R, Yogev L, Amnon B, Kleiman S, Hauser R, Lessing JB, Paz G, Yavetz H, "The expression of mannose-ligand receptor is correlated with sperm morphology," (*Arch Androl.* 2002 Nov-Dec; 48(6):475-80).

The study on reducing chronic urinary infections with juice extracts is: Kontiokari T, Sundqvist K, Nuutinen M, Pokka T, Koskela M, Uhari M, "Randomised trial of cranberry-lingonberry juice and Lactobacillus GG drink for the prevention of urinary tract infections in women," (*BMJ* 2001 Jun 30; 322(7302): 1571). The reason for the effectiveness of these extracts is given in a letter from Ofek I, Goldhar J, Zafriri D, *et al.*, relating their findings of changes in bowel flora following repeated exposures to these juices: "Anti-Escherichia coli adhesion activity of cranberry and blueberry juices," (*NEJM.* 1991 May 30; 324(22): 1599). Their study with fructose inhibiting this adhesion is: Zafriri D, Ofek I, Adar R, Pocino M, Sharon N, "Inhibitory activity of cranberry juice on adherence of type 1 and type P fimbriated Escherichia coli to eucaryotic cells," (*Antimicrob Agents Chemother* 1989 Jan; 33(1): 92-8).

A group at Laval University in Quebec has done the most work with xylitol induced mutation of oral bacteria: L. Trahan, G. Bourgeau and R. Breton, "Emergence of multiple xylitol-resistant (fructose PTS-) mutants from human isolates of mutans streptococci during growth on dietary sugars in the presence of xylitol," (*J Dent Res.* 1996 Nov; 75(11): 1892-1900). One of the best examples of the long-term benefits seen with repeated exposure to xylitol is: Soderling E, Isokangas P, Pienihakkinen K, et al., "Influence of maternal xylitol consumption on mother-child transmission of mutans streptococci: 6 year follow-up," (*Caries Res.* 2001 May-June; 35(3): 173-7). A study looking at xylitol resistant bacteria in children is: Meurman P, Merilainen L, Pienihakkinen K, *et al.*, "Xylitol-resistant mutans streptococci strains and the frequency of xylitol consumption in young children," (*Acta Odontol Scand.* 2005 Oct; 63(5): 314-6). The Belize studies are those most clearly demonstrating long-term benefits in caries prevention. The initial study was done in an early school setting and lasted for 2 years. It was designed to test the efficacy of various mixes of sugar alcohols in the gums. This first Belize study (Mäkinen KK, Bennett CA, Hujoel PP, Isokangas PJ, Isotupa KP, Pape HR Jr, Mäkinen PL, "Xylitol chewing gums and caries rates: a 40-month cohort study," (*J Dent Res.* 1995 Dec; 74(12): 1904-13)) clearly showed the superiority of xylitol only chewing gums, but it was even further demonstrated when they retuned to look at the children's teeth five years later, with no xylitol during this interval. The permanent teeth that had erupted a year after the child began regularly chewing xylitol sweetened gum were found to have 93% less tooth decay in those teeth five years later. (Hujoel PP, Mäkinen KK, Bennett CA, Isotupa KP, Isokangas PJ, Allen P, Mäkinen PL, "The optimum time to initiate habitual xylitol gum-chewing for obtaining long-term caries prevention," (*J Dent Res.* 1999 Mar; 78(3): 797-803)). The most likely reason for this benefit goes back to the ability of xylitol to block adhesion. If the adherence of S. mutans is blocked while the dental biofilm is forming they are not going to be a part of that biofilm and these teeth are not going to be as open to decay.

The role of xylitol in bacterial adherence was studied by Paul Naaber for Clostridium difficile (Naaber P, Mikelsaar RH, Salminen S, Mikelsaar M, "Inhibition of adhesion of Clostridium difficile to Caco-2 cells," *FEMS Immuno Med Microbiol.* 1996 Jul; 14(4): 205-9.). Its effect on nasal pathogens was first demonstrated in the study mentioned earlier done by the same group that did the cranberry-lingonberry study to prevent urinary infections (Kontiokari T, Uhari M, Koskela M. "Antiadhesive effects of xylitol on otopathogenic bacteria," *J Antimicrob Chemother.* 1998 May; 41(5): 563-5). Its greatest effect was on the bacteria *Streptococcus pneumoniae*, which is the major pathogen for upper respiratory infections as well as pneumonia. This family of bacteria is responsible for thousands of deaths annually in the U.S. and many more around the world, and taming it would be a major blessing for mankind. And it is possible because Trahan and his colleagues at Laval showed that it shares the same genetic makeup for dealing with xylitol as does its cousin *S. mutans*, which dental researchers have tamed (Benchabane H, Lortie LA, Buckley ND, Trahan L, Frenette M, "Inactivation of the Streptococcus mutans fxpC gene confers resistance to xylitol, a caries-preventive natural carbohydrate sweetener," J Dent Res. 2002 Jun; 81(6): 380-6). Further research with xylitol is being done currently by Garth James and his colleagues at the biofilm engineering group at the University of Montana, who report that it has a broad spectrum ability to disrupt bacterial biofilm (personal communication October, 2006). They also have an informative web site on the nature of biofilms at www.erc.

montana.edu. M.-C. Badet presented a paper on the "Effect of xylitol on a model of oral biofilm" at the conference for the International Association of Dental Research, March 22, 2007, in New Orleans with information confirming that of the group at Montana in respect specifically to dental bacteria. The abstract is available at http://iadr.confex.com/iadr/2007orleans/techprogram/abstract_88048.htm. (Accessed 6 Feb 2007). The most recent summary of information about xylitol's success at preventing caries is: Peldyak J, Mäkinen KK, "Xylitol for caries prevention," (*J Dent Hyg*. 2002 Fall; 76(4): 276-85). My article (Jones AH, "The next step in infectious disease: taming bacteria," *Medical Hypotheses*. 2003 Feb; 60(2): 171-4) is based on the published works already mentioned.

The usefulness of milk in decreasing bacterial adherence is from Itzhak Ofek, David Hasty, and Ron Doyle, *Bacterial Adhesion to Animal Cells and Tissues,* which was referenced earlier when introducing the importance of bacterial adhesion. The information about the funding of the research being cut for galactose and B. pertussis was from a 2001 conversation with David Zopf, chief scientific officer at Neose Technologies until January, 2008.

Chapter 5: Symptoms, Symptoms, and more Symptoms

The China Study is an interesting read not only for its dietary advice, but for its accounting of the barriers presented by our profitable food industries to any information seen as hostile to their profits and because our food is a major part of the context to which we all adapt (T. Colin Campbell, Thomas M. Campbell II, John Robbins, and Howard Lyman. *The China Study: The Most Comprehensive Study of Nutrition Ever Conducted and the Startling Implications for Diet, Weight Loss and Long-term Health.* Benbella Books, 2006).

An excellent discussion of some of our many adaptations is in George C. Williams and Randolph M. Nesse, *Why We Get Sick: The New Science of Darwinian Medicine.*

1994. Because Dr. Nesse is a psychiatrist much of the book looks at the place of depression in promoting adaptation. It's introduction of symptoms as defensive adaptations, manipulations by infecting agents, or side effects is a key concept in understanding evolutionary medicine.

The account of Osteopathic Medicine's success at treating the flu is documented by Smith, R. Kendrick, M.D., D.O. "One Hundred Thousand Cases of Influenza with a Death Rate of One–Fortieth of that Officially reported under conventional medical treatment." The paper was read at the Annual Convention of the American Association of Clinical Research, New York City, Oct. 18, 1919, and published in Journal of the American Osteopathic Association 1920, 19: 172-175. It was reprinted in that journal in 2000, (100: 320–323). There has been criticism as to whether or not manipulation was the only difference and Harold Magoun Jr, DO, FAAO, FCA, DO, ED (Hon) in his letter: "More About the Use of OMT During Influenza Epidemics," published in the *Journal of the American Osteopathic Association*, October 2004, 104;(10):406-407, pointed out the difference in the use of drugs that block our normal defenses. Osteopathic medicine also had few hospitals at that time so patients were not as likely to be put in large wards as would be the case in larger cities.

Using electron micrographs Christer Svensson and his colleagues in Sweden looked at the tissues in the back of the nose during and after a histamine challenge and concluded—it's a defense; (Svensson C, Andersson M, Grieff L, Persson CG. Nasal mucosal endorgan hyperresponsiveness. American Journal of Rhinology, 1998, Jan-Feb; 12(1):37-43).

More than any other person the demise of bloodletting was due to studies by Pierre Charles Alexandre Louis in 1835. He looked at its use in cases of pneumonia, definitely in the infection causing inflammation side of the spectrum. More on this subject is at: http://www.jameslindlibrary.org/trial_records/19th_Century/louis/louis_commentary.html

Chapter 6: GO! Defense

Gastrointestinal defenses

The World Health Organizations publications on the treatment of diarrhea include: *The management of diarrhoea and use of oral rehydration therapy,* (1985); and *The rational use of drugs in the management of acute diarrhoea in children,* 1990; and many others reflecting the serious and ongoing severity of this problem, especially in developing nations. The pumping nature of the sodium-glucose transport system and the molecular proportions needed to turn it on were reported in: Meinild A, Klaerke DA, Loo DD, Wright EM, Zeuthen T. "The human Na+-glucose cotransporter is a molecular water pump." *J Physiol.* 1998 Apr 1; 508(Pt 1): 15-21. The initial study showing the benefits of oral rehydration in Bangladesh is: Sack RB, Cassells J, Mitra R, *et al.* "The use of oral replacement solutions in the treatment of cholera and other severe diarrhoeal disorders." *Bull World Health Organ.* 1970; 43(3): 351-60. "Water with sugar and salt." *Lancet.* 1978 Aug 5; 2(8083): 264, is where the Lancet editors speak of oral rehydration as one of the most significant medical advances of the 20th Century, and its lamentable use in the United States is reported in: Reis EC, Goepp JG, Katz S, Santosham M. "Barriers to the use of oral rehydration therapy." *Pediatrics.* 1994 May; 93(5): 708-11.

Genitourianry defenses

The role of bacterial biofilm in protecting the female genital tract was first noted by PA Domingue, K Sadhu, JW Costerton, K Bartlett and AW Chow: "The human vagina: normal flora considered as an in situ tissue-associated, adherent biofilm." *Genitourinary Medicine*, 1991 Jun; 67(3):226-231. Recognition of the beneficial effects of this biofilm led to looking at what happens when it is removed by Scholes D, Daling JR, Stergachis A, Weiss NS, Wang SP, Grayston JT, "Vaginal douching as a risk factor for acute pelvic inflammatory disease." *Obstet Gynecol.* 1993 Apr; 81(4): 601-6. The production of defense factors by this biofilm is discussed in Aroutcheva A, Gariti D, Simon M, *et al.* "Defense factors of vaginal lactobacilli." *Am J Ob & Gyne.* 2001, Jan 20; 185(2): 261-354. To quote from their results: "Bacteriocin activity was tested on 4 strains of Gardnerella vaginalis. Approximately 80% of the lactobacilli tested produced bacteriocin that inhibited growth of G vaginalis. Six of the strains did not produce bacteriocin. Thirteen strains produced all 3 defense factors, whereas the others lacked 1 or 2 properties."

The position paper from the Society for Adolescent Medicine on sex education is: Santelli J, Ott MA, Lyon M, Rogers J, Summers D. "Abstinence-only education policies and programs: A position paper of the Society for Adolescent Medicine." *J Adoles Health.* 2006 Jan; 38(1): 83-87. A fact that underscores the importance of education is that while most young people are interested in preserving their fertility a Toronto, Canada study in 18 of their high schools showed that 94% of their seniors did not know that sexually transmitted diseases often cause sterility. This study was done by Susan Quach and Clifford Librach: "Infertility knowledge and attitudes in urban high school students." *Fertil Steril.* 2008 Mar 3, (E published ahead of print).

See www.janeelliott.com for more about her teaching the basics of discrimination, and www.prisonexp.org, or Zimbardo's book, *The Lucifer Effect: Understanding how Good People Turn Evil*, for more about his prison experiment. Hilgard's experience with conjoint hypnosis at Stanford is mentioned in Araoz, Daniel L, "Hypnosis in group-therapy. *International Journal of Clinical and Experimental Hypnosis,*" 1979 Jan; 27 (1), 1-13.

Respiratory defenses

Maggie Profet made a name for herself when she pointed out that morning sickness was the woman's body telling her what food was bad for the baby. We believe that her model of asthma as a defense is just as revolutionary, but less known. (Profet M. "The function of allergy: immunological defense against toxins." *Q Rev Biol.* 1991

Mar;66(1):23-62.)

David Edwards showed that some people exhale high volumes of bacteria and that the inhalation of saline was adequate to prevent this epidemiologic problem. (Edwards DA, Man JC, Brand P, Katstra JP, *et al.* "Inhaling to mitigate bioaerosols." *PNAS* Dec. 14, 2004, 101(50): 17383-388.) The role of environmental humidity in respiratory conditions is well documented in Arundel AV, Sterling EM, Biggin JH, Sterling TD. "Indirect health effects of relative humidity in indoor environments." *Environ Health Perspect* 1986; 65:351–61.

Information on the ear infections among the native children in Alaska is mostly from interviews with hearing specialists in Nome and Kotzebue who listen to and deal with the indigenous people there as they try to cope with the results of those infections.

The side-effect study showing the doubling of infection and asthma rates was done for the drug Loratadine. It was in the *Physician's Desk Reference* under Loratadine until the 2002 edition.

The Dade County Coroner's study of drowning victims is reported in: Copeland AR. "An assessment of lung weights in drowning cases. The Metro Dade County experience from 1978 to 1982." *Am J Forensic Med Pathol.* 1985 Dec; 6(4): 301-4. I am not aware of anyone reflecting on the identical mechanisms of the bronchoconstriction found in these drowning victims and that of asthma. The major epidemiologic study looking at asthma is from the CDC (Mannino DM, Homa DM, Pertowski CA, Ashizawa A, Nixon LL, Johnson CA, Ball LB, Jack E, Kang DS. Surveillance for asthma—United States, 1960-1995. MMWR CDC Surveill Summ. 1998 Apr 24; 47(1): 1-27), but their data doesn't extend to before 1970. A study from Charleston went back further (Crater DD, Heise S, Perzanowski M, Herbert R, Morse CG, Hulsey TC, Platts-Mills T. Asthma hospitalization trends in Charleston, South Carolina, 1956 to 1997: twenty-fold increase among black children during a 30-year period. Pediatrics 2001

Dec; 108(6): E97). They showed a stable baseline from 1956 to 1970.

David Edwards' study of vaporized saline and exhaled bacteria is: "Inhaling to mitigate bioaerosols." *PNAS* Dec. 14, 2004, 101(50): 17383-388.

Jerry Klein heads the Boston group that studies many aspects of otitis and is a leading researcher in pediatric infectious disease. His article, "The Burden of Otitis," which discusses the healthcare costs of this illness and alludes to the educational ones is in *Vaccine.* 2000 Dec 8; 19 Suppl 1:S2-8.

Several long term studies on the minimal effect of tubes on hearing impairment are summarized in: Lous J, Burton MJ, Felding JU, *et al.* "Grommets (ventilation tubes) for hearing loss associated with otitis media with effusion in children." *Cochrane Database Syst Rev.* 2005 Jan 25; (1): CD001801.

Matti Uhari was the lead researcher looking at chewing gum and ear infections: Uhari M. *et al.* "Xylitol chewing gum in prevention of otitis media. *British Medical Journal.* 1996 Nov 9; 313(7066): 1180-84. His group was also the one that looked at the use of cranberry and lingonberry extracts to prevent recurrent UTIs. The only criticism to his chewing gum study was that he used sugar sweetened gum, known to cause tooth decay, as the blind. Unfortunately chewing enough xylitol sweetened gum to prevent only 42% of ear infections winds up costing more for the gum than treating the ear infections with antibiotics, but this was the study that got us thinking about how to improve its delivery.

Xylitol

The first of the Turku sugar studies is: Scheinin A, Makinen KK, Ylitalo K. *et al.* "Turku sugar studies. I. An intermediate report on the effect of sucrose, fructose and xylitol diets on the caries incidence in man." *Acta Odontol Scand.* 1974; 32(6): 383-412. An excellent summary of the intervening research is found in: Peldyak J. Makinen

KK. "Xylitol for caries prevention." *J Dent Hyg.* 2002 Fall; 76(4): 276-85.

The Finnish researchers' study of adherence of pathogens in the nose is reported in, Kontiokari T, Uhari M, Koskela M. "Antiadhesive effects of xylitol on otopathogenic bacteria." *J Antimicrob Chemother.* 1998 May; 41(5): 563-5. When researchers at the University of Iowa read this study they thought using xylitol nasally may help children with cystic fibrosis. The report of their findings is: Zabner J, Seler MP, Launspach JL et al. "The osmolyte xylitol reduces the salt concentration of airway surface fluid and may enhance bacterial killing." *Proceedings of the National Academy of Sciences USA.* 2000 Oct 10; 97(21): 11614-9.

The study looking at concentrated solutions that wind up stimulating our own normal washing is: Silber G, Proud D, Warner J, *et al.* "In vivo release of inflammatory mediators by hyperosmolar solutions." *Am Rev Respir Dis.* 1988 Mar; 137(3): 606-12. It is important to remember that the "inflammatory mediators" are those that trigger the washing, and that this response, like the inflammatory response we blocked with blood-letting, is a defense.

Chapter 7: Shopping for Healthcare: Shop 'til you Drop

Barbara Starfield is a capable critic of our system. She goes beyond the well known shortcomings to shed light on some of its more hidden faults. She points out that treatment in the system was the third leading cause of death in the U. S. (Starfield, B. "Is U. S. Health Really the Best?" *JAMA* 2000 Jul 26: 284(4): 483-85.) She also compared our health care system with that of eleven others using sixteen different indicators of health care efficiency showing that we are consistently among the worst. (Starfield B. *Primary Care: Balancing Health Needs, Services and Technology.* New York, NY. Oxford Univ. Press.1998.) The fact that our health is not as good at that in socialized England is born out in Banks J, Marmot M, Oldfield Z,

Smith JP. "Disease and disadvantage in the United States and England." *JAMA*. 2006 May 3; 295(17): 2037-45. The conclusions of the Institute of Medicine regarding the problems in our systems are reported in their publication: *Crossing the Quality Chasm*, referenced earlier. The World Health Organization compared all nations in their "World Health Report 2000" accessed on their web site at http://www.who.int. There are many published reports comparing performance of developed countries in a variety of health related areas. Most are available at the OECD (Organization of Economically Developed Countries) web site www.oecd.org. One of the more up-to-date surveys of health indicators in the U. S. is the Commonwealth Fund's report: "Why Not the Best? Results from a National Scorecard on U.S. Health System Performance," available at http://www.cmwf.org/publications/publications_show.htm?doc_id=401577 (accessed 12/1/2006). The CIA data on comparative health measures, which include infant mortality, is at https://www.cia.gov/cia/publications/factbook/rankorder/2091rank.html (accessed 12/1/2006).

Sara Jo Baker's account of the Brooklyn pediatricians is on page 157 of her book *Fighting for Life*, referenced earlier.

The problems associated with health insurance are well covered by Rick Mayes', *Universal Coverage: The Elusive Quest for National Health Insurance.* Ann Arbor, MI. Univ. of Michigan Press: 2005.

Boid rules in the marketplace

The play on Acton's aphorism is from John Patrick Diggins, "The -Ism that failed" in *The American Prospect*, 1 Dec 2003. The benefits of marketplace medicine are recounted in *Market-Driven Healthcare: Who Wins, Who Loses in the Transformation of America's Largest Service Industry*, by Regina E. Herzlinger (Perseus Books: New York, NY. 1997), and one aspect of the down side, the challenge to academic medical centers, is explained in

"Marketplace medicine: Rx for disaster," by Leon Eisenberg (*Academe*, Nov/Dec 1999). More information on the shadow side of capitalism is "The Good Company: A sceptical look at corporate social responsibility," a special report in *The Economist* (January 22, 2005). See especially "Profit and the public good," (15-19) for a theoretical discussion of the beneficial aspects of Adam Smith's invisible hand. For an argument that the hand is not functioning today see Joseph Stiglitz "There is no Invisible Hand," an op-ed piece published in *The Guardian* (20 December 2002). The role of good governance in empowering the "voice and accountability" that deals with transparency and the limitations on the abuses that so often accompany asymmetric information is in: Daniel Kaufmann, Aart Kraay, and Massimo Mastruzzi. "Governance Matters VI: Aggregate and Individual Governance Indicators 1996-2006." The World Bank. Washington, DC.

Local Support and the Plasmid Model

The Ornish program for reversing heart disease is currently being tested by a major insurance company, but referrals to it remain few when one considers the size of the problem. His program is presented in: Ornish, Dean. *Doctor Dean Ornish's Program for Reversing Heart Disease.* Random House, New York: 1990.

Yaneer Bar-Yam's ideas on healthcare are found in his "Understanding the Healthcare/Medical System Crisis," a report from his New England Complex Systems Institute in June of 2003 (NECSI Technical Report 2003-06-01), and from his *Making Things Work* (Knowledge Press, 2004), Chapters 10 and 11. A significant part of his solution is to have two sections to our healthcare system.

Regarding the causes of autism the reference for facial recognition as the only anatomic defect consistent to the autism spectrum disorders see: Schultz RT. "Developmental deficits in social perception in autism: the role of the amygdala and fusiform face area," *Int J Dev Neurosci* 2005 Apr-May; 23(2-3): 125-41. A recent study looking at the association of autism with exposure to television is: "Does Television Cause Autism?" By Michael Waldman of the Johnson Graduate School of Management at Cornell University. This report is published on the Internet at: http://www.johnson.cornell.edu/faculty/profiles/waldman/autpaper.html (accessed 3 Dec 2006). The recommendation of the American Academy of Pediatricians regarding early television exposure was made in 1998. The discussion continues with a recent review: Certain LK, Kahn RS. Prevalence, correlates, and trajectory of television viewing among infants and toddlers. *Pediatrics.* 2002 Apr; 109(4): 634-42.

Many have criticized the waste in our healthcare system, but few have come close to putting a dollar amount to it. This is well done by these alternative oriented primary care physicians as recorded by Sarnat RL, Winterstein J, & Cambron JA in "Clinical Utilization and Cost Outcomes from an Integrative Medicine Independent Physician Association: An additional 3 year update," published in *Journal of Manipulative and Physiological Therapeutics.* 2007, May; 30(4): 263-269.

The Canadian study looking at the increased mortality of "for profit hospitals" is in the *Canadian Medical Journal* (2002 May 28; 166(11): 1399–1406.) led by P.J. Devereaux and entitled, "A systematic review and meta-analysis of studies comparing mortality rates of private for-profit and private not-for-profit hospitals."

The story of water as a critical commodity is the subject of, *Water Wars: privatization, pollution, and profit,* by Vandana Shiva (South End Press. Cambridge, MA. 2002)

The value and problems of "evidence based medicine" and "randomized clinical trials" are presented well in: Mant D. "Can randomized trials inform clinical decisions about individual patients?" *Lancet* (1999 Feb 27; 353(9154): 743-6), and van Weel C, Knottnerus JA. "Evidence based interventions and comprehensive treatment." *Lancet* (1999 Mar 13; 353(9156): 916-18). The

Citizen's Council on Health Care has looked at evidence based medicine and concluded: "The public should not be fooled by the nifty-sounding names. Evidence-based medicine is managed care masquerading as science." Their report is available online: http://www.cchconline.org/pdfreport/, (accessed 2/4/2005).

Dr. Angell's comments on the commodification of healthcare are in: "The Forgotten Domestic Crisis," by Marcia Angell (*New York Times.* Op-Ed, Oct. 13, 2002). The physician response to regulatory changes in the medical marketplace is the topic of the study done for Medicare and found at Centers for Medicare & Medicaid Services (CMS) http://www.cms.hhs.gov/statistics/actuary/physicianresponse/ (Accessed 10/9/2004).

Newt Gingrich's comment on the failure of the third party payer system is quoted by Peter Grier in his *Christian Science Monitor* article of 9 Dec 2003 "Bush signature won't end Medicare debate."

More on the economic pressures to game our systems for our own benefit is discussed in John Kenneth Galbraith. *The Economics of Innocent Fraud.* Houghton Mifflin. 2004.

A few of those looking at the sociological or cultural aspects of illness include: Antonovsky A, "The structural sources of salutogenic strengths," pages 67-104 in C.L. Cooper & R. Payne (Eds.), *Personality and stress: Individual differences in the stress process* (1991) and Kobasa, S. "Personality and resistance to illness," in *American Journal of Community Psychology*, 1979 Aug. 1; 7(4): 413-423.

Chapter 8: No Lab-Rat Left Behind—Education

Peter Levine and Ann Frederick tell the story of the cheetah in the opening paragraphs of their *Waking the Tiger : Healing Trauma : The Innate Capacity to Transform Overwhelming Experiences* (North Atlantic Books, 1997), and Bruce Perry and Maia Szalavitz describe its various stages and its expression in traumatized children in *The Boy Who*

Was Raised as a Dog: And Other Stories from a Child Psychiatrist's Notebook—What Traumatized Children Can Teach Us About Loss, Love, and Healing, (Basic Books, 2007).

John Taylor Gatto. "Against School: How Public Education Cripples our Schools and Why." *Harpers*. 2003, Sep;307(1840):33-38.

Harris's quote is taken from William H. Goetzmann. *The American Hegelians: An Intellectual Episode in the History of Western America*, (Alfred A. Knopf Inc. New York. 1973). The Johns Hopkins lectures are included on pages 300-309. The quote on the subsumption of the individual is from the first lecture; the explanation of how this subsumption is the part of informal and not formal education extends from the first to the second lectures. There is also an excellent account of the influence of this socialist paradigm applied to education by J. Michael Bodi on the web site for the American Association of Behavioral and Social Sciences. It is found at http://aabss.org/journal1998/bodi.htm. (Accessed 11/10/2005).

Reisman. David, Reuel Denney, Nathan Glazer. *The Lonely Crowd A Study of the Changing American Character.* Yale Univ. Press. 1961.

The connection between child rearing practices in Germany and the rise and acceptance of the Nazi party and the holocaust that followed is a theme of psychologists looking at history. It likely begins with Erik Eriksen's *Young Man Luther*, which showed Luther's strict and abusive childhood. It carried on into the 18th and 19th Centuries as witnessed by their school systems; and into the 20th Century as witnessed by the sale of 40 editions of Dr. Daniel Schreber's advice on raising children. Alice Miller refers to Dr. Schreber's principles as poisonous pedagogy, showing how they were devoid of any love and treated the child strictly as an object to be molded into society. Of Dr. Schreber's own children one was a manic depressive written about by Freud, and one committed suicide as a young adult. Miller's article can be found at the web page for the

Journal of Psychohistory at http://www.psychohistory.com/htm/06_politic.html (accessed 19 Dec 2007).

Steven D. Levitt (*Freakonomics*. New York: Harper Collins Pub. Inc. 2005) discusses test statistics showing that teachers cheat for their students when the stakes are high enough.

Feynman, Richard. *Surely Your Joking Mr. Feynman.* Bantam. 1985. Reminiscences edited by Edward Hutchings.

Peter Senge's comments on the importance of loving relationships in a learning environment are from his comments in *Unifying Themes in Complex Systems.* An earlier reference in Chapter 2 includes a quote of the material. Arthur Zajonc is the director of the Center for Contemplative Mind in Society at Amherst College. While there are many articles describing his work they are well summarized in, "Cognitive-Affective Connections in Teaching and Learning: The Relationship between Love and Knowledge," in the Fall, 2006 *Journal of Cognitive Affective Learning*, 3(1):1-9.

Resa Steindel Brown. *A Call to Brilliance.* Fredric press. Thousand Oaks, CA 2006. This book is an odyssey that tells the story of her challenges dealing with her children and their education. Her oldest son learned to read at age nine, but entered college three years later. Her second son outdid that by learning to read at age ten and entering college at eleven. Had they been educated in the public schools they would have been labeled as dyslexic, dysgraphic, and with ADHD. They would have spent their school years drugged and in special education. Her story shows that there are better options, and that they can be included in Public Education. Ms. Brown was involved for several years with the award winning G. T. Waters school in Thousand Oaks, California. Many other students at this school had similar patterns of rapid advancement and early university admission—her story is not just about her own gifted and challenged children.

Jay Boyd Best and his colleague Irvin Rubinstein began their experiments with learning in planarian worms in 1958. The article relating planaria's abilities and their optimal learning environment is, "Protopsychology" in *Scientific American*, Feb. 1962; 208(2): 54-62.

Arne Dietrich teaches at the American University in Beirut, Lebanon and has a major interest in creative thought processes. Most of his articles are available from his web page at http://wwwlb.aub.edu.lb/~ad12/. Of his articles on the subject we found most useful, "The cognitive neuroscience of creativity," in *Psychonomic Bulletin & Review*, 2004, 11: 1011-1026. His work shows that creativity is linked to the cortical structures of the temporal, parietal and occipital lobes which seem to come together in the prefrontal cortex, the part of the brain that is peculiarly human. It should be contrasted with the work of those looking at the neuroanatomy of conditioned learning which show such learning as associated with the basal brain structures. See for example: Zahm DS, Trimble M. "The dopaminergic projection system, basal forebrain macrosystems, and conditioned stimuli." *CNS Spectr.* 2008 Jan; 13(1): 32-40.

Paolo Freire's work is from his *The Pedagogy of the Oppressed* (Herder and Herder. 1972), and Ruby Payne's is from her *A Framework for Understanding Poverty,* (Aha Process, Inc. 2005).

A review of early childhood education and intervention, "Life Chances: The Case for Early Investment in Our Kids," is the focus of the December 2007 issue of *The American Prospect.* Early intervention programs and their results are also well summarized by Dr. Robert Slavin, co-director for the Center of Research and Education for Students Placed at Risk at Johns Hopkins University and chairman of the Success for All Foundation. His comments (at the Second Annual Symposium of the Berkeley Center for the Development of Peace & Well-being sponsored by the Institute for Human Development, UC Berkeley, May 9-10, 2003) are summarized on the Internet at http://

peacecenter.berkeley.edu/Hierarchy_synopsis.pdf. (Accessed Sept. 9, 2006.)

Rosamund S. and Benjamin Zander's argument about the stress of grades is from their *The Art of Possibility* (Penguin, 2002). Alfie Kohn's writing on the same problem is in *The Case Against Standardized Testing: Raising the Scores, Ruining the Schools*, (Heinemann, 2000), and *The Schools Our Children Deserve: Moving Beyond Traditional Classrooms and "Tougher Standards"* (Houghton Mifflin, 1999).

O. Fred Donaldson (*Playing by Heart: The Vision and Practice of Belonging.* Health Communications Inc. Deerfield Beach, FL. 1993) talks about the play of a child being 'authentic play'. The golf story is told by Michael Mendizza of Touch the Future.

"A First Look at the Literacy of America's Adults in the 21st Century," released in Dec. 2205, looks at our nation's literary abilities. It comes from the National Center for Educational Statistics at http://nces.ed.gov/pubsearch/pubsinfo.asp?pubid=2006470.

The estimate of civilian casualties in Iraq is by Gilbert Burnham, Riyadh Lafta, Shannon Doocy, Les Roberts, "Mortality after the 2003 invasion of Iraq: a cross-sectional cluster sample survey." *Lancet.* 2006 Oct 21; 368(9545): 1421-8.

Paul, Gregory S. "Cross-National Correlations of Quantifiable Societal Health with Popular Religiosity and Secularism in the Prosperous Democracies." *Journal of Religion & Society.* Vol. 7, 2005; available on line at: http://moses.creighton.edu/jrs/2005/2005-11.html (accessed 15 April 2008).

James W. Prescott's "Body Pleasure and the Origins of Violence," was published in *The Futurist,* April, 1975. Most of Prescott's writings are available on line through the group touchthefuture.org. The studies looking at the bonobo are in: Frans de Waal, "Bonobo Sex and Society" in *Scientific American* (March 1995), p. 82ff; and those of Alice Miller, referenced above, are from the *Journal of Psy-*

chohistory, Fall 1998 Vol. 20, No. 2. Margaret Mead's work is in her *Coming of Age in Samoa: A Study of Adolescence and Sex in Primitive Societies.* New York: Penguin, 1965.

The study looking at the beneficial effect of cohesion on internal violence is by Robert J. Sampson, Stephen W. Raudenbush, and Felton Earls, "Neighborhoods and Violent Crime: A Multilevel Study of Collective Efficacy," in *Science,* 1997 August 15; 277: 918-924.

The American Academy of Pediatrician's report on the importance of play is by Kenneth Ginsburg M.D., MS.Ed., and the Committee on Communications and Committee on Psychosocial Aspects of Child and Family Health: "The Importance of Play in Promoting Healthy Child Development and Maintaining Strong Parent-Child Bonds," in *Pediatrics,* 2007 Jan; 119(1): 182-191.

Chapter 9: A "Boids" Eye View of Society

Chris Lucas is a British physicist who has written a great deal about the application of complexity in the social world. His web page is calresco.org and this particular quote is from http://www.calresco.org/wp/attrsoc.htm.

Sharansky, Natan. *The Case for Democracy: the power of freedom to overcome tyranny and terror.* Public Affairs, 2004.

Karl Wittfogel. *Oriental Despotism.* 1963. Wittfogel's theme is the association of the geographical context of water use in farming, either irrigation or flooding, with the necessity of a strong central government to control the sharing of the water and/or the reestablishment of flooded property boundaries. The Landmark article, "The Tragedy of the Commons," by Garrett Hardin is in *Science*, (1968 December 13; 162(3859):1243-1248). It is also reprinted at a website maintained by Joseph Tainter and his group at at http://dieoff.org/page95.htm. (Accessed 5/28/07.)

Tainter, Joseph. *The Collapse of Complex Societies.* Cambridge University Press. 1988. There is also much information on the Tainter framework at his website www.dieoff.org. Jared Diamond's work in this area is *Collapse:*

How Societies Choose to Fail or Succeed. Viking. New York. 2005. Gilberto Gallopín's comment is from "Planning for Resilience: Scenarios, Surprises and Branch Points," in *Panarchy: Understanding Transformations in Human and Natural Systems*, edited by Lance Gunderson and C. S. Holling. Island Press. Washington. 2002.

Just how rapidly the economically available fossil fuels are getting priced out is reflected by data from the Natural Resources Defense Council, U. S. Energy Information Administration, U. S. Environmental Protection Agency, and the U. S. Department of Energy. For the cost of a barrel of oil in 1940 one could pump 100 barrels. In the 1990's one barrel of oil could pump 3 barrels in the U. S. and 10 in Saudi Arabia. Biofuels don't provide much relief. Switchgrass to ethanol is the most efficient so far, but requires 420,000 square miles of switchgrass to cover our current needs. Our total cropland is 625,000 square miles. Thanks to *Yes!* Magazine for putting these figures together. See: It Takes Energy to Get Energy, in *Yes!* Summer, 2006: 39. The use of bacteria to generate electricity is told by researchers from the University of Arizona at Tempe at http://www.renewableenergyworld.com/rea/news/story?id=51072 (accessed 2 June 2008).

Marcus Borg. *The Heart of Christianity: Rediscovering a Life of Faith.* Harper Collins. San Francisco, 2003:190.

Carol Gilligan's *In a Different Voice: Psychological Theory and Women's Development* (Harvard Univ. Press. 1982), shows how men and women see their world differently, at least in the west.

The setup of the Iroquois League and how it contributed to our Constitution is the theme of *Indian Givers: How the Indians of the Americas Transformed the World*, by J. Weatherford, see especially Chapter 8, (New York: Fawcett Columbine, 1988.). Bruce Johansen's *Native American Political Systems and the Evolution of Democracy: An Annotated Bibliography,* available online at http://www.ratical.org/many_worlds/6Nations/NAPSnEoD91.html, includes much material on the forgotten importance of the Iroquois on our nation's founding. One of the best studies of the issue is done by Renee Jacobs in "The Iroquois Great Law of Peace and the U.S. Constitution: How the Founding Fathers Ignored the Clan Mothers" (*American Indian Law Review.* 16 (1991):497-531). Johansen comments on her work: "While the founders adapted some aspects of Iroquois law, Jacobs makes a strong case that they were nearly totally blind to the equity of the sexes that was woven into Haudenosaunee fundamental law and political life." But if one looks at the correspondence between John and Abigail Adams, which is included in Jacob's article, one must conclude that, at least in his case, the omission of women and their rights from the Constitution was understood and intentional. This correspondence is in *The Book of Abigail and John: Selected Letters from the Adams Family, 1762-1784,* edited by Lyman Butterfield, Marc Friedlaender, and Mary-Jo Kline (Harvard Univ. Press, 1975). The particular correspondence was dated March 31, and April 14, 1776 and is on pages 120-122.

Acton is credited with the statement by the Reverend F. Forrester Church in his conversation with Bill Moyers, published by Public Affairs Television and Doubleday in 1989 as *Bill Moyers: A World of Ideas.* Revered Church, the son of the late Senator, recalled the statement from an unnamed Harvard professor (personal communication). I have not been able to trace it to Acton.

Fair analyses of the cold war and its part in the soviet collapse are: Jonathan Schell, *The Seventh Decade: The New Shape of Nuclear Danger.* (Metropolitan Books/Henry Holt & Co. 2007); John Lewis Gaddis, *The Cold War: A New History* (Penguin Press, 2005); and Richard Rhodes, *Arsenals of Folly: The Making of the Nuclear Arms Race* (Alfred A Knopf. 2007.)

Amy Chua's observations on the dangers inherent on combining the inequities of capitalism with the equities of democracy are in *World on Fire: How Exporting Free Market Democracy Breeds Ethnic Hatred and Global*

Instability. (Doubleday, 2003). Greenspan's comments on the dangers inherent in inequality are in *Christian Science Monitor*. June 14, 2005.

The importance of addressing the context of ailing ecosystems rather than their analytically determined unbalanced elements is the work of Boris Worm and his colleagues in: "Impacts of biodiversity loss on ocean ecosystem services" in *Science*. 2006 Nov 3; 314(5800): 787-90. See also *Panarchy: Understanding Transformations in Human and Natural Systems* by Lance Gunderson and C. S. Holling (Island Press, 2002), where this concept is a central theme in why our efforts fail.

Written by Daniel Kaufmann, Aart Kraay, and Massimo Mastruzzi, "Governance Matters IV: Governance Indicators for 1996-2004" was published by The World Bank in May 2005. It is available on line at: http://siteresources.worldbank.org/INTRES/Resources/469232-1107449512766/GovMattersIV_main.pdf. (accessed 26 May 2008).

The problem of inequality among the sexes in early cultures is addressed by Steven Kuhn and Mary Steiner who propose a benefit for the division of labor in the Neandertals: "What's a Mother to Do? The Division of Labor among Neandertals and Modern Humans in Eurasia," *Current Anthropology*, 2006 Dec; 47(6): 953-980.

Hernando de Soto in his *The Mystery of Capital: Why Capitalism Triumphs in the West and Fails Everywhere Else* (Basic Books, 2003) shows that capitalism is built on other elements like the idea of private property and its protection by the government.

Greenspan's comments and apologies were to the Congressional committee investigating his role in the deregulation of the financial industry and the part that played in the financial crisis of the fall of 2008. They are reported in the *New York Times*, 24 October, 2008 in: "Greenspan Concedes Error on Regulation."

The influence of language on thought patterns is forcefully presented in Whorf's *Language, Thought, and*

Reality: Selected Writings of Benjamin Lee Whorf (edited by John Carroll, MIT Press, 1956) when he compares Navaho language and thinking processes with those of the typical American. See also Lev Vygotsky's *Thought and Language* (Mishchlenia i Rech, (1934)). Translated by A. Kozulin. MIT Press, 1962. This book has been retranslated by Eugenia Hanfmann and Gertrude Vakar, transcribed, and put online at http://www.marxists.org/archive/vygotsky/works/words/index.htm. (Accessed 5/30/07). Of particular interest to our theme, but not particularly to this point, are Vygotsky's support for the idea of play as organizing the developing brain in children.

For a discussion of the power of these other new media few works surpass Marshal McLuhan's *Understanding Media: The Extensions of Man* (McGraw Hill: New York. 1964.), and to see how they are used to manipulate society few surpass *Manufacturing Consent: The Political Economy of the Mass Media* by Edward S. Herman and Noam Chomsky (Pantheon (January 15, 2002).

The quote from William Sloan Coffin comes from my own notebook entry dated in 1992, but I did not record a primary reference.

Chris Hedges' account of the Bosnian war is: *War is a Force that Gives Us Meaning*. (Public Affairs Press. 2002.) and information on the group originating in South African, *Search for Common Ground*, is available at www.sfcg.org.

'Fuzzy it up' is the phrase used by Daniel Ellsburg, in an interview with Errol Morris of the New York Times, as he quotes Bobby Kennedy explaining how his brother would have gotten us out of Viet Nam. As described by Morris: Fuzzing it up is a common practice in government. "You hide intention and responsibility. You have one person say one thing, and another person the exact opposite. You create a blizzard of paper, so much paper that actual evidence is lost in the glut. And of course, you deny anything and everything you can deny—particularly the obvious. (Denying the obvious is always popular.) You produce noise, distraction and confusion. People rarely think of this as a well-established bureaucratic technique, but it is a tried and true methodology." Morris' interview with Ellsburg was on November 13, 2003 and recorded on the web site at http://morris.blogs.nytimes.com/2008/05/19/the_most_curious_thing/ (accessed 21 May 2008).

John Perkins' *Confessions of an Economic Hit Man* (Berrett-Koehler Publishers. San Francisco: 2004.) reveals the easy transition in conventional wisdom when it is associated with profits. Jürgen Habermas' transition from a creative to a consumer society is in his, *The Structural Transformation of the Public Sphere: An Inquiry into a Category of Bourgeois Society*. MIT Press: Cambridge, MA, 1989, (English Translation of the German original, *Strukturwandel der Öffentlichkeit. Untersuchungen zu einer Kategorie der bürgerlichen Gesellschaft,* 1962). It is equally a record of the survival of those profiting.

The Downing Street Memo records a meeting on 23 July 2002 of British defense leaders and shows how a leader's perceptions, albeit faulty, can dominate facts. It is available online at http://www.downingstreetmemo.com/docs/memotext.pdf (accessed 21 Dec 2007). The best analysis of this memo is that of Mark Danner posted on the Internet at www.tomdispatch.com/post/2486/mark_danner_on_the_british_smoking_gun_memo (accessed 21 Dec 2007).

Bruce Lipton records several instances where perceptions effect DNA expression in his *The Biology of Belief: Unleashing the Power of Consciousness Matter and Miracles* (Santa Rosa, CA: Mountain of Love, 2005).

Governor Perry's foibles have been ably recorded by Amy Smith at the *Austin Chronicle.* They can be found in its archives beginning in February, 2007. She credits the Associated Press with the most telling fumble: the combination of a staff meeting with Merck representatives to discuss the vaccine with a same day contribution of $5,000.00 to Perry's campaign fund.

The bit of information on Nike's CEO and Duke's coach is among many tidbits found in Chuck Collins' and Felice Yeskel's *Economic Apartheid in America*, (New Press, 2000).

The Institute of Heart Math (www.heartmath.org) is dedicated to the understanding that heart rate variability—the beat to beat variability in heart rate like that evaluated in fetal heart rate monitoring—signals a healthy heart, and that there are ways to increase one's own variability, which results in improved health. Dean Ornish's metaphor for how his group meetings opened the heart was a personal communication. His work is in: *Doctor Dean Ornish's Program for Reversing Heart Disease.* (Random House, New York: 1990.)

Easterly, William. *The White Man's Burden: Why the West's Efforts to Aid the Rest Have Done so Much Ill and so Little Good.* New York: Penguin Press, 2006. The Southwest Industrial Areas Foundation is a cooperative enterprise of industry and faith-based groups aimed at increasing community and providing the education and services necessary for people and families to better function in society; they provide the community. See Ernesto Cortas' "Faith, Charity, and Justice" in *The American Prospect*, Special report on Poverty. May, 2007.

The *Report from Iron Mountain on the Possibility and Desirability of Peace* (Delta, 1967) was supposedly leaked according to Leonard Lewin's introduction. A later edition by Lewin and Victor Navasky confessed the satire, but satire or not the benefits of the defensive alignment are clear to any government agent.

In regard of Roosevelt's wait and see approach to the Japanese fleet see: Robert Stinnett's *Day of Deceit: The Truth about FDR and Pearl Harbor* (New York, Free Press, 1999). Stinnett maintains that the attack was a carefully orchestrated design, initiated at the highest levels of the American government. Less vituperative is *Pearl Harbor: The Final Judgment* (New York: Crown, 1992) by the late Henry C. Clausen and Bruce Lee. Of all those pursuing the truth about how much was known and when, Clausen had the greatest access to the classified documents. His conclusion is that it was known that something was going on and that the leadership waited to see. The 9/11 Commission Report for the rest of the world is *The War on Freedom: Why America was Attacked on September 1, 2001*, by Nafeez Mosaddeq Ahmed, (Progressive Press: 2002).

Chapter 10: As American as Apple Pie—The Military

Statistics of U. S. involvement in arming other nations is from Noam Chomsky, "The United States and the 'Challenge of Relativity,'" in Tony Evans (ed.), *Human Rights Fifty Years on: A Reappraisal*, Manchester University Press, November, 1998. Alan Greenspan's comment on oil is from his memoir *The Age of Turbulence: Adventures in a New World,* (Penguin Press. 2007).

Gregory D. Foster's article on the use of force and different methods of interaction with others is, "Strategy and the Search for Peace." *The Futurist.* Nov.-Dec. 2006. Walter Wink used *The Third Way* as the subtitle for his book, *Jesus and Nonviolence: A Third Way* (Fortress Press, 2003). The information on dealing with bullies comes mostly from Jerry's own program in her elementary school where bullying was included in her part of the curriculum. When everyone knew the psychological nature of the bully no one wanted to go there and bullying disappeared. Her program also included many of the elements included in the program "bullies to buddies" which is focused on changing the responses of those bullied to get a more cognitive response (See their web site at www.bullies2buddies.com).

Eugene Gendlin. *Focusing.* Everest House. 1978.

Chapter 11: Religion: An Attractor That Needs To Be Stranger

Julian Jaynes. *The Origin of Consciousness in the Breakdown of the Bicameral Mind.* Houghton Mifflin. 1976.

Joseph Campbell, *The Masks of God,* is in three volumes covering primitive, oriental, and occidental mythology.

Kolata, Gina. "Remembering a 'Magical Genius': Ramanujan was born 100 years ago and grew up poor and uneducated, but his work continues to draw and inspire mathematicians." *Science* 19 June 1987 236: 1519-1521. Bruce Berndt in his *Ramanujan: Letters and Commentary (History of Mathematics, V. 9,* (American Mathematical Society, 1995) is more supportive of Ramanujan's mathematical abilities, but it was Ramanujan himself who gave credit to the goddess.

Bertrand Russell. *The Conquest of Happiness.* Liveright: New York and London, 1930. The references to authentic play (Donaldson) and child-directed play are included in the chapter on Education.

Fundamentalism is the focus of Fall, 2005 issue of *Parabola.* Both Christian and Islamic brands are covered in this issue. Of interest also is "Keeping the Faith," pages 9-10, in "A Long Walk: a survey of Saudi Arabia." *Economist.* January 7, 2006.

See: de Waal's "Bonobo Sex and Society" in *Scientific American* (March 1995), cited earlier.

Ervin Laszlo. *Science and the Akashic Field: An Integral Theory of Everything.* Inner Traditions. Vermont. 2004.

Wilber, Ken. *Integral Spirituality: A Startling New Role for Religion in the Modern and Postmodern World.* Integral Books: Boston and London, 2006.

Grof, Stanislav M.D. *The Holotropic Mind: The Three Levels of Human Consciousness and How They Shape Our Lives.* Harper Collins: New York, 1990.

INDEX

A

B

C

D

E

F

G

H

I

L

M

N

O

P

R

S

T

U

V

W

X

www.ingramcontent.com/pod-product-compliance
Lightning Source LLC
LaVergne TN
LVHW040824090826
845145LV00001BA/147

9780984216413